# THE
# INSIDE
# TRACK
## THE PROFESSIONAL APPROACH

by
**Alan Potts**

RP
ROWTON PRESS

## Acknowledgements

Grateful acknowledgement is given to the Timeform Organisation for permission to quote from *Timeform Perspective*.

**Jacket design by Pure Design & Advertising Ltd, Shrewsbury.**

---

© Rowton Press Ltd 1998
First Published 1998
by Rowton Press Ltd,
P.O.Box 10, Oswestry,
Shropshire SY11.

1st reprint December 1999

Typeset by Rowton Press using MICROSOFT WORD FOR WINDOWS
Output on a Hewlett Packard HP Laserjet 4000.

Printed and bound in Great Britain by Redwood Books, Bath
Jacket printed by Wincanton Print

1-871093-18-X

# Foreword

## Ian Carnaby

"No-one wins at betting," my wife assures my curious, non-betting friends. "Well, apart from Ian's friend, Alan Potts. He's different, isn't he darling?"

Yes, he certainly is. I happened to be with him at Bath races when he placed £24,000 on Labour (at 1-6 with Tote Credit) to win the 1997 General Election. It was not a typical Potts bet but he viewed it as writing himself a cheque for £4,000. I remember his words at the time: "However strongly you feel about a horse, something can always go wrong in the race. But nothing can go wrong with this," he said. The wager made the front page of *The Sporting Life* and prompted much comment.

I am delighted to write a few words about Alan's new book, *The Inside Track*, which delves further into the methods of a professional punter, first outlined in *Against The Crowd*. This foreword is about the author, not me, although I must say the General Election bet had a sobering effect on me.

Of course, not everyone wants to lay out that sort of money, however infinitesimal the risk. But how many of us with a lifetime's punting stretching back into the dim and distant past could come up with the stake anyway? Alan has put himself in an enviable position through sheer hard work and, above all, a determination to learn from his mistakes. He has become a successful backer of horses - and I surprise myself by writing that down. Because, as a failed punter myself, having realised one day that scribbling, not betting, would get me and mine through to the end, I am the last person willingly to acknowledge the successful methods of others.

Some things change hardly at all in gambling. There were

roulette systems when Dostoyevsky was doing his pieces in Wiesbaden a hundred years ago, and there was someone called 'The Major' offering inside information in the racing press.

Today's advertisements are along the same lines, but gaudier. Many of them claim a strike-rate which, if accurate, would enable the loyal follower to retire well before his fortieth birthday. Unless he happened to join in at the start of a losing streak, of course. When that happens, very few punters have the mental toughness, or indeed the bank balance, to go on investing purely on someone else's say so.

Alan is well aware of this, and it gave him a refreshingly balanced view of his role as a partner in Mark Holder's successful telephone tipping service. The work with Holder offered him a guaranteed income, covering all his racing and travelling expenses, while ensuring that he brought even more discipline to bear on his betting.

However, he admitted to me recently that advising other people brought its own pressure. Potts knows there will be losing runs, but he cannot be sure how clients will handle them. And that worries him. Too many backers think that somehow, somewhere, there must be a magic formula. There isn't of course. There is patience, and faith, and, if all else fails, pushing off for a week or so and doing something else. Alan admits as much.

Like *Against The Crowd*, *The Inside Track* is written in a wry, self-knowing style. Middle-aged readers may concede that they, too, always seemed to be on the roundabouts when the sexual revolution of the sixties was in full swing. But there is also a welter of detail. Why was the summer of 1995 so disappointing for him? How could the losing run on turf reach 20 at one stage? Alan could handle that, because a couple of short-heads made all the difference, but he identified an additional problem - a shortage of winners in high-quality handicaps, which had previously been more than kind to him.

Unfortunately, value had dried up, partly because of the growth of price-related tipping - Pricewise and Beat the Book - in the racing press. So, it was time for an alternative strategy, and we are off on a journey through American pro-punting literature and the possibility of combining systems on the All-weather tracks, with aspects of Alan's own previous experience to bring about a more successful 1996.

Most informative of all is the Speed Figures section (even allowing for the vagaries of British conditions), where Alan requires a speed figure to be at least 12 points better than the horse's handicap mark. This gave him the prolific Grey Kingdom, who won a Nottingham six-furlong handicap by six lengths, with a speed figure of 69 against a mark of 41. What must Alan have thought when the horse went to Carlisle next time for a similar contest, with the same 7lb claimer in the saddle? Backed from 4-1 to 11-4, Grey Kingdom bolted up by four lengths.

Then we have fascinating chapters on the importance of pace in a race - Bosra Sham could not possibly have won the Coral-Eclipse in 1997, irrespective of Kieren Fallon's possible error, because the gallop was so pedestrian - the effect of the draw, British All-weather racing, which is something of a Potts speciality, and even his approach to spread betting, insofar as it affects racing. He writes that no expert has explained it satisfactorily - which is fairly wounding if you happen to be a spread betting writer. With Alan, you soon learn to accept constructive criticism.

As he is at pains to point out, he is not trying to set out a plan enabling readers to pop around the corner and make an immediate profit. Rather, he wants to eliminate as many unnecessary mistakes as possible. He cheerfully acknowledges that most betting office regulars are unlikely to read the book, and will never understand - or WANT to understand - the concept of value, let alone how claiming races work. But it's all there, just in case.

Everyone who DOES read it carefully will have an immeasurably better chance of showing ahead. He argues convincingly, for example, that an each-way bet is a weak bet (you don't really expect the horse to win) and virtually rules out multiple investments, even doubles. If you have a £20 win double on two 5-1 shots, and start off well, you will effectively be putting six times as much on the second horse as the first. Do you really fancy it six times as much? Ever looked at it that way?

If you go to the races and fill out a Placepot, that's up to you. But never kid yourself that it's anything more than an 'interest' bet, because the Tote takes out far too much from the pool for it to be anything else. As you turn the pages of *Inside Track*, be prepared for some illusions to be shattered, and listen to a few home truths. Even if you eliminate only one glaring weakness from your own strategy. *The Inside Track* will pay for itself over and over again.

I have known Alan Potts for some years now, ever since he wandered down to the two-furlong pole at Salisbury for a chat. Is he an obsessive? No. He works hard at betting, but talks equally well on other subjects. Why is he such a good punter? Because he used to be an indifferent one, and decided to change things. What makes him so relaxed and confident about his approach? A steady profit has something to do with it, no doubt. But also, I think, it's because it's what he wants to do.

That may seem an obvious thing to say, but any punter who looks longingly at the life of a professional should ask himself whether it is really for him. Even if I made horse racing pay, I would still have the uneasy feeling that I should be doing something else. It's a lot of days, a lot of years, watching them run round in circles. As soon as you think that, you can't be a professional.

But Potts is not like that. Racing is right for him - and I feel envious, the way I always do when something will clearly last someone a lifetime.

I could quote any number of paragraphs to sum up his philosophy, but I like this best, because it is both shrewd and gently ironic.

"Beating the most challenging, intellectual pastime available to man is a goal worth pursuing. But it will be a private pleasure, because your claim to beat the bookies will either be dismissed as lies, or ignored as worthless." This is a self-sufficient man with few illusions.

Read the book, and see what you think.

# CONTENTS

## Other books published by Rowton Press Ltd

**Against The Crowd** by Alan Potts

**McGovern on Sports Betting and How To Make It Pay**
by Derek McGovern

**Market Speculating** by Andrew Burke
**Spread Betting** by Andrew Burke

**Betting for a Living** by Nick Mordin
**Mordin on Time** by Nick Mordin
**The Winning Look** by Nick Mordin

**One Hundred Hints for Better Betting** by Mark Coton

**Coups and Cons** by Graham Sharpe

**For further details, credit card orders or information on forthcoming titles please call Rowton Press on:**

**01691 679111**

or write to:

**Rowton Press Ltd, PO Box 10, Oswestry, Salop SY11 1RB**

RP
ROWTON PRESS

# INTRODUCTION

## Only fools back horses

"This time next year Rodney, we'll be millionaires."

Unless you've spent most of the past fifteen years exploring the darker reaches of the Amazon jungle, you can probably hear David Jason uttering the catchphrase of his character Derek 'Delboy' Trotter. Del's ambition is much the same as most gamblers – a big return for the minimum of effort and outlay. It's why millions of people buy National Lottery tickets each week; they're not after the £10 prize. Delboy is also the same as most gamblers, in that he always loses. He wants to win, but he's only interested in short-cuts and quick returns. His idea of long-term planning is posting Rodney on lookout when he's flogging bent gear down the market. Delboy is never going to be a winner, because he isn't prepared to put in the necessary work, he isn't willing to listen to experts and he never, ever learns from past mistakes.

Winning money consistently by betting on horses isn't easy. It can only be achieved by a small percentage of punters, since it's the losses incurred by the majority that keep the whole business afloat. This is hardly a new revelation, but it consistently seems to escape the attention of the average betting shop customer.

Consider the financial equation that supports these businesses – they have fixed expenses for rent, business rates, staff, SIS, heating and lighting, insurance, newspapers and security. A standard high street shop is probably looking at a minimum of £1,000 per week in a decent location. That's how much they have to win off their punters before they start to show a profit.

Try dividing that figure by the number of people you found in attendance the last time you visited your local bookies and you'll have some idea of the task you face in trying to make money from betting – and that's before taking the betting tax into account.

It's reasonable to ask, therefore, whether it's actually possible to make a living from betting. I can only speak from personal experience, but, in my case, the answer is yes. In fact in the year under discussion in this book, 1997, I exceeded my own fairly modest targets to a degree that left me feeling I had moved to a new level of betting.

There were several factors that contributed to my profits, not least the discovery of the virtues of spread betting, and each factor will be addressed in the book. It is not my intention to produce a set of rules, nor a series of systems that readers can follow, but rather to persuade punters to think about their approach to backing horses.

As most serious punters will already realise, the world is divided into two categories – punters and the rest. I can talk to other punters, confident they will understand the language of my business. But to the 'rest' of the world, the announcement that I am a professional gambler usually produces much the same response as if I'd said "Mafia hit man", or "international cocaine dealer". A professional gambler is someone they only expect to meet in the pages of fiction, not at a party or in their office. Especially when the person claiming this occupation is, in the words of one journalist:

"A nondescript figure in his late forties, dressed in routine chain store clothing, who melts easily into a crowd".

As this was written by a man who could have passed an audition for the role of Worzel Gummidge, it seems a clear case of the kettle calling the Potts black.

Once strangers are persuaded that I really do make my living from betting, they invariably pull out that old chestnut about 'nobody beating the bookies'. I sometimes think that this must be the only piece of parental moralising that survived the swinging sixties – it certainly seems to have had more impact on most members of my generation than any of the dire warnings about the dangers of drink, drugs or unsafe sex! Not that the latter ever featured in my teenage lifestyle. The sixties may be retrospectively viewed as an era of free love, but in common with most of my friends, I missed the swings and spent the entire decade on the roundabouts.

The question of how I could make the game pay arose so often that, eventually, I came up with a parable to explain it, using the example of golf as a parallel with betting. The two activities do in fact have much in common. Both are entirely individual and results can't be blamed on anyone else. Both have short periods of action interspersed with long intervals of inaction, leaving far too much time for analysis of what's going wrong. In both betting and golf, problems are more likely to arise from the mental side of the game, rather than the actual execution. And, in both, the final score is the only measure of success or failure, regardless of how it was achieved.

Tens of thousands of people in this country play golf, at least in the sense that they go to a golf course and hit a few balls. Most of these 'golfers' play once or twice each week, never practice and never expect to play the game anything like a professional. In just the same way, large numbers of people bet on the horses. Like the casual golfers, they simply turn up at the betting shop, without any preparation, and start placing bets. They have no more chance of making it pay than their golfing counterparts do of becoming Nick Faldo.

I use Faldo as my golfing example, not because I see myself as his punting equivalent, but because for a few years in the late eighties and early nineties, he came as close as any man to making golf look easy. It wasn't just that his swing was perfectly grooved, or that he practised from dawn to dusk. What I really admired was his mental toughness. A leading amateur golfer remarked during this golden period, that hundreds of players could hit the ball as well as Faldo, but they couldn't match his scores, because they lacked his course management skills. They would always go straight for the pin, trying for a birdie on every hole, whereas Faldo knew when to cut his losses, hit the middle of the green and accept two putts.

The comparison with punting is clear – the losing punter finds winners but doesn't make the right bets. He backs the horse regardless of its price, while the professional knows when to stand aside and wait for another opportunity.

Faldo always played a course in the same way, whether he was ten over par or ten under. He had a game plan and he would stick to it. If the plan said use a two iron from the tee, he would do so, even if John Daly was playing his second from 100 yards closer to the green. He knew his own strengths and weaknesses, and he wasn't bothered what others were doing, even in his own group. In the same way, a professional punter lives or dies on his own opinion. If I've decided that a horse is worth a bet at 3-1, nothing anybody says to me on the racecourse is going to change that bet, unless it's a bookmaker shouting 11-4 the field.

There is one major difference between Faldo and punters. Everybody knows exactly how Faldo has performed every time he sets foot on a golf course, and they also know how much prize money he has won. Professional punters live in a world wreathed in secrecy, in which the financial success or failure of the players is a purely personal matter. The only criterion by which we are measured is our continued presence on the racecourse. If you are still there and still punting, it is assumed you are making profits, but nobody really knows.

If you are an amateur golfer, you can step on to the first tee at St Andrews knowing the exact score that Faldo achieved on his last visit. You can play over the same ground, compare your performance with his, and discover again that he inhabits a different world. Amateur punters, likewise, play the same races, facing the same bookmakers, but they have no idea how their performance measures up against the professionals. Of course there are occasional stories about the bets placed by the likes of Michael Tabor, J.P. McManus and Robert Sangster. But they are not men who bet for a living, they are rich men indulging in a hobby. In golfing terms they match up with the star names who turn out for celebrity golf tournaments, when Faldo might find himself playing a round with Jimmy Tarbuck. (I could have expressed that better, but you know what I mean.)

In this book, I hope to give punters some idea of how one professional set about playing the game, and the results achieved.

It is not my intention to lay down a set of rules that can be followed by any reader as a path to riches. It took me twenty years to progress from a mug to a profitable punter, and another ten after that before I was confident I could always make a living from my betting. If, along the way, I had discovered a short-cut to profits, I wouldn't be passing it on to all and sundry for less than twenty quid! If you buy an instructional book or video produced by Nick Faldo, you don't expect it to turn you into an Open Champion overnight, but you do anticipate picking up enough ideas to improve your golf handicap. I can no more provide a guarantee of success than Faldo, but I hope this book will at least provide an appreciation of what is involved in punting for a living and prompt you to think about new ideas for your own betting in future.

The book is divided into six main sections, which can be read separately. The first four cover Flat racing on turf, on the All-weather, NH racing and spread betting. The final two provide more general material that is relevant to all forms of racing. Each of the four specific sections concludes with a workshop, detailing bets I have made and designed to demonstrate the practical application of the ideas discussed. There are also plenty of examples contained within the main text. All the bets are taken from my own records for the calendar year of 1997, unless otherwise stated.

There has been one other significant change to my professional life as a result of the publication of my first book, *Against The Crowd*, which had a marked effect on my betting. Following a talk I gave at a racing club meeting in Cheltenham, I met the brothers Paul and Mark Holder, sons of the late Richard Holder, who trained just outside Bristol. As a result of that meeting, I later joined Mark as a partner in his business, advising clients on betting, via a daily telephone message.

From the first time I started to provide that service, in August 1996, my own punting has become more profitable. It might be a coincidence, but I don't believe in them. What I do believe is that the imposition of a daily schedule on my previously free-flowing existence provided a more disciplined approach, which helped me to eliminate the less successful parts of my betting. When you have to explain and justify each bet you recommend to a paying audience, it soon exposes any cracks in your thinking.

The common question put to anybody who works on such a service is – if you're so good, why sell your bets to other people? I'm not going to pretend that I had any altruistic mission to educate the punters, or that I felt it my duty to help people beat the bookies, both of which answers have been given by others in the same line of business. I started working with Mark because it offered me a guaranteed income that would cover all my racing and travelling expenses, with something to spare. Since that time, my personal betting profits have been better than in the previous two years, but that couldn't be relied upon, and even a gambler can see the advantage of a 'bird in the hand'.

# PART 1

## FLAT (TURF)

### On the wrong track

Bath racecourse, 25 September 1995. I haven't had a bet for nine days and my confidence is shot to pieces after a dreadful summer's punting that has produced a deficit of over £15,000. At the paddock prior to the ten-furlong maiden for two-year-olds, a big, rangy colt really takes my eye. When he floats to post on the fast ground, 12-1 is simply too big to resist and a bet of £3,000/240 is soon arranged. Always in the front rank, Flyfisher looks home and dry at the furlong pole, but in the shadow of the post he's caught by the odds-on favourite Gentilhomme – the margin is a short-head.

The race epitomises the summer, a story of nearly, maybe, should have been - and biased stewards! But there was more to it than that. The methods I had used successfully for many years were no longer working. I had found my fair share of winners during the summer, but had passed on backing a good many of them because the price was too short. Every time I found a value bet that paid off, I either messed up the staking, or gave back the profits within days. For example, a £2,700/300 on Sherman at York on May 18 was followed by a £2,900 deficit from the following three days at Newbury. Two winners on June 15, which netted a £3,250 profit, merely funded £4,000 lost on the first two days at Royal Ascot, where I found lots of big prices on the Tote, but no winners.

My first crisis of confidence came at the end of the Newmarket July meeting. On the Monday evening at Windsor, I backed the well-drawn and consistent Court Nap to the tune of £4,000/320, only to see him touched off by a whisker in a photo-finish that took the judge fifteen minutes to resolve. My mood was not improved by the trainer's reported comment that Court Nap was always at a disadvantage in a photo as he had such a short neck! My first six bets at Newmarket produced three more seconds and a third, before a £2,500/500 about Twilight Patrol in the one-mile handicap run just prior to the July Cup. She also finished second, but she was carried across the width of the July Course by the winner, Nordinex, and I thought that retribution for the disqualification of Cuff Link at York in 1994 was about to arrive. But not in 1995! The stewards accepted that interference had taken place, but decided that it hadn't affected the result. Having greeted the loudspeaker announcement of this gross injustice with a high decibel imitation of J. P. (McEnroe not McManus), I stomped off to the car park without even waiting to watch the feature race of the meeting.

Every punter will have experienced a week like the one I had at Newmarket, and it certainly wasn't my first. My personal remedy is to take a break and get away from racing and betting for at least a week. In fact I didn't return until the first day of the Glorious Goodwood meeting, when the apparent wisdom of the move was highlighted by a couple of winners, including a £6,000/300 on Brief Glimpse in the fillies Listed event over seven furlongs. Surely this represented the turning of the tide? Well, not exactly: my next 20 bets on the turf were all losers! The gloom was lifted during that barren period by a couple of decent wins at the Wolverhampton All-weather track, but once again the major meetings that had seen me successful in previous seasons were a disaster area.

At York in August, six bets produced the usual proportion of placings, ending with Foundry Lane's third in the Ebor Handicap (£3,500/500). My betting at the York meeting ended at that point, as, in temperatures in the 90s, I succumbed to the heat and found myself being revived in the first aid tent by a succession of maternally minded St Johns Ambulance staff. Friends who had read my views on the effect of the draw on the Ebor, unkindly suggested that I had fainted at the sight of a horse drawn 21 winning the race. Another ten-day break followed, but I arrived at Doncaster for the St Leger meeting still without a turf winner since Goodwood. I broke the sequence by backing Grey Shot on the opening day, but more seconds and thirds left me £2,000 adrift by the end of the week. And so to Flyfisher...

Having written in *Against The Crowd* that "nobody is immune to losing runs or to loss of confidence", I could now see those words coming back to haunt me in spades! At the end of September, I sat down to analyse what had gone wrong. The figures didn't make pretty reading. I divided the bets into categories according to price, and considered each group separately. The longshots (10-1 and over) that had provided my profits in previous years, produced a return of one winner from 30 bets. However, they would have shown a profit if either Court Nap or Flyfisher had prevailed by a short-head rather than finishing second, so that didn't seem to be a major problem. One Flat season is a short period over which to judge a type of bet that requires long-term patience.

The real damage had been done in what I called the 'everyday' group – bets at prices between 3-1 and 6-1. I would expect around a 20 per cent strike-rate at those odds, with a profit that would at least fund the stakes on the longshot bets. The reality was six winners from 48 bets, with five of those six backed only to a minimum £300 stake. This group cost me just over £9,000 and that marked it out as the prime cause of the deficit on the season. More detailed analysis showed that most of those 48 bets had been in the good class handicaps that had always been my strength, but clearly no more.

I eventually concluded that there were two main reasons for this slump. The first seemed to be the improvement in the accuracy of the official handicappers. I had struggled all season to find horses who looked to me to be well-handicapped, whereas in previous years something would often leap off the page when I looked at the declarations. The reasons for the improvement probably don't matter, although the increased availability of race films must be a factor, and probably the competitive racing initiative had also helped to provide the officials with better information. The second problem was the growth of price-related tipping in the trade papers. Several times during that summer, I had analysed a race overnight, only to find that Pricewise or Beat The Book had reached the same conclusion and were broadcasting it to the nation. Since they were inevitably concentrating their efforts on the bookmakers' early price races, we were operating in the same territory, and their followers were picking off the best prices.

By mid-October I had switched my attention to the jumping, but it was obvious that I needed a new approach for the 1996 turf season, although at that stage I had no clear idea what it might be. During the winter, I read a number of relevant books by American authors, and re-read some others that had already pointed me in the right direction for All-weather racing. It took a while for the penny to drop, and then I realised that the most significant thing about all these American punters was not what they wrote about, but what they never mentioned. They seemed to have no interest in form in the sense that it is understood in this country. When writing about an individual horse, they rarely mentioned the horses it had run against. They simply weren't interested in who had beaten it, or whom it had beaten, let alone the distances or weights involved.

Although different writers placed the greatest emphasis on different factors, the principal concerns of all of them were the same – speed figures, pace and track bias. In general terms, when looking at past performances, they were much more interested in the way the race had been run, than who took part. When analysing future races, they were searching for clues as to the shape of the race. Who would lead? How fast would they go? How many front-runners? Where is the fastest strip on the track? And is the track favouring front-runners, or fast finishers?

During the winter of 1995, I started to apply this sort of thinking to my All-weather betting, and it soon became clear that I had an edge. I produced my own speed figures for the first time and, after a period of testing without betting, I acquired enough confidence to invest purely on what they told me. When I backed six All-weather winners during two weeks in February 1996, I knew that I would never go back to the type of form analysis that still characterised 99 per cent of the media pundits in Britain.

But I still wasn't convinced that the same methods could be applied on the turf. American turf racing is limited to one or two races per day at those tracks with grass, and many offer only an unrelieved diet of dirt racing. The American authors who wrote about turf racing all emphasised that they found it more difficult than dirt racing. Their methods didn't work as well on turf, and many simply ignored it. Others looked for specific ideas that could be used for turf races, such as a concentration on breeding. Their biggest problem was with speed figures. They couldn't produce an accurate figure because the small number of races each day provided insufficient data to calculate the variant (i.e. how much faster or slower than normal the track was riding on a specific day).

Andy Beyer (the doyen of American writers and a must read for any serious All-weather punter) reported in *Beyer On Speed*, that he had finally realised that turf racing was different when he found anomalies in his nationally distributed speed figures for horses who had run on both dirt and turf.

Computer analysis persuaded him that the error arose from the adjustment made to the speed figure to allow for the number of lengths that each horse had finished behind the winner. Beaten horses in turf races appeared to be earning figures that were too high when compared with their dirt figures. He concluded this meant that in turf races, the field were generally more bunched up at the finish than in dirt races – something any British punter with 20/20 eyesight could have told him after the first season of All-weather racing here.

Beyer admitted that, with what he described as "typical American arrogance", he had thought the slow pace, fast-finish style of British racing was due to a lack of intelligence among our trainers and jockeys, who didn't appreciate the value of early speed. He now realised that the key factor in grass races is the finishing kick and that "perhaps speed figures have limited usefulness because they measure a horse's overall performance, instead of placing an emphasis on the final fraction".

Here in an American book, I found a line of thinking that coincided almost exactly with the 'power' theory I described in *Against The Crowd*. Beyer went on to outline the methods of a California-based professional called Andy Cylke, who was beating turf races in that state using a speed figure system in which the time for the final quarter-mile was the key component – a system he called Sustained Pace. It made interesting reading, but couldn't be applied in the dinosaur state of British racing, since we have no access to accurate sectional timing.

Boosted by my success on the All-weather during the early months of 1996, I determined that I would try these new methods during the 1996 turf season. Clearly, I wouldn't be able to translate the American ideas directly to the turf, but by mixing them with my own past experience, I hoped I could find a way forward that would eliminate the difficulties I had encountered during 1995. At the very least I would be working in ways that were entirely alien to most punters, and if I could produce results, they were likely to be very profitable. I only hope I don't have to do the same again in 1999, after giving you the benefit of my research!

# Speed figures on turf

The idea of calculating my own speed figures for turf racing has never had any appeal. I've always felt there were simply too many variables involved for such figures to be anything more than an educated guess. Consider a single card from my local track at Newbury, say the first of the season on Friday April 18. There were seven races scheduled, of which four were run on the straight course and three on the round course, so the first problem is to equate times run over different stretches of ground. One race is for two-year-olds, three are for three-year-olds and three for older horses, so the second problem is to make allowance for the maturity of the different age groups.

The distances range from five-furlongs to two miles, and whilst the straight course races can be assumed to be run over the advertised distance, those on the round course can be significantly affected by the positioning of the rail on the long home turn. Add to that the issues of rain during the meeting, a headwind, and a slow early pace in at least two of the races, and the number of imponderables leaves me wondering if the effort would be worth my while. And, of course, the effort would be considerable, with up to six meetings being staged on some days during the summer. The work involved would impact on my ability to go racing, in itself a time consuming activity - especially travelling around the M25 on a Friday evening, when a speed figure of zero generally prevails!

I have been a subscriber to *Timeform Perspective* since it's inception in the late eighties, and in recent years that form book has included the Timeform speed figure (they use time figure, but I'll stick to speed figure for consistency) for the first six home in each race. Since Timeform have fifty years of experience and fifty years of data, it seems illogical for me to try to improve on the figures they produce – as ridiculous as hoping that I could sew better underpants than Marks & Spencer. *The Perspective* also provides an explanation of the basis on which their figures are calculated, so that it is reasonably easy to see how the figure is reached.

With several years of figures and race results to hand in back issues of *Timeform Perspective*, I settled down to look for ways in which I could use the figures. I investigated a number of approaches, but there was one that stood out, producing a good percentage of winners, often at reasonable prices. The examples that follow are all based on Timeform speed figures, but I think it should be possible to adapt any source of figures, so long as it is possible to adjust them to match the official handicap scale.

This line of research had been prompted by a comment made by Andy Beyer, to the effect that his personal speed figures enabled him to identify horses that could successfully step up in class after a win. In the American racing programme, he was looking for horses who could repeat a win when competing at a higher claiming level. I had often wondered if there was a way of spotting horses who could defy a penalty or a weight rise in British handicaps, and the Timeform figures looked to offer a method.

They are adjusted so that they operate on the same scale as the official BHB handicap mark, i.e. a Timeform speed figure of 100 indicates a horse capable of running off a handicap mark of 100, and similarly across the scale from 30 (Donkey) to 130 (Entrepreneur). I looked for the winner of a handicap who had recorded a speed figure significantly higher than his current handicap mark, and then checked out his subsequent results. If the speed figure was an accurate assessment of his merit, then the horse should be able to win again off a higher mark and/or in higher class. It soon became clear that this method did indeed highlight future winners, and on occasions, winners at exceptional prices. I worked backwards through the 1995 and 1994 seasons and found enough evidence to confirm this was one approach that I should adopt for 1996.

The first winner I backed that season was Primo Lara, who hacked-up in a seven-furlong handicap at Thirsk on April 19. He had won at Beverley seven days earlier, recording a speed figure of 77 when running off a handicap mark of 65. Under a 6lb penalty he confirmed he was better than his handicap mark suggested, winning by three and a half lengths despite being eased inside the final furlong. The SP of 5-4 (I took the opening show of 7-4) was nothing to write home about; but then again he never looked like getting beaten. Not surprisingly, it didn't always work as smoothly as that, and in a couple of cases I missed good opportunities before I got to grips with the best way to use this information.

A gelding called Scharnhorst started the season with a win over seven furlongs at Leicester. The speed figure was 79 for a horse running off a mark of 66. In the terminology I adopted this was referred to as a 'plus 13' – i.e. a speed figure 13 points higher than the handicap mark. I had already decided that qualifiers should only be backed if they ran under similar circumstances, so when Scharnhorst was dropped to six furlongs at Kempton, I left him alone and he finished in mid division in a field of 16. His next run came in a 0-70 limited stakes, back over seven furlongs, at Folkestone. I was at Chepstow for a NH meeting, and simply didn't know that he was running (not very professional, eh?). In an inevitable application of Murphy's Law, he made all to win at 10-1. He also recorded a speed figure of 79, which again suggested he could cope with better company than a 0-70 class race. When he stepped up to a 0-90 handicap at the Chester May meeting, I took the early 14-1 with a bet of £250 each-way. Scharnhorst tried to make all, and although headed inside the final furlong still looked odds-on to reward the place part of the bet. He was in a three-way photo for third place, and the judge eventually decided he'd finished fifth, beaten two short-heads by the third placed horse. It was, of course, an 18-runner handicap and the bookmakers were paying out on fourth place!

Another missed opportunity was Orinoco River. He won a 12-furlong handicap on the final day of the Chester meeting, producing a plus 12 (speed figure 84, handicap mark 72). On the strength of that, I backed him in a similar race at Newbury (£4,000/480), but he finished a well-beaten sixth. Deterred by that run, I ignored his next start, at Pontefract, when he bounced back to win at 10-1 and record a speed figure of 90. With hindsight, the race at Newbury probably came too soon after Chester, as there was just an eight-day gap. It was a useful reminder that speed figures cannot and should not be used in isolation, but as part of an overall consideration of a race.

Despite those misses, the 1996 turf season increased my confidence in the merits of this approach, and with some more research looking back at previous seasons, I eventually set down some guidelines for 1997. I use the word 'guidelines' rather than 'rules' advisedly. Although there is no doubt speed figures can provide a useful edge, the vagaries of racing on turf are such that they are nowhere near as clear cut as they are on the All-weather tracks. Whilst a good speed figure could highlight a solid contender, I still wanted to use that in conjunction with other criteria before I would decide to bet – not least the question of price. The guidelines were as follows:

- The speed figure should be at least 12 points greater than the handicap mark. The evidence pointed to this being a cut off point above which the strike-rate was significantly higher. It also meant that the speed figure achieved would usually be higher than the revised handicap mark for the next race.

- The subsequent race should be over the same distance, or not more than one furlong farther. I'm in no doubt that the performance of most handicap class horses on turf is very distance-sensitive, and the evidence from previous years supported this view.

- If an apprentice rode when the good figure was achieved, consider whether his weight allowance was an important factor, especially if he isn't riding this time.

- Concentrate on plus figures achieved in sprint handicaps. Not surprisingly, fast sprint figures were more likely to be reproduced, given that sprints are more likely to be run at a true pace.

- Don't support a horse on speed figures alone if other factors suggest there is a doubt about the figure being reproduced. Factors such as the ground, the nature of the track and the size of the field also need to be considered.

Bearing those points in mind, let's look at the results achieved by some of the horses who produced fast figures early in the 1997 season. Experience has shown, by the way, that big differences between speed figure and handicap mark, are more likely to emerge in the first two months of the season. By mid-summer, the handicappers have got the measure of most horses.

One of the first qualifiers in 1997 was Grey Kingdom, and his subsequent running demonstrates almost every one of the guidelines given above. He ran seven races between April 21 and June 14.

**April 21     Nottingham          6f hcp**
*Won by 6l recording a speed figure of 69 against a handicap mark of 41. Ridden by 7lb claiming apprentice D Mernagh. This 'plus 28' made him look invulnerable under a penalty.*

**April 25     Carlisle            6f hcp**
*Won by 4l recording a speed figure of 70 against a handicap mark of 48 (41 + 7lb penalty), again ridden by D Mernagh. Starting price was 11-4 from opening 4-1, and 5-1 had been offered prior to racing.*

**April 28     Pontefract          6f hcp**
*Finished third, beaten over 4l, running off a mark of 49. Started 5-4 favourite, but set off too quickly and couldn't last home. The speed figure of 36 confirms a below-par performance.*

**May 2       Musselburgh         7f hcp**
*Won by 1l off a handicap mark of 48, again with D Mernagh claiming 7lbs. No speed figure available, due to distance changes at the track after realignment of the final bend. Starting price was 9-4 favourite.*

**May 22      Goodwood            7f hcp**
*Finished in the ruck, running off a handicap mark of 62. Had no chance here as a front-runner drawn one in a field of 15 on a track with a strong bias to high numbers. Ridden by G Bardwell, so had lost the 7lb allowance as well.*

**June 7      Doncaster           7f hcp**
*Finished third off a mark of 62, again ridden by G Bardwell. Starting price 10-1 from early 12-1.*

**June 14     York                6f hcp**
*Won by one and a half lengths, again off a mark of 62, but reunited with D Mernagh. Starting price 16-1 in a field of 23.*

Even after that, Grey Kingdom wasn't finished, managing another win over seven furlongs at Epsom in July, this time off a handicap

mark of 69 – the exact speed figure he'd produced in that initial win
at Nottingham.

As you can see from this sequence of runs, the massive plus
figure at Nottingham clearly marked Grey Kingdom as a horse likely
to stay ahead of the handicapper for some time. He also signalled
that the first run was no flash in the pan by repeating the speed
figure almost exactly when winning at Carlisle. Not every horse can
reproduce its best form over more than two or three races. Another
big plus figure was recorded by Meranti.

### April 8     Nottingham          6f hcp
*Won by 4l recording a speed figure of 68, running off a handicap
mark of 44, ridden by 7lb claiming apprentice R Ffrench.*

### April 17    Ripon               5f hcp
*Finished 4th of 19, beaten 2 lengths off a mark of 50, ridden this
time by Victoria Appleby who was unable to claim in this apprentice
race. The drop in trip didn't help here, but neither did a middle draw
in stall 11.*

### April 18    Thirsk              7f hcp
*Won by three-quarters of a length off a mark of 49, with Ffrench
back in the saddle. Backed down from 4-1 to 2-1 favourite. The
speed figure this time was 55, so only a plus 6, which suggested
he'd struggle to follow up this win.*

So it proved, with Meranti a well-beaten favourite at Nottingham
next time, with no apparent excuse. The right day to back him was
at Thirsk, where he had a favourable low draw and a stable
companion to make the early running, and then let him through on
the inside three furlongs from home! Next, let's look at another
sprinter: Runs In The Family.

She recorded a 'plus 24' when winning at Lingfield, though the
possibility existed that she had been flattered by a high draw, which
gave her a rail to run against and suited her front-running style. She
was beaten on each of her next four starts, although running
consistently, but in none of those races did she get the combination
of five-furlongs, a good draw and cut in the ground that seemed
ideal. Everything fell into place again at Warwick, when she was
allocated stall one in a five-furlong fillies' handicap run on good-to-

soft ground. Always in the first two, she led a furlong out and went to score by two and a half lengths, returning a 'plus 16' this time. The starting price was 7-2, after 9-2 had been available in the ring. She ran well again on her next start at Chepstow, finishing a close second under similar conditions, but her speed figure that day was only 62, less than her handicap mark of 64, and that pointed to the slight decline that followed.

Sometimes a deal of patience is required – Kinnescash produced a 'plus 17' in a ten-furlong handicap at Leicester, but was then sent back over hurdles by trainer Peter Bowen. He reappeared on the Flat at Windsor, and led at halfway in a 12-furlong handicap to win at 4-1. And sometimes the good figure is just an apparent one-off, as with Rockforce. He produced a 'plus 16' in a ten-furlong handicap at Newbury, in what looked a competitive twenty two runner contest, but that 25-1 success was one of the very few bright spots in a pretty dismal season for the stable of Mick Channon. Rockforce ran a fair fourth next time at Chester, but looked out of his depth at Epsom and Royal Ascot.

From a personal point of view, my biggest betting success from speed figures came later in the season with Cross The Border. This sprint handicapper had been a useful two-year-old, and had been rated in the 90's by the official handicapper at the start of his three-year-old season with Richard Hannon. Now a four-year-old and in the stable of David Nicholls, Cross The Border had dropped down to the basement level mark of 54. Between July 16 and August 28, he produced five victories, all signalled by the speed figures he produced in that period.

### July 16    Doncaster          5f hcp
*Won off a mark of 54, recording a speed figure of 73, Ridden by apprentice P Roberts, but no weight allowance as this was an apprentice race.*

### July 23    Catterick          5f hcp
*Won off the same mark of 54, ridden by trainer's wife Alex Greaves and recording a speed figure of 68. Backed from 7-4 to 11-10 favourite. A good thing, made more so by having the perfect draw in stall one.*

**August 18   Windsor                5f hcp**
*After a short break, well beaten in another apprentice race, this
time ridden by the trainer's son, running off a mark of 62. His draw
in stall 11 looked good in a field of 12, but runners came down the
middle that day at Windsor, and Cross The Border saw too much
daylight on rail and probably raced on slower ground.*

**August 22   Thirsk                 5f hcp**
*Won another apprentice handicap off 62, ridden by P Roberts,
recording a speed figure of 82 and returned at an astonishing 11-2,
having drifted from 7-2.*

**August 23   Beverley               5f hcp**
*Won again off 62 (no penalty for the apprentice race win), this time
under Alex Greaves again, and returned at 11-8 favourite. The
speed figure for this race was 72, but he never came off the bridle.*

**August 25   Epsom                  5f hcp**
*A big step up in class and a poor draw in stall 2, but he managed
third off a mark of 68 and returned a generous 6-1 for each-way
supporters, having opened at 3-1. The speed figure was 77, hardly
suggesting he was about to stop winning.*

**August 28   Musselburgh            5f hcp**
*Won again off a mark of 69, overcoming a poor draw under P
Roberts in yet another apprentice race. Given his Epsom form in
0-95 class just three days earlier, his starting price of 5-2 in this 0-
65 contest was amazing.*

That marked the end of his winning run as the handicapper took his
revenge, but he did manage a creditable third in a big field at
Doncaster off a mark of 76. He was then raised to a mark of 80 but
he couldn't handle that, as his earlier speed figures would suggest.
This string of runs by Cross The Border also highlighted another
theme that I found in several American texts – that of 'back-class'.
Translated into UK English, I take that to mean past evidence that a
horse could compete in a higher class of race. When such a horse
shows signs of a return to something like his best form, then he's
worth following, as he's going to be competing against horses who
have never shown his level of ability.

   Another sprint handicapper with a similar background,
Blessingindisguise, also enjoyed a run of success during 1997.

Having started his three-year-old season saddled with a handicap mark of 85, he failed to win during 1996 and things looked no better on his first two starts in 1997. He eventually won off a mark of 58 at Redcar in May, and then fulfilled the potential that his initial mark had suggested, winning another four races. The last of those came at Ascot in July, when he took a rated stakes off a mark of 86.

During that period he twice produced speed figures that met the criteria listed earlier, and his Ascot win was preceded by a 'plus 14' that highlighted his chance, even from 7lbs out of the handicap. However, unlike Cross The Border and Grey Kingdom, he didn't produce a big plus figure at the start of his run of success that would have marked him as one to follow. That was probably due to the way he was ridden from off the pace, doing just enough to win each time. The speed figure such a winner produces inevitably then depends on how fast the runner-up can go.

Having looked at finding winners from speed figures, I then asked myself if they would be just as useful in highlighting losers. If a horse who wins and produces a good 'plus' figure is worth supporting next time, would the reverse also hold true? If I noted those winners who produced a speed figure significantly lower than their handicap mark, would those horses be outclassed next time off a higher mark? And if so, could I produce a profit by opposing them?

In theory this sounds good – a winner producing a slow time has probably been flattered and quite possibly has benefited from holding a good position throughout. In practice it didn't work out that well. The fact that a winner has recorded a slow time isn't a firm indicator that he couldn't have gone faster if necessary.

I can point to examples that would support the theory, such as Tregaron, who recorded a 'minus 8' in winning the Victoria Cup at Ascot, a race that might be expected to be run in a fast time. He was well fancied for the Hunt Cup on the strength of that win, but ran poorly (admittedly after adverse rumours in the week prior to the race).

The enigmatic staying handicapper Top Cees won the Chester Cup, recording a 'minus 29', and was then a beaten 5-2 favourite for the Northumberland Plate on his next start. But both those races were run in atrocious conditions, and punters could be forgiven for thinking that speed figures don't have much relevance in testing ground. The Chester Cup runners finished spread out all over the Roodeye, with fifty lengths between the first and sixth horses home.

If there are other reasons for opposing a fancied horse, then a negative speed figure would provide further evidence for consideration, but I wouldn't want to oppose a horse simply on the evidence of a slow time – at least not on turf.

# The pace of the race

On July 5, the running of the Eclipse Stakes at Sandown Park produced one of the most controversial and most discussed incidents of the entire Flat season. The line-up was:

| 1 | PILSUDSKI | 5-9-07 | M Stoute | M J Kinane |
|---|---|---|---|---|
| 2 | ALLIED FORCES | 4-9-07 | S Bin Suroor | L Dettori |
| 3 | SASURU | 4-9-07 | G Wragg | M Hills |
| 4 | BOSRA SHAM | 4-9-04 | H Cecil | K Fallon |
| 5 | BENNY THE DIP | 3-8-10 | J Gosden | W Ryan |

The build-up to this contest had included all the usual overblown analysis afforded to Group 1 class races. Even ageing pundits, who normally only use the word 'pace' as a prefix of 'maker' when visiting their doctor, felt able to discuss the likelihood of a slowly run race. Since Bosra Sham had shown a tremendously powerful finish when given a good pace in her previous race at Royal Ascot, I could see no reason why any of the other four contestants would choose to commit suicide by setting up the race for the favourite. I didn't think that a slow race was likely, I thought it was certain.

Some of the discussion centred on which of the runners would be suited by a slow pace. This was palpable nonsense, in that the key factor in a slow race is racetrack position, and that can rarely be predicted in advance in a race of this nature. If the early pace is so slow that the front-runner can conserve his resources and complete the final quarter mile in less than 24 seconds, then any horse behind the leader at the two-furlong pole has to run faster than that to win. Even for a horse with the ability of Bosra Sham, that is close to impossible. In a race run at a normal pace, the apparent fast-finisher is overtaking horses that are slowing down. In a slowly run contest like the Eclipse, the horse in front never gets tired, and doesn't slow down – and, as subsequent events confirmed, getting past Pilsudski wasn't easy, even if he was flat to the boards!

In this field test of the importance of pace, Pilsudski got the best ride and won the race as a result. Sitting close in second, he was the first to go for home, and never looked likely to be caught. Fallon on Bosra Sham was widely criticised for attempting to go for a gap on the inside three furlongs from the finish, and failing to get through. His problems had been apparent from the start, once he had settled two or three lengths off the pace.

This race was a perfect demonstration of the sort of thing that happens every day of the Flat season, especially in races with small fields, but it was a rare example of pace actually being discussed in the racing media. When the pace is mentioned, it usually only happens after a slowly run race, when one or more trainers will utter that priceless cliché, "We could have done with a stronger pace". There is an obvious response to that, but it ignores the fact that, for most horses, setting their own pace isn't an option that allows them to produce their best. After two hundred years of turf racing, if front-running had been proven to win more races than it lost, then the tactic would be more common.

There is an intriguing parallel between this aspect of turf racing and human athletics. In common with any sports enthusiast, I've lost count of the number of one-paced British front-runners I've seen swamped in the closing stages of championship races. At the top level of athletics, beyond the sprint distances, it is the runners who can produce the fastest final lap that reign supreme. And it is also the pattern that predominates in turf racing. But in both cases, a slowly run race can change the situation – then it pays to hold a good position when the final sprint begins. Think of those 1,500 metre finals in which the runners are tripping over each other for the first two laps, with David Coleman repeatedly telling us that "somebody will have to make a break soon". Someone does (usually the plucky Brit with no finishing kick!) and the race immediately spreads out, leaving those at the back with no hope of making up ground.

The comparison with athletics also highlights the difficulty of pace analysis in this country. Whereas David Coleman can call on lap times for the race in progress, and a vast database of past evidence, punters are limited to the subjective estimates of the racereaders for the major form guides. In view of that, I don't think it's worth attempting anything subtler than grading races in three categories for pace – fast, average and slow.

**Fast** Also called a strong pace and usually results in all the front-runners finishing well beaten. Suits a certain type of horse, which explains why the winners of the big handicaps at the major meetings often can't reproduce that form when running in a smaller field elsewhere. Don't be fooled by a race in which one or two horses establish a big early lead. The remainder of the field ignore them, and most of the runners are setting only an average pace. This sort of race is easily identified if Derek Thompson is commentating, as he'll invariably say "They're not messing about here", before the runners have covered a furlong.

**Average** Runners bunched, but not falling over each other. Winner can come from front or behind, and form is likely to work out in future races.

**Slow** Nobody willing to make the running, several horses fighting for their head, positions changing frequently. If the slow pace persists beyond the first two or three furlongs, then the horse in front has a considerable advantage when the pace does eventually quicken. The result is likely to be false.

None of that is very scientific, but it's all we have! Knowing the pace after the event helps with analysing results, especially when a slowly run race is the explanation for a winner that you didn't expect. But from a punting point of view, the ideal is to be able to predict the pace in advance. Sadly, few slow races are as easy to spot as the Eclipse Stakes.

I look for two possible pace outcomes that can produce good bets, or avoid bad ones:

- I try to avoid betting in any race at seven furlongs or farther unless I can find at least one probable pacesetter in the field. In general, sprints and most two-year-old races are run at a proper pace, but any field of eight runners or less should ring alarm bells in all other races.

- I look for races in which there is just one regular front-runner with form good enough to suggest he can win. Even on turf, an unopposed front-runner able to set an average or slow pace has a tactical advantage.

A good example of the lone front-runner was the performance of Fahris at Goodwood in the Group 3 Select Stakes. With just five runners, this was a prime candidate for a slow pace, but Fahris had shown the ability to run well from the front in previous races, and had never been out of the first two when winning at Newmarket in April. His three main rivals looked equally certain to be held up, whatever the pace.

Desert Story was sent off the 5-4 favourite, but was untried at this ten-furlong trip, and likely therefore to be patiently ridden. Green Card and Amid Albadu were the other contenders, with the latter the only possible challenger for the lead, but in my view flattered by his all-the-way win in lesser company at Epsom last time. Fahris drifted from 9-4 to 100-30, when I bet £2,000/600.

He jumped out smartly and was five lengths ahead after a furlong, even though he was only setting an average pace. I thought the race was already decided at that point, and so it proved. Ray Cochrane dictated the pace, kicked on three furlongs out and nothing ever looked likely to find the speed necessary to cut back his lead. He won by six lengths from Desert Story, a performance that persuaded punters to make him a 9-2 shot next time at Ascot. But in that race, he was meeting other front-runners and faded into fourth place behind Kingfisher Mill.

It's the nature of pace analysis that it doesn't always work out as planned. Faced with the seven-furlong conditions race at Newbury on July 18, I identified a probable lack of pace which might work to the advantage of Easy Dollar. He was a habitual front-runner, well drawn in stall two, ridden by that excellent judge of pace, Jason Weaver, and a seven-furlong specialist.

He set off in front as expected, but my script didn't include a scene in which the 20-1 shot Mithali would take him on. The pair were probably eight lengths clear by the time they reached the turn for home, and I had already mentally torn up my ticket. The pace was much too fast to be sustainable and, sure enough, they finished sixth and seventh, well behind the five who had been held up, with only the 100-1 shot Raheen unable to catch them. It's a defining moment in the education of a punter when you finally realise that being ten lengths in front at halfway (in a turf Flat race at least) is a bad sign, not a promise of victory.

The Goodwood winner, Fahris, also featured in a race that demonstrated the likelihood of a false result in a race with a small field and a slow pace. The Group 3 Scottish Classic attracted just three runners, with Fahris as the 5-6 favourite, Even Top at 11-8 and Crystal Hearted at 8-1. The latter was allowed to dawdle along in front for the first two furlongs and as a result had the best position when the sprint for home began, and held on by a neck from Fahris. The trainers of the beaten horses both offered the usual excuse that they would have preferred a stronger pace, but what did they expect before the race was run? At least with Fahris, the lesson was learnt, leading to the win described above.

Pace alone isn't going to identify that many betting opportunities, but it can highlight winners. More importantly, the identification of a lack of pace can avoid wasted bets in races producing a false result.

# Quick on the draw

When I wrote about the effect of the draw in *Against The Crowd,* it was at a fairly basic level of understanding – a sort of GCSE pass but no higher. Looking at past statistics, I could identify whether it was better, over a specific course and distance, to be drawn high or low, but I was only looking at the winners. I stressed the need to concentrate on recent results, rather than a survey of the past ten years, emphasising that things can change that might reverse the effect of the draw. Those ideas are quite adequate, and can at least avoid a punter consistently backing horses who have little chance because of their draw. But I felt at the end of 1995 that I could gain more by further work.

Over the past two years, I have developed my understanding by watching how races are run and observing how a jockey's tactics may be forced on him by the vagaries of the draw. I think I can best explain this by giving a couple of examples.

First consider a six-furlong handicap run at Salisbury in June. Talking with Ian Carnaby before racing, he asked if I expected the favourite, Sir Joey, from his local stable of Pat Murphy, to win. I explained that I felt Kieren Fallon had a problem as a result of his number one draw. With the stalls on the far side at Salisbury that meant he would start on the outside, but with only eight runners, I wouldn't have seen that as a problem a few years back. By trying to envisage how the race would be run, I could foresee that Fallon would be faced with two, equally unsatisfactory choices. He could break quickly, in which case Sir Joey would see too much daylight and almost certainly wouldn't run his race. Or he could deliberately miss the break and then switch to his right soon after the start. This would give Sir Joey the cover he needs to produce his best, but would cost him three or four lengths in the first hundred yards. With no guarantee of a strong pace, that could leave Fallon with a tight bunch in front of him, with a furlong to run and no space to manoeuvre. Either way, he would look poor value at around 2-1.

Fallon took the second option and suffered a nightmare run, squeezed out between the first two home inside the final fifty yards, and getting no sympathy from the stewards. Stall one wouldn't have been ideal for any of the runners in the race, but for Sir Joey it was the worst possible draw.

A race that many more readers will have seen was the Group 1 Queen Elizabeth Stakes over the round mile at Ascot in September 1995. The winner was Bahri, ridden by Willie Carson, who took the horse to the outside of the track on the run up from Swinley Bottom. He found some faster ground there, thanks to the tree cover that keeps most of the rain off the course. Meanwhile, his 'pacemaker' Muhab was leading the group who were taking the normal route along the inside rail, and Richard Hills was ensuring that the pace they were going was a shade slower than Bahri! Once Bahri had cut the corner and joined the others, the race was over, as he was clear, and went on to win by six lengths, with the 8-13 favourite Ridgewood Pearl held in second. That the tactics had decided the result was reinforced when that mare went on to win the Breeders' Cup Mile on her next start. But Carson was only able to deploy his plan thanks to the draw.

Bahri was allocated stall one, nearest the outside fence at the start, so that he could move under the trees without any other rider being involuntarily taken across with him. And to complete the perfect set-up, Muhab, the pacemaker, was in stall two and could thus ensure that every other runner was taken to the inside rail. The unfortunate Johnny Murtagh on Ridgewood Pearl had drawn stall five and couldn't have followed Bahri, even if he had been aware of the tactics that Carson would use. A classic example of tactics dictated by the draw, in the sense that only the draw made them possible.

In trying to anticipate how the draw will affect the way a race is run, I use a sequence of questions, as follows:

- What is the draw advantage over this course and distance, and how important is a good draw?
- What is the ideal way to ride this horse in this race?
- Does the draw make it easier or harder for the jockey to execute the ideal tactics?
- Can I estimate the loss or gain in lengths?

To demonstrate this in practice, let's look at the Group 3 Hungerford Stakes, run over seven furlongs 64 yards at Newbury on August 15. This race is run on the round track, starting in the chute halfway round the home turn. The horses run about one and a half furlongs before making the final turn into the home straight. The two main contenders were Dazzle (7-4 fav) and Decorated Hero (11-4) – nothing else started at less than 8-1. The advantage over the round seven furlongs at Newbury generally lies with the low numbers in the draw, who have the inside on the turn, but the bias is not that strong. On a scale of one to ten, I would place the importance of a low draw at five.

Then look at the next three points for each horse in turn, starting with Dazzle:

> *Dazzle can pull hard and needs to be covered up and delivered as late as possible.*

> *Dazzle is drawn nine of ten, on the outside, which gives Reid more problems in getting her settled than if she was drawn nearer the middle to inside.*

> *If Dazzle runs wide throughout the race it will cost her two to three lengths.*

And then Decorated Hero:

> *Decorated Hero can front-run, or sit close to the pace and challenge late.*

> *Decorated Hero is drawn two of ten and Dettori should be able to dictate his chosen tactic, with Bin Rosie in stall one highly unlikely to take him on if he decides to lead.*

> *Decorated Hero should be on the rail and is likely to save at least one length.*

In a strong market at Newbury, Decorated Hero was available at 7-2 and 100-30 shortly before the off and I bet £2,400/700. He sat on the rail behind a medium pace, with Bin Rosie boxed in behind him, pulled out and quickened one-furlong out for a comfortable win. It was a simple plan, perfectly executed and made to look easy

– Dettori at his best. I suspect he can do the sort of analysis I've described above, almost without knowing how it's achieved. Dazzle refuse to settle, was always at least four or five horses wide of the rail and had an impossible task by halfway.

I have found that running through these questions can produce benefits, even on a track where it would be normal to assume that the draw confers no advantage on any particular horse. Of course, sitting in my study at home, deciding the ideal tactics that a jockey should use to take advantage of a good draw, or to overcome a bad draw, doesn't mean that the race will be run exactly as I envisaged it! Always remember the American professional punter who declared that:

"If jockeys had brains, their heads wouldn't fit into those size four hats."

Indeed, it should come as no surprise to learn that it's the top men, such as Dettori, who seem to have considered the possibilities – or perhaps the genius for being in the right place throughout a race is instinctive.

One track at which the draw has a particular importance is Goodwood. Races over the round course have always tended to favour those drawn high. But during 1997, the influence seemed to be greater then ever. A poor draw can be overcome, but only by a jockey who has noted the importance of being close to the far rail by the time the horses turn for home with just over three furlongs to run.

During the final three two-day meetings in August and September, if you could predict the horse who would be leading past the three-furlong pole in all races of seven furlongs and over, you would have achieved a better than 50 per cent strike-rate. Watching from the usual side-on position from the stands, or on television, it is difficult to see why the position on the rail is so important. But a walk down to the gate where the horses come out onto the course, just beyond the winning post, changes the perspective.

From side-on the course appears to be straight throughout the final three furlongs, but looking back up the course from the finish, it becomes clear that it is shaped more like an EEC non-approved banana. The turn into the 'straight' is about two furlongs in duration, and the turn is approximately 90 degrees. But from the three-furlong pole to the finish, the course continues to curve gently in the same direction, with a noticeable elbow just before the one-furlong pole. Seen from this position, it becomes crystal clear that the wider a horse has to move to make its challenge, the more ground it will have to cover.

In addition, the natural lie of the land falls sharply away on the other side of the rail during the final two furlongs. This is visible on TV, if you look at the cars parked on the inside of the course near the finish. I'm no gardener, but it seems likely that when the course is watered, the ground closest to the rail must drain quickly, given the slope down which the water can run. I did study geography, and I do know why you don't find rivers at the top of a hill!

So the horse on the far rail has less distance to cover, is running on faster ground than his rivals, and of course has the rail to keep him straight. He can only be challenged on one side, so his rider has no problem deciding where to carry his whip. And being in front, he isn't subject to the interference that those behind him often suffer in tight finishes at Goodwood. No wonder that horses who look likely to be swallowed up passing the two-furlong pole, regularly run on 'gamely' to repel all challenges.

A good example of this effect could be seen in the performance of Gadge in a seven-furlong handicap on May 22.

Gadge had won his last two starts, at Bath and Thirsk, prominent throughout and leading over two furlongs from home in both of those one-mile handicaps. I had seen the race at Bath, where he looked to me to have more in hand than the winning margin of one and a half lengths would suggest. But what made him a really good bet here was his draw in stall 12 of the 15 runners.

With the three runners drawn higher all being hold-up horses, he looked almost certain to have a clear run in front and to obtain the vital position on the far rail. A price of 9-2 doesn't often look attractive in a handicap with so many runners, but I had no doubt that it was value in this case, and bet £2,700/600. Gadge made all the running, taken on early by the poorly-drawn Grey Kingdom (stall one), and holding on from Dancing Image, who did well to take second from his draw in stall three, but was forced to make his challenge very wide.

The performance of Dancing Image suggested he was the horse to follow from this race, and he did eventually reward supporters when winning over course and distance in August, having previously finished fourth in the Royal Hunt Cup and sixth in the Hong Kong Trophy at Sandown, when again poorly drawn. He was well backed in each of those races, although I suspect that had more to do with the presence of Dettori in the saddle than in any wider appreciation of his efforts to overcome the disadvantage of stall three against Gadge. But he does highlight the potential benefit of noting horses who run well against the bias, whether from a poor draw, or by running on the slower part of the track, or both.

Another aspect of betting on the strength of a bias, is the opportunity to take advantage of something seen in the early races on the card. I attended Newbury in May, and with the ground riding very soft, it was clear that the stand rail was the best place to be on the straight course.

The second race on Saturday was a six-furlong maiden for two-year-olds, in which the three highest drawn runners in a field of 14 filled the first three places. A group of four on the stand rail finished nine lengths clear of those running down the centre. The fifth race was a six-furlong handicap for three-year-olds, which, at first glance, I had dismissed as a possible betting event. But with the form horse, Sharp Hat (fourth and fifth in big fields at Newmarket) drawn 13 of the 13 runners, a trip to the ring was in order. Even then, I expected that my analysis would hardly be unique, and I anticipated a price of 5-2 or less about Sharp Hat. To my surprise he drifted from early 11-4 out to 4-1, at which point I took £2,000/500.

He won by three lengths, with the runners drawn 12 and ten following him home. As with Gadge, I had backed the form horse, but the value came from the considerable advantage they both gained from the track bias. Sharp Hat was raised 7lbs for that win, and not surprisingly failed to record another success in seven starts.

That bias at Newbury was only clear after watching the races. It is by no means certain that it will be repeated the next time there is soft ground, as I've seen plenty of occasions when the middle is favoured under similar conditions.

Much the same problem arises at Haydock, York and Doncaster, all of which seem to favour high numbers on the straight course at times. But it wouldn't be profitable to back apparently well-drawn horses blindly at any of those tracks. One of the big advantages of the arrival of SIS and the Racing Channel, is the opportunity to see races for yourself and make your own judgement as to the prevailing bias.

# Ideas for different races

In addition to the theories already discussed, I also use some specific approaches for the different types of race run on the Flat. These ideas apply equally on the turf and the AW tracks, but are included here to avoid duplication in later chapters.

## 1 Maiden Races

I don't often bet in maiden races – a check on my records for 1997 shows just 12 such wagers – although, as they included five winners, perhaps I should play more often. In general, confronted with a field of maidens, I'm all too painfully aware of my lack of knowledge about breeding and conformation to want to step in, especially at a short price. Certainly there have been occasions when I've picked out a winner from paddock inspection, but it's easy to forget all the other good looking types who turned out to have the pedigree of a BMW but the speed of a Reliant Robin. Maiden races are the favoured playground of the inside information specialists, and I'm happy to leave them to their own devices and concentrate on races where the form is more settled.

Of those five winners in 1997, four were backed because they showed me something special, either in the paddock or on the way to the start (or both), and one was a simple value bet on a 6-1 shot against a very beatable short-priced favourite. In every case, the bet was only possible because I was actually at the track, as the evidence that prompted me to play wouldn't have been available elsewhere.

Although I might not bet in most maidens, I certainly watch them carefully as they will provide clues that form the basis of bets on later races. I try to second guess the official handicapper by making my own assessment for each maiden race winner, giving a personal handicap mark and a prediction of the type of race the horse might be capable of winning, or not as the case may be. To do this I take into account several factors:

- The ease of the win
- The grade of the track and the value of the race

- The speed figure
- The distances between the first six home
- The breeding of the winner
- The trainer

Here's an example of a maiden race winner who produced a winning bet next time he ran – Ghalib at Newbury on September 19. A three-year-old maiden that late in the season wouldn't normally be expected to throw up a useful horse, but the analysis suggested otherwise:

- He won more easily than the one-length margin would suggest and overcame inexperience on his debut
- Newbury is a Grade 1 track and the race was Class D and worth £5,000 added
- The winner's speed figure was 89
- The sixth horse in a field of 12 was beaten 15 lengths over one mile
- The winner is a son of Group 1 miler Soviet Star, out of a dam who won at a mile and a half
- Trained by Dick Hern

The important clues here are the way the field was spread out – if they finish in a bunch it's unlikely that all of them are useful – and the fact that Ghalib had been kept in training despite presumably having problems that had kept him off the track until this late in his three-year-old season. He had also seemed very green in the paddock before the race, and I had dismissed him as a probable winner on that basis. I concluded that Ghalib was likely to run up to a BHB mark of at least 100, and possibly better.

His next run was in a conditions race at Ascot on October 10, in a small field, again over one mile. Obviously I wasn't alone in my assessment of his Newbury win, as he was sent off 11-8 favourite, though I did find a little 13-8 and 6-4 to produce a bet of £1,250/800. This was one of the few occasions during the year that I broke my usual rule of not betting under 2-1, but he looked gilt-edged in this company and justified support by an easy two lengths. He went on to finish a close fourth in a Listed race at Newmarket, suggesting that a mark of about 105 represented his merit at the end of 1997. If he stays in training, I'll be watching out for him at ten furlongs on soft ground during 1998.

Another example from Newbury demonstrates the opposite result – a maiden race winner who I felt was over-rated. In fact the race at Newbury on July 18 was a novice stakes and thus open to previous winners, but nine of the ten runners were making their racecourse debut. There were several well-bred and expensive youngsters on display, but the hype was all for the winner, Ariant, a £675,000 yearling now with John Gosden. He was sent off the 4-11 favourite and won by a neck. Post-race reports suggested that the winner would move up to Group class for his next race, but that looked optimistic to me. The race had been slowly run, the first eight home were covered by only six lengths, and the speed figure was a modest 57. On this evidence I would only rate Ariant at about 80 on the BHB-scale - good enough to win a nursery, but he obviously wasn't going to run in that sort of race!

The winner returned in the Gimcrack Stakes at York, went off at 6-1 with Dettori on board, and finished tailed off last of eight, beaten almost fifteen lengths. He didn't reappear after that, and the horses he beat at Newbury did nothing to suggest that wasn't his true form, as between them they failed to win a single race before the end of the year.

It's a lesson that, of course, applies to all races, but even if you're not having a bet, always watch maiden races with an eye to the future. If you predict a top class future for a maiden winner and it makes its next appearance in a 0-60 handicap, you've either found the bet of the year, or you need a new pair of binoculars.

## 2 Claiming Races

Claiming races have been a part of the Flat race programme in Britain for many years, but their numbers have increased in the nineties as the number of meetings has expanded to meet the demands of the off-course bookmakers. The concept has been imported from the USA, where claimers make up the majority of races on most cards. Whereas an ordinary class of horse in this country might be referred to as a 70-rated handicapper, in the

States the same horse would be a $15,000 claimer – the claiming price becomes the marker by which the animal's merit is measured.

A claiming race provides the opportunity for the trainer to allocate the weight the horse will carry, rather than leaving it to the official handicapper. The conditions for a typical British claimer read as follows:

For three-year-olds and upward, each claimable at their advertised claiming price. Weights: Colts and geldings 9st 5lb; fillies 9st. Allowances: for each £500 below the maximum advertised claiming price of £10,000 1lb. (Minimum advertised claiming price £2,000.)

Translating that into plain (well plainer anyway) English, the trainer declares the valuation he puts on his horse at the time of entry, and the weight the horse carries depends on that price. If the trainer values his horse at the maximum price of £10,000, then he carries 9st 5lb (or 9st if a filly or mare). If he puts a price of £7,000, then his horse carries 6lbs less than the top weight, based on the condition of one pound less for each £500 drop in the price. The minimum weight in this race is 8st 3lb for a colt or gelding valued at £2,000, or 7st 12lb for a filly/mare.

So we have a race specifically designed for moderate horses, whose connections are prepared to lose them after the race if anyone is willing to pay the asking price. Clearly, if you think your horse is worth more than £10,000, you don't enter for this race in the first place. Equally, if you have a horse capable of winning any sort of race, you are sure to value it at more than £2,000, so that entering on bottom weight might ensure a victory in this race but would also guarantee that somebody else takes the horse home.

The assumption upon which the conditions of the race are based is that weight can bring together horses worth £2,000 with those worth £10,000.

That is a false assumption, and punters can benefit by concentrating their attention on the higher-priced, and therefore higher weighted horses, in claiming races. This is better understood in the USA, where claimers are restricted to a much narrower price range, thus bringing together horses of approximately equal merit at more or less level weights. So I'd offer three general pieces of advice for betting in claiming races:

- Concentrate on the horses entered for a price within £5,000 of the maximum price in the conditions. The lower the maximum, the more this applies.

- Give preference to previous form in claiming races over form in maidens or handicaps.

- Be wary of apparently top class horses running in claimers – they probably have a problem; else why are connections willing to let them go cheaply?

A good example of that last category was at Sandown on September 17, when the very useful sprinter Venture Capitalist ran in a five-furlong claimer and was sent off 6-4 favourite in a field of 20. His previous run had been in the valuable Portland Handicap at Doncaster, and his handicap mark of 98 made him look a good thing at Sandown. Venture Capitalist was hampered by a moderate draw in stall nine, and could only manage fourth, beaten by horses who would have been receiving much more weight in a handicap. Subsequent defeats in conditions events at Hamilton and Redcar seemed to confirm that Venture Capitalist was well below his best, but his trainer had provided punters with that information for free when he entered him in a claiming race.

I managed a winning bet in a claimer at Newbury on May 28 by applying the second and third points above. Favourite for this fairly valuable claimer was Mr Bombastique, from the Barry Hills yard, seventh in a rated stakes at York off 87 on his previous start. Already wary of this apparently good thing, I was further encouraged to oppose him at odds-on when he pottered to start on the prevailing fast ground. The second favourite, Double Gold, had won a claimer at Warwick by eight lengths just five days earlier, and a bet of £1,600/500 was rewarded with a five-length win here. It's worth noting that the trainer of Double Gold, Brian Meehan, has shown himself a shrewd user of claiming races to find opportunities for his lesser horses.

## 3 Limited Stakes

Whenever the BHB race planning department come up with a new type of contest, punters should make every effort to understand the conditions and to identify the type of horse that will produce the winners. In doing so they will place themselves at an advantage over other punters and usually be better informed than the trainers as to what is required. Limited stakes were introduced to the programme in 1993, and during their early days provided some excellent betting opportunities. Even today, I rate them a valuable source of bets and well worth some research.

To demonstrate how a shrewd trainer can take advantage of the conditions of a limited stakes and at the same time provide a gilt-edged bet, let's look back to that first season, to one of the first bets I had in this type of race. It was at Bath on 12 June, 1993. The race was a 0-60 limited stakes for three-year-olds over the extended 11-furlong trip. The standard conditions of entry for these races are quite simple – any horse with an official rating equal to or less than the limit on the date of entry can run. Penalties are applied for every win during the six months prior to the race, and fillies and mares receive an allowance, usually of 5lbs. These conditions clearly favour a filly, who will receive weight from a colt or gelding who she would meet on level terms in a handicap. They don't favour a colt or gelding who has won three or four races in the last six months, as his accumulated penalty for those wins will mean that he is much worse off at the weights than he would be in a handicap.

When I studied these races, I soon realised that the likeliest winner was a horse who was unpenalised for recent wins but had shown form that suggested he was capable of earning a handicap mark higher than the top limit for the race. If the selection was a filly in receipt of a sex allowance, all the better. I also spotted that there was an anomaly in the conditions, in the fact that a horse qualified for the race on the basis of the official rating that applied on the date of entry. The current Flat handicap system provides for ratings to be adjusted once each week, with the revised rating taking effect on a Saturday. Any horse running in a handicap on a Saturday, runs off the mark he acquires on that day, not the mark that applied when he was entered for the race. The race at Bath in 1993 showed perfectly how this provided an opening for a trainer who got his timing right.

By the end of May, Allesca had run several times and had been allocated a handicap mark of 60 after running fourth in a 0-65 limited stakes at Doncaster over ten furlongs. On Monday 31 May, she won a 12-furlong maiden at Chepstow on soft ground, by one and a half lengths and ten lengths.

When the handicapper assessed this performance, he revised Allesca's mark up to 70, to take effect from Saturday 12 June. However, when trainer Mark Usher entered Allesca for the 0-60 race at Bath, she qualified to run as the entry was made on the previous Monday, June 7, at which time she still had her old mark of 60. Thus on June 12, I found myself looking at a filly with an official rating of 70 running in a race in which no other runner was rated higher than 60, and yet meeting them on level weight terms. Her penalty for the Chepstow win was balanced by her fillies' allowance. Not only were the weights massively in her favour, she was also proven over the trip and on the prevailing good-to-soft ground. On the Friday evening, I had no doubt that all this would be equally clear to everybody else, so I was amazed to find that Allesca wasn't even predicted as favourite in the Saturday trade papers. That honour went to the Martin Pipe-trained Buglet, a gelding that the stable had claimed after he finished second in a ten-furlong selling handicap at Nottingham, running off a mark of 56.

In the event, Buglet was sent off 2-1 favourite, with Allesca at 11-4 after support at 3-1 (guess who!). Allesca was ten lengths clear as they entered the final furlong, but jockey Nick Adams proceeded to terrify punters by easing down to a walk and almost being caught out as Buglet finished well to get within one length at the line. Off her new mark Allesca went on to emphasise what a good thing she had been at Bath by reappearing five days later at Royal Ascot and running fourth of sixteen in the valuable 12-furlong handicap for three-year-olds run on Gold Cup day. That sort of golden opportunity doesn't appear often, as trainers have become more adept at placing horses in these races and punters have latched on to the anomaly I've described. But even in 1997, there have still been cases of horses running in this type of race when their revised handicap mark would render them ineligible.

The best example from my own 1997 betting record concerns a sprinting filly called Songsheet. The sequence of changes to her handicap mark is quite complex, so pay attention at the back and take notes!

On Tuesday 27 May, following a series of defeats, the handicapper dropped her mark from 62 to 60, with the change to take effect on Saturday 31 May. On Wednesday 28 May, Songsheet, running off her old mark of 62, won a five-furlong handicap at Folkestone in good style, with recent winner Runs In The Family over two lengths back in third. On the following Tuesday, June 3, the handicapper again revised her rating, putting her up to 69, the change to take effect on Saturday 7 June.

On Wednesday 4 June, her trainer entered her for a 0-60 limited stakes to be run at Windsor on Monday 9 June. Although she never ran in a race off a mark of 60, that was her official rating from May 31 until June 6, and thus she was qualified to run in the 0-60 contest. On Monday 9 June 9, she ran in that 0-60 limited stakes, although by then she had an official mark of 69, which would have applied if she had been running in a handicap on the same date. Once again the penalty for her recent win was wiped out by her fillies' allowance.

With several front runners in the race to provide the strong pace that suits her, and a prime draw in stall ten of the 11 runners, I made her an odds-on shot to win the race. I still don't know why she was available at 15-8, before going off as 7-4 favourite – perhaps the defeat of five previous favourites at the meeting had left backers potless, but she won like an odds-on shot. By the way, her prospects in a 0-60 contest were further advertised by a speed figure of 74 for her Folkestone win. I breached my usual rule of not betting under 2-1 for this special case and collected on a £1,050/600 wager.

## 4 Pattern Races

Moving to the opposite end of the racing scale, let's start with the cream in the Group 1 races that provide the championships for the various age groups and distances. I don't often bet in Group 1 contests, simply because they tend to be analysed to death, both on the day and for weeks in advance. By the time the race is run every tiny detail of each horse's form and training routine has been considered, and the ante-post market will ensure that any value has been squeezed out by the Big Three (or probably Two by the time you read this). In fact, this media hype can lead to excessively short prices about the favourites in Group 1 races, with the betting tending to reflect the number of column inches attracted by each horse.

During the 1997 season, a number of short-priced hot-shots were turned over:

| | | |
|---|---|---|
| 2,000 Guineas | Revoque | 10-3 |
| 1,000 Guineas | Pas De Reponse | 5-2 |
| Lockinge Stakes | Spinning World | 6-4 |
| Derby | Entrepreneur | 4-6 |
| St James Palace Stakes | Desert King | 2-1 |
| Coronation Stakes | Sleepytime | 5-6 |
| Eclipse Stakes | Bosra Sham | 4-7 |
| July Cup | Royal Applause | 11-10 |
| King George & Queen Elizabeth | Helissio | 11-10 |
| Sussex Stakes | Starborough | 9-4 |
| International Stakes | Bosra Sham | 4-5 |
| Yorkshire Oaks | Reams Of Verse | 4-7 |
| Queen Elizabeth II Stakes | Revoque | 9-4 |
| Cheveley Park | Cape Verdi | 11-8 |
| Middle Park | Arkadian Hero | 10-11 |

If that list hasn't convinced you that Group 1 races are generally much more competitive than the media pundits would have you believe, then you'd better stick to the National Lottery. Knowing that those horses might be beaten was a help, but you still need to find the winners to make a profit in the fixed-odds market. However, most Group 1 races attract the attention of the spread betting firms, and it was certainly possible to make money by selling any favourite starting at less then 2-1 in a Group 1 contest last season.

I would like to follow that with some equivalent pearl of wisdom about Group 2 races, but frankly I can't see any trends in them that are worthy of note. As their title suggests, they seem just to fall between Group 1 and Group 3 (that may win the prize for the most blindingly obvious comment in the entire book!). So let's move on to the Group 3 and Listed races, where I can offer some advice:

- Any horse capable of winning a handicap or Rated Stakes from a mark of more than 100 is worthy of consideration in these races, especially if backed up by a 100+ speed figure.

- The weight penalties imposed for previous pattern race wins really make a difference. These minor Group races are often contested by horses who would run at more or less level weights in a handicap, so an additional four or seven pounds penalty significantly reduces the chances of success.

- It can pay to note past patterns of winners, as to age, penalties and previous races.

- Be very wary of a Group 1 winner appearing in these races. Apart from having to carry a large penalty, you have to ask whether they are merely using the race as preparation for bigger things.

I had one of my very best bets of the entire Flat season by following that last suggestion. The race was one of three new Listed contests staged at Newbury on September 18. They lined up as follows for the one-mile three-furlong Doubleprint Arc Trial:

| 1 | SWAIN | 5-9-9 | Saeeed Bin Suroor | L Dettori |
|---|---|---|---|---|
| 2 | ARABIAN STORY | 4-9-2 | Lord Huntingdon | K Fallon |
| 3 | CLERKENWELL | 4-9-2 | M Stoute | J Reid |
| 4 | POSIDONAS | 5-9-2 | P Cole | T Quinn |
| 5 | SUNBEAM DANCE | 3-8-9 | Saeed Bin Suroor | R Hills |

Sunbeam Dance, running as a pacemaker for Swain, could be dismissed. Clerkenwell was being prepared for a possible trip to Australia to run in the Melbourne Cup, and looked to have no chance over this trip. That left me with the question of how hard would connections be trying with Swain. His last run had been a victory in the King George at Ascot, worth almost £300,000 in prizemoney, and much more in prestige. He was also in line to run in the Prix de l'Arc de Triomphe at Longchamp, just seventeen days after this Newbury race, again for massive money and reputation. If things got tight in the final furlong, would we really expect to see Frankie put Swain under pressure for the sake of a £50,000 Listed race? I was confident that the answer must be no. Add into the equation a trip short of his best and ground faster than at Ascot and I rated Swain just about the worst 1-2 favourite of the year.

Left with choice of Arabian Story and Posidonas, I plumped unhesitatingly for the former at this trip. He had finished second in a similar contest in Sweden last time, form that might be worth anything, or nothing. But his win in a ten-furlong Listed race here at Newbury in July had been impressive, and had been achieved in a fast time (speed figure 118) despite the small field. I backed Arabian Story at 13-2 and 11-2 as he quickly closed in to 9-2 at the off. From the start, Dettori set Swain a stiff task by ignoring his pacemaker and settling in last place. He still looked sure to win when challenging at the furlong pole, but although he edged in front, Dettori didn't go for everything and was caught in the final fifty yards – by both Arabian Story and Posidonas, with the latter prevailing by a short-head. Well, I said it was one of the best bets of the year, but I didn't say it had won!

With the benefit of hindsight, the obvious question is why didn't I back both Posidonas and Arabian Story, accepting odds of around 11-4 the pair against Swain? There are several professionals who adopt exactly this sort of policy, and often back two, three or even more horses in the same race. I'll discuss this in more detail in the later chapter on staking.

# What is your edge?

One of the most surprising, but least discussed things about a horse race, is that anyone should ever think it possible to predict the result. If the thoroughbred horse wasn't supremely consistent, the entire sport would collapse, at least as a betting proposition. It's well worth taking a moment to consider just how narrow the margin can be between success and failure.

In a Flat race over one mile, if we award the winner a performance figure of 100 per cent, then a runner beaten by one length at the finish has finished just nine feet behind over a total distance of five thousand, two hundred and eighty feet. That means that the second horse has run 99.8 per cent, and even a horse beaten five lengths has run 99 per cent as well as the winner. Just a one per cent difference in the level of performance - but in common with most punters, I'd expect the two horses to finish in the same order if they met again under similar conditions. Certainly, looked at in this way, the common remark by a trainer that his horse was "only 90 per cent today – he'll improve" takes a bit of believing.

The racing authorities set out to reinforce the closeness of the competition in several ways. The first and most obvious is the handicap mark, but the 'competitive racing' initiative of recent years was designed with the same objective in mind. I mentioned both of these as factors that helped to persuade me at the end of 1995, that I needed to review my methods for turf Flat racing. Having concluded that traditional form analysis no longer produced profitable bets, I now approach every race asking a single question – what is my edge? Or in simple terms, what do I know (or think I know!) about this race that gives me an advantage over other punters?

In the previous chapters, I've discussed the use of speed figures, pace analysis and track bias. All of these provide me with a way of looking at a race that is not in common use. As the authorities are trying to make the races as close as possible, it becomes more difficult to separate the runners by means of traditional form study.

The alternative methods I now use provide me with a way of dividing the runners once more into contenders and those who can be ignored. They offer me an edge that means I find winners at prices that look amazingly generous – but only from my viewpoint. The hardest thing to handle when making this switch was to accept that mechanical approaches could be more successful than the intellectual effort involved in analysing pure form. Backing a winner simply because he recorded a big speed figure last time doesn't require hours of study, and that 'feels' wrong. I always operated on the basis that the harder I worked, the luckier I became – now the effort is expended in looking for the ideas, not in time spent on a specific race.

Let's look at an example of a race that might have cost me an hour or two to analyse a few years ago – in 1997, the probable winner jumped off the page as clearly as if I'd already seen the next day's results in the paper. The horse concerned was an ordinary handicapper called Thatchmaster. I had seen his last three races in 1996, which produced a second at Salisbury and a win and a third at Goodwood. He established himself in my mind as a consistent front-runner, well suited to a right-hand track and fast ground over one mile, or one mile and a quarter. Although he ran well in 0-70 grade handicaps, his win had been in a claiming handicap, nominally also a 0-70 race, but clearly of lesser class given the conditions of entry. As a five-year-old in 1996, it was unlikely that he would show any great improvement, or that he would change his ideal pattern.

He began the 1997 season by running in a 0-90 grade handicap at Goodwood, when the class of the race clearly ruled him out as a contender, but he ran well to finish fourth, though flattered as he had made the running in a slow contest. He then took in a 0-75 one-mile handicap at Sandown and caught my eye when finishing third, staying on well after being headed early in the home straight. This confirmed he had retained the ability to win back in his correct class, especially over ten furlongs. However, circumstances were all wrong for his next race, a 0-80 ten-furlong handicap at Bath. The track at Bath is left-handed, and he also looked sure to be taken on for the lead in a race with several potential front-runners. He was sent off at 9-2 second-favourite, and, after running fast for one mile, dropped out to finish last. This set up the ideal scenario for a bet next time – a poor run that would look terrible to a form student, but which I was confident could be ignored.

The opportunity came on August 23, when Thatchmaster appeared in the same ten-furlong claiming handicap at Goodwood that he had won the previous year. The main opposition came from Statajack, Wentbridge Lad and The Executor, but they all faced the problem of coming from off the pace against a lone front-runner on a track which was clearly favouring the leaders in the home straight. I checked all the other 11 runners, but couldn't find a single one likely to take on Thatchmaster in front. The conditions could hardly have been better if I'd sat down with the trainer and designed the race specifically for the horse. The Saturday crowd entered into the spirit of the occasion by backing Statajack and Wentbridge Lad, leaving Thatchmaster to drift from 7-2 out to 11-2. I bet £3,300/600 and he was returned 5-1.

In front from the start, the jockey was able to give Thatchmaster a breather at the top of the hill, and then kicked on three out, at which point his three main rivals were all at least six lengths off the pace. He was still five lengths clear passing the furlong pole and although Harlequin Walk came through to close on him near the finish, it was only on sufferance. Thatchmaster recorded a fast time for a race of this class, but that was no surprise given the ideal circumstances – he had never been under any pressure at any stage of the race.

A subsequent run in a limited stakes at Nottingham gave him all the same problems he had faced at Bath – left-hand track and other front-runners. Taken on for the lead, he was headed two out, but kept on really well to hold fourth on the line and still looked to me to be in the best form of his life. His last run of the season came at Salisbury in an ideal 0-70 ten-furlong handicap, but his chance looked negligible when he was drawn two of the 18 runners. The ten-furlong start at Salisbury is at the beginning of the loop at the far end of the course, so that the runners negotiate about 270 degrees of turn in the first three furlongs. Stall two is on the outside of the turn and presents a front-runner with an insuperable problem. If he doesn't lead he won't produce his form, but in order to lead he has to use up too much energy in the early stages of the race and won't get home – a classic Catch 22 that you won't discover in the formbook. Thatchmaster couldn't get to the front and wasn't given a hard time to come home in eighth place. The seven horses in front of him were drawn 17-13-7-16-11-14-15, which confirms the impossibility of the task he faced. He didn't run again during the turf season, probably because there were no suitable races on a right-hand track, but I'll look forward to following him in the 1998 season.

As you can see, the understanding of the requirements for the horse – his ideal race – combined with the prior knowledge of conditions at Goodwood to highlight his chance. But the issue of the class of the race was still paramount. The traditional methods of separating horses still have their place, but the identification of value stems from the rest of the analysis. In this example, the race went exactly as I had envisaged it would, almost as if I'd been allowed to issue the riding instructions to every jockey. When it all clicks into place as neatly as that, the satisfaction of the prediction is almost as great as the financial reward – the satisfying feeling that every punter will recognise of being proved right.

Of course it doesn't always work out quite so well. Earlier in the year, again at Goodwood, I was equally confident, perhaps more so, about the prospects of Blue Imperial in a nine-furlong handicap at the July meeting. He had won at Bath over eight furlongs the previous week, always up with the pace in what looked a fast race, recording a good speed figure and winning by three lengths. At Goodwood he had a 6lb penalty, but he also had the ideal running style for the track and a perfect draw in stall 17 of the 18 runners. I bet the early morning 6-1, and when that price was available again in the ring, I stepped in again, accumulating a total bet of £7,000/1140. As anticipated, Blue Imperial jumped out quickly and settled in second close to the pacemaking Mantles Prince, who had started from stall 18. But soon after the home turn, he came under pressure and dropped tamely away to finish 15th. The theory that the pace had been too strong wasn't supported by the performance of Mantles Prince, who stayed on into sixth place, beaten about two lengths. I had become so confident using these new methods that this result really shook me. I was back at Goodwood the next day, but functioning at about 50 per cent efficiency and placed a couple of really duff bets before recognising that I was on auto-pilot and heading for home. That Friday wasn't so much a case of 'what is your edge', as 'totally over the edge'.

It no longer matters how much I 'fancy' a horse in traditional terms – if I can't identify an edge, I don't make a bet. It doesn't matter what your edge is, or how you identify it, so long as it enables you to separate the runners in a way that is different from the mass of punters. Having reached this position, I no longer worry so much about price. The concepts of value still apply, but finding an edge should automatically guarantee value, simply because it views the race differently. If your edge identifies winners everybody else is backing, then it's blunt! In the next section we'll look at a cross section of bets from one month during the 1997 turf season, to see how different races were analysed. It will also confirm that the losers remain in the majority. But overall the season was my best ever in terms of ordinary win betting (excluding such exotic items as the Jackpot). The final figures were as follows:

| Month | Winners/Bets | Profit/Loss | Overall Total |
|---|---|---|---|
| March | 1/1 | + 500 | + 500 |
| April | 3/10 | + 980 | + 1,480 |
| May | 6/22 | +6,660 | + 8,140 |
| June | 9/32 | +4,210 | +12,350 |
| July | 10/44 | -5,880 | + 6,470 |
| August | 8/31 | +5,620 | +12,090 |
| September | 9/32 | +5,120 | +17,210 |
| October | 2/14 | -2,065 | +15,145 |
| Total | 48/176 | | Profit £15,145 |

# Turf workshop

I've no intention of boring readers rigid by detailing every bet placed during the Flat season - and in fact the writing of such a lengthy diary would bore me more than you! However, most of the examples I've quoted in the earlier chapters of this section have been winning bets, and that impression of constant success needs to be rectified. If you've got this far without the phrase "smug git" (or something stronger) passing through your mind, I admire your fortitude. So here is the background to ten representative bets, that demonstrate the practical use of the ideas discussed in this section of the book, but also confirm that losers remain much more common than winners.

| 29/04 Bath 5f Hcp | BEAU VENTURE | Unpl SP 3-1 £1600/500 |
|---|---|---|

*Principally a speed figure bet, supported by a good draw. Beau Venture had run consecutive races at Nottingham and Folkestone, recording a speed figure of 76 (plus 12) in both contests. Running here off 69, he's a front runner drawn close to the inside and meeting rivals who are fully exposed as ordinary 0-70 sprint handicappers. Although a nine-year-old, Beau Venture appears to be in the best form of recent years and can make all.*

*Actually he led for just over three furlongs and then curled up quicker than a hedgehog. He was taken on for the lead, which I hadn't anticipated, and the early pace was too fast to be sustained. Later in the season, Mark (Holder) pointed out that front runners rarely seemed to win sprints at Bath, despite the apparent advantage they should have from racing on the inside of the bend, three furlongs out, and the elbow just before the furlong marker. I watched some films and concluded that front runners were losing momentum at the elbow by changing their legs. Having used their speed to be in front at that point, they couldn't pick up again during the final furlong. A horse challenging on the outside wouldn't notice the elbow at all and wouldn't check its stride at any stage. This is just a theory, but I find it helps to think in such terms about apparently contradictory racecourse evidence – even if I'm totally wrong. It's all part of trying to predict how races will be run. In 1998, I'll be looking for finishers in the sprints at Bath, and if I back a couple of winners, then the thinking will pay off.*

**20/05  Gdwd  1m Hcp        SHARP SHUFFLE        2nd  SP 10-1**
                                                           **£5100/500**

*In a field of 11, I was only interested in those drawn eight to 11.
Sharp Shuffle had stall 10. He'd run third in the competitive Spring
Mile at Doncaster in March, then done well to win a mickey mouse
event at Brighton, coming from behind off a slow pace, which is
never easy. He'd patently failed to stay ten furlongs at Kempton on
his latest start and looked a big price here back over his best trip.
The presence of the confirmed front-runner Artexerxes in stall 11
ensured a sound pace, to suit the hold-up style of Sharp Shuffle.*

*Dane O'Neill sensibly kept on the far rail, but struggled to find a
way through as the field bunched two furlongs out, and by the time
he got clear, the favourite Gold Spats had the race won. He took
second inside the final furlong without coming under strong
pressure, but was never going to catch the winner, who was drawn
in stall 7. I stuck to my guns all year long concerning the
importance of a high draw over seven furlongs and a mile at
Goodwood and it paid dividends later in the season.*

**18/06  Ascot  1m Group 1    MOONLIGHT PARADISE Unpl  SP 6-1**
                                                           **£2800/400**

*I wrote about the potential value to be found in opposing the hyped
up favourites in Group 1 races, and the Coronation Stakes provided
a good example. I had seen Sleepytime beaten in her trial for the
1,000 Guineas at Newbury on the round seven-furlong course
there, and she had also found trouble in running over this course
and distance in the Fillies' Mile as a two-year-old. The evidence
pointed to her being a long-striding filly, definitely at her best on a
straight course. Moonlight Paradise had impressed me as a two-
year-old and although she had disappointed behind Sleepytime at
Newmarket, having been 7-2 there, I was happy to take 7-1 in this
smaller field.*

*I was right to oppose Sleepytime, who again looked unsuited to
the short straight at Ascot, but wrong to opt for Moonlight Paradise,
who seemed not to stay the trip. However, I'd have needed a
crystal ball to find the winner, Rebecca Sharp, a 25-1 shot, who'd
finished behind even Moonlight Paradise at Newmarket.*

**27/06  Folks  10f Hcp       BAKERS DAUGHTER       2nd  SP 3-1**
                                                           **£2000/600**

*Front runner, happiest at this trip, consistent and predictable. She
had been running well in big fields in much better races than this,
including second in a 0-80 handicap at Newbury and a close fourth*

*in a 0-70 at Windsor. Although this was nominally another 0-70 race, the top weight was only rated 63, and four of her ten opponents were in the handicap basement with ratings under 35. There didn't appear to be any other front runners in the field and she looked certain to have an unopposed run in front. I bet with confidence, which then diminished as I watched an ex-French horse called Bold Faith being backed from 7-1 into 11-4 favouritism. Willie Musson, who isn't known for making too many mistakes at this game, trained this one.*

*Sure enough, Bakers Daughter was able to lead at a sensible pace but it was no surprise when Bold Faith came to challenge entering the final furlong. As usual she ran on perfectly gamely, but the dark horse prevailed by a short-head.*

*No matter how clearly you analyse a race in advance, there is always the chance of something unexpected to spoil the party.*

| 8/07 | Newm 6f Hcp | ELNADIM | 2nd | SP 5-1 |
| | | | | £3300/600 |

*This was the fifth race on the day, and earlier races had suggested strongly that the nearside rail was providing an advantage over the centre of the track. In the mile handicap, the winner Ben Gunn had come from a long way back at halfway, weaving a passage along the stand rail. In this sprint handicap, Elnadim had stall ten of 11, one off the rail, whilst the favourite Danetime was drawn in stall one.*

*Elnadim had impressed me when winning his maiden at Pontefract by four lengths and I had him marked as a possible for Listed races, so that his handicap mark here of 93 seemed generous.*

*I had under-estimated Danetime and he overcame the draw to win by two lengths from Elnadim, who ran a perfectly competent race under the rail in second.*

*These two horses continued to haunt me as the season progressed. Danetime went on to win the Stewards Cup narrowly from my choice, My Best Valentine, but was beaten under a dismal ride when I finally backed him in the Haydock Park Sprint Cup.*

*Elnadim went on to justify my support by winning his next three starts, including a Listed race back at Newmarket and the Group 2 Diadem Stakes at Ascot. Did I back him in any or all of those three races? What a stupid question to ask a competent professional punter with nothing to do all day but study the racing and keep on top of what's running! Of course I didn't back him, although I confess I've no idea why not, though I probably had very good reasons at the time.*

**30/07  Gdwd  5F Hcp      DANDE FLYER        4th   SP 11-2**
**£3500/460**

*There are periods when a low draw on the straight course at Goodwood is just as important as a high draw on the round course. The first day's results at the five-day July meeting had provided enough evidence that the stand rail was favoured, and my approach to this sprint handicap was to concentrate on the horses drawn one to five in a field of 16.*

*From those, Dande Flyer looked the one most likely to benefit from the presence of three tearaway front runners drawn low. The presence of the exceptional Royston Ffrench in the saddle was an additional incentive to bet. I had no trouble obtaining 8-1 and 7-1, but he was very well backed on course and went off the 11-2 favourite.*

*This race provided another demonstration of the uncertainty that keeps bookmakers in Rollers and punters like me in Renaults. Dande Flyer was in stall two, with The Wad, one of the probable front runners in stall one. As the stalls opened, The Wad unshipped his jockey, and running loose he swerved across the horses drawn two to five. The runners drawn in the middle of the track were given a two- or three-length start, with Lady Sheriff taking advantage to make all from stall 13.*

**21/08  Salis  8f Hcp      SWORD ARM         3rd   SP 4-1**
**£2700/600**

*All three factors were in favour of Sword Arm in this race. He was drawn in stall ten right against the far rail in a field of ten. That should ensure he could be covered up but close to the pace as he preferred, and there were a couple of likely pace-setters to prevent a slow race. He had also shown good speed when winning at Bath, recording a figure of 89 in a 0-80 Limited Stakes. As a bonus, I felt that the joint 4-1 favourite Strazo was unlikely to be suited by the firm ground.*

*Everything went according to plan until just inside the final furlong. Sword Arm had held the rail position in third early on, took the lead passing the two-furlong pole and looked to have the race secured as he went a couple of lengths clear. Passing me about 150 yards from home, he faltered and was passed by the strong finishing Conspicuous, who went on to win by three lengths. I* suspect something went wrong physically with Sword Arm (burst blood vessel or a breathing problem perhaps), a view underlined by his losing second to the original front runner Orange Place, who had looked well held with a furlong to run.

**22/08  Gdwd  7f Group 3     ALIGNMENT               2nd   SP 7-1**
**£3750/460**

At this meeting, I was concentrating on trying to work out which horse would be in front passing the three-furlong pole and thus in possession of the prime spot on the far rail. Alignment, drawn five of six, looked the likeliest candidate, as she had led in her only run to date, a seven-furlong maiden at Sandown. Although still a maiden, I was prepared to accept the view of Michael Stoute that she was a Group class filly – he's trained more of them than anyone bar Henry Cecil.

I'd been impressed with the favourite, Elshamms, on her debut at Newmarket, but not so impressed that I wanted to back her at 5-4. Remember that pattern races are never that uncompetitive.

Alignment led as I'd hoped, and looked to have the challengers held at the furlong marker, but was caught on the line by Midnight Line, trained by - you guessed - Henry Cecil. Commentator for the day, Simon Holt, called Alignment as the winner, so I retained hope of payment throughout the twenty minutes it took the judge to separate the first two.

The decision went against me, and when I saw the print on the noticeboard, I could only envy the brilliance of the judge's eyesight. In common with everyone else, except the backers of Midnight Line, I was certain I was looking at a dead-heat.

Later in the afternoon, I encountered Simon Holt cantering across the courtyard behind the stands. He told me he was going to the SIS van in order to 're-voice' his commentary on the finish, because the film would be used in future whenever Midnight Line was running. An interesting concept, but I suppose it would be too much to expect the bookies to allow us to 're-voice' our bets!

**3/09   Bright 12f Hcp      BATHE IN LIGHT          2nd   SP 10-1**
**£4000/400**

I have made no secret of the fact that I never bet on races at Brighton, so this entry in the log is going to surprise plenty of people. One of the smartest punters I know says he has just one golden rule – 'Don't have any rules'. I might not go that far, but certainly rules are made to be broken. I dislike betting at Brighton *because the racing is poor quality, the ground is usually rock hard, and the slopes and cambers of the track almost guarantee that the races are rough and stewards' inquiries common. On this day, the ground was officially good after heavy rain and the runners were coming over to the stand rail, thus reducing the prospect of trouble in running.*

*Bathe In Light was a filly I'd recommended punters to back on her previous start at Salisbury, although I failed to get on that day as she was supported down from 3-1 to 6-4 favourite and I missed the fancy prices waiting to see her move to post. In that race, she'd cruised into the lead looking all over the winner passing the two-furlong pole, but seemed not to stay and faded to finish sixth.*

*I'm always prepared to give another chance to a horse who goes easily through a race on the bridle, especially when the price is as big as it was here. I was actually at York on September 3, but bet anyway when I found that Bathe In Light was 10-1 – I'd expected she would be half that price.*

*This time Bathe In Light was allowed to stride on at a modest pace and looked the likely winner until Mono Lady produced a strong finish to go clear inside the final furlong. Bathe In Light turned around the form with two fillies who had finished in front of her at Salisbury, but still found one too good.*

## 2/10   Newm 1m Listed   INTIKHAB   1st   SP 11-4
**£2475/900**

*This was a pace analysis that highlighted the strong probability of a falsely run race in which Intikhab would be best placed to take advantage. The favourite was Bin Rosie, a long-standing dodgepot who had to be held up and delivered in the final strides. Fallon wasn't going to find that easy in a small field, with no guaranteed pace and an outside draw in stall one. His price of even-money compelled a bet in this race.*

*Third favourite was Swiss Law, another hold-up horse, as I knew to my cost, having backed him at Goodwood when he was disqualified after forcing a passage on the far rail. Intikhab had an admirable record of never finishing out of the first two in nine career starts – the sort of horse punters should love. As the stake would indicate, I thought this was one of the best bets of the season.*

*This time the race went just as I'd hoped (you had to allow me one winner in this chapter!), with Intikhab tracking the moderate pace set by Polish Rhythm, kicking into the dip and never looking likely to be caught once in front. Bin Rosie could never get any cover and had no chance of giving the winner a six-length start with three furlongs to run – he trailed in last.*

## Summary

Combined with the examples contained in the earlier chapters, you've now seen the full story behind at least 20 per cent of my bets during the Flat season. Obviously the purpose is to help you look at races in the same way, and in many cases come to the same conclusion. But if you see me on the racecourse after reading this, I'd appreciate it if you'd let me have first crack at the best prices - after all I've got a living to make. There's only one author writing about racing who doesn't have to bet to supplement his income, and he's called Dick Francis!

# PART 2

## FLAT (AW)

### Here be dragons

When our mediaeval ancestors set out to explore and map the globe, there remained plenty of places where no European had ever set foot. The crude maps of that era indicated the mixture of fear and ignorance concerning these uncharted lands by using the symbol 'Here Be Dragons'. As far as most punters are concerned, the three areas on the British racing map occupied by the All-weather tracks could be marked by the same legend. They avoid betting on All-weather races because they don't understand that this surface offers some of the most consistent and predictable racing in the country.

A BHB survey carried out during 1997 confirmed that All-weather meetings were viewed as a disincentive to bet by most regular punters. In the same year, even as distinguished a journalist as Henry Rix, the inspirational tipster previously employed by the *Racing Post*, wrote that he preferred to pass on the All-weather racing whenever possible.

When All-weather racing began in the late eighties, I shared the view that it was an unattractive side-show, lacking in star horses, with weak markets and no obvious way of finding an edge. Once Wolverhampton opened, I soon became aware that the draw provided a short-cut to profitable betting at that track and I wrote briefly about that track in my previous book, *Against The Crowd*.

With that knowledge, I returned to a number of American-written books in my library and started to use their experience of dirt tracks to establish my own methods.

The Americans focussed on three main ways of analysing races – speed figures, draw bias and pace analysis. As I've already explained, having started using these techniques to help with the All-weather racing, I became sufficiently convinced of their power to transfer them to the turf. However, the application of these ideas to the All-weather tracks is quite different in many ways and well worth an in-depth look.

In this section of the book, I'll explain how I create my own speed figures for All-weather racing, how I use the draw and pace analyses, and emphasise the differences between turf and All-weather races that punters need to understand.

# All-weather opportunities

The first, and most important thing to grasp about racing on the All-weather surfaces, is that it is completely and utterly different from racing on turf. The media still try in vain to establish links between the two, with comments such as "he acts on soft ground, so this surface should suit", or "he looks different class based on his turf form". These are so far wide of the mark that the writer might as well be recommending a horse for the Grand National on the basis of previous form as a show jumper. Let's look at a couple of examples that highlight the gulf.

On 6 December 1997, Wolverhampton staged their feature race of the year, the Listed Wulfrun Stakes. Seven runners went to post, with the four-year-old Centre Stalls sent off as the 6-5 favourite, despite his lack of previous All-weather experience. Typical of the pre-race comments were:

- Confidence runneth over at Fulke Johnson-Houghton's Didcot yard as Centre Stalls bids to cut down the opposition. He ran a super race in the Queen Anne, the best of his career; and with another 100 yards would have won it.

- Centre Stalls must take a great deal of beating in a race where he is 9lb clear on official ratings.

- An outstanding betting proposition at Wolverhampton is Centre Stalls, who has always been viewed as the type who would excel on the All-weather.

Presumably the punters who bet £500/400, £1,100/1,000 (x2) and £550/500 (x2) shared this confidence. Centre Stalls finished last, 25 lengths behind the winner, Farmost, a horse with plenty of previous form on the All-weather, and winner last time over course and distance. Supporters of Centre Stalls were expecting that his superior class on turf would automatically translate to the All-weather, but in fact he is a prime example of the type of turf runner who almost never handles the sand. He highlights one of the key differences between turf and All-weather racing.

On turf, Centre Stalls had established himself as a horse well suited by a strong pace that would enable him to use the finishing power that marked him as a class horse. Prior to the Royal Ascot race, Centre Stalls had won a top-notch Rated Stakes at York over one mile. That race was run at a terrific pace, and Centre Stalls was able to run on strongly to improve from a midfield position three furlongs out to lead at the one-furlong pole and draw clear. It would have been hard to identify a better example during the year of the type of horse I described in *Against The Crowd* as possessing the 'power' – i.e. the ability to sustain his finishing speed throughout the final quarter-mile.

At Royal Ascot, in the opening race over the straight mile, Centre Stalls again had the race run to suit him. With the leaders going off too fast for their own good (the first three were all held up), he took second in this Group 2 race, beaten just a neck. In both those races, Centre Stalls showed his best quality – the ability to quicken off a strong pace. But that doesn't work on the All-weather surfaces. It's certainly true that most All-weather races are run at a good pace – indeed in the Wolverhampton race, Farmost made all and produced the best speed figure of the year on the All-weather. But it simply isn't possible to quicken on sand in the way that it is on turf. Although we don't have sectional timing (so the figures have to be guesswork) it's reasonable to assume that Centre Stalls would have covered the penultimate furlong in his turf races in around 11.5 seconds – the total time at Ascot was 1m 40s which equates to an average of 12.5 seconds per furlong from a standing start.

The All-weather surfaces don't provide sufficient grip to allow any horse to gallop that quickly, especially at Wolverhampton, where the final bend inevitably slows the horses down at around the three-furlong pole. The time for the 9.3 furlongs at Wolverhampton was 2m 0.7s, a more sedate 13 seconds per furlong. In the Wolverhampton race, Centre Stalls was close enough with half a mile to run. If he could have run the remaining half-mile in 47-48 seconds, he would almost certainly have been an easy winner. Instead he floundered on the surface, which just slips away from under the feet of the horse as he tries to accelerate. If you want more evidence, try running from a standing start on a grass field, and then on a beach above the tide line (as an asthmatic overweight fifty-year-old, my personal experience of this experiment is approximately forty years out of date!).

Whilst the evidence is entirely subjective, my own view is that the ideal turf profile (if such a thing exists) for an All-weather runner, is the type who often looks one-paced in the final two furlongs, after holding a prominent position. Certainly this fits the second example I'm going to use to highlight the difference - a horse called South Eastern Fred. There are plenty of other horses who I could use to make this point, but who could resist that name!

By 1997, South Eastern Fred was firmly established as an All-weather specialist, with several wins at both Lingfield and Wolverhampton on his record. He ended the 96/97 winter season with an All-weather handicap mark of 93, a figure that placed him amongst the ten best horses to run during that period. When he was returned to turf racing at Folkestone in March 1997, he ran in a modest Class E handicap off a mark of 49. Despite meeting horses who wouldn't get within twenty lengths of him on sand, on favourable weight terms, he could only manage a one-paced third, with Timeform reporting "handily positioned throughout and held every chance until the winner sprinted by".

Ten years ago, a horse like South Eastern Fred would have been condemned to spending his summers galloping unsuccessfully around Folkestone, and his winters plodding round Plumpton over hurdles. Now, trainers have the third option of trying their charges on the All-weather; and if they take to that, there is the prospect of picking up plenty of prizemoney. In fact, given the way the system operates, it is actually advantageous for a horse to be established as terrible on turf, before the switch to the sand. At present, a horse who has had three runs on turf qualifies for an official handicap rating, which will follow him to the All-weather. If he proves to be more proficient on sand, then he starts from an artificially low handicap mark and has every chance of running up a string of successes.

A typical example of this can be seen in the running of Mansab during the early part of 1997. He began his career on turf as part of the Maktoum empire, trained by John Dunlop. As such he was unlikely to be tried on the All-weather, although he was perfectly bred for dirt racing, being a son of the Breeders' Cup Sprint winner and American sprint champion Housebuster. After a number of disappointments, he was culled by the Maktoums and bought at the 1996 July sales by Pat Murphy. Belatedly switched to the surface he was born for, he hacked up in a 0-55 Limited Stakes over six furlongs at Southwell and followed that up with handicap wins off marks of 66 and 72. All three races were run in fast times, and if he had returned to the All-weather tracks there was probably further improvement in him. Back on turf later in 1997, he beat just one horse home in three starts. In common with several other horses who have shown ability on our All-weather tracks, Mansab has now been sold to race in Dubai, where his opportunities will be much greater.

All the horses I've discussed in this section have been better on the All-weather than on turf, and you won't see many examples of the opposite. If a horse is established with a rating of 80+ on turf, but turns out to be only a 50-60 class horse on the sand, then it is fairly pointless running him on the All-weather. He can race for much better prizemoney on turf, and the only type of race he can win on sand will be claiming or selling races – but his value as a turf horse would render that economic suicide.

Having, I hope, firmly established that form on turf has no relevance to form on All-weather, let's move on to consider the differences in the way races are run on the two surfaces. Most races on turf are run at a steady early pace, with the runners still in a bunch well past halfway, seeking a position for the sprint to the finish. Even in relatively small fields, it is quite common for horses to be hampered, boxed in, denied a run, or in one way or another prevented from obtaining a clear run. This is accepted as part of the natural way of things, with the tactical skill of the jockey a major factor in producing a horse at the right moment. Because of the sprint finish style of racing, it is also normal for the winning distances to be small and for horses to take the lead in the final strides of the race. And one of the most impressive sights that turf racing can offer, is the class horse cruising upsides his rivals, still 'on the bridle', and just needing to be let down to win hard held.

None of those pictures of turf racing would be familiar to an All-weather enthusiast. The great majority of races are run at a strong early pace, increasingly so in the last two years, as jockeys recognise the value of a good early position in All-weather races. By halfway, the field is invariably well spread out, and that means it is quite rare for a horse to be denied a winning chance by failing to get a clear run. Whereas the biggest crime for a jockey on turf is to 'hit the front too soon', the exact opposite is true on sand. Quite simply, you never see a horse still on the bridle inside the final furlong of an All-weather race, unless he's already well clear and has the race won. Horses who appear to be finishing fast on sand are merely galloping on at the same speed, catching rivals who are tiring after setting a faster early pace.

Winning distances are much greater on the All-weather, partly because the horses aren't just contesting a two-furlong final sprint, and also because the underfoot surface seems to make it much harder for a beaten horse to keep going. Because of this I have opted to ignore the form of horses outside the first three in All-weather races, treating a fourth-place finisher in the same way as the last horse home. As long as the horse has shown good form previously, a defeat by twenty or thirty lengths, that would look inexcusable on turf, can be ignored on sand. The stewards at the All-weather tracks don't yet seem to have cottoned on to this fact! Come to that, they still haven't really worked out that turf and All-weather are different beasts either. Connections of Centre Stalls were called in to explain his performance at Wolverhampton. They told the stewards that the horse didn't act on the bends, which was true up to a point. It just glossed over the fact that he didn't act on the straights either!

# All-weather speed figures

I have explained earlier why I don't feel it is worthwhile producing my own speed figures for turf racing. But the All-weather tracks remove many of the problems, and once I had started on speed figures, I quickly realised the value of placing my own interpretation on the numbers. The method I use is, I think, uniquely my own. When I first made the attempt, I was concerned that producing the figures should not take up too much time, as time at home is a valuable commodity for a regular traveller to the races. I can now produce figures for a single All-weather meeting in less than fifteen minutes, and there is no reason why any reader shouldn't be able to do the same. Fortunately the method contains plenty of scope for subjective input, so that we won't all come up with the same results every time.

I made three early decisions that simplified the work and ensured my figures were sufficiently individual to give me an edge:

1 I work only on races run at distances up to and including ten furlongs.

2 I ignore the weight carried by each horse.

3 I based my standard times on the speed of a horse with a BHB rating of 70.

The first decision eliminates the races around two turns at Southwell and three turns at Wolverhampton, plus the staying races at Lingfield. There are fewer of these races, so that establishing an accurate standard time is more difficult. The longer races tend to be contested by a poorer class of horse than those between five and ten furlongs and the winning distances at the two Fibresand tracks (Southwell and Wolverhampton) are frequently into double figures, with tired horses barely able to put one foot in front of another at the finish.

On the question of weight, I strongly believe that All-weather races are barely affected by the weight carried. I will produce several examples of horses, who once established as suited by the All-weather surface, were able to run up a sequence of wins regardless of increasing weight. As in turf racing, any horse will eventually rise to a class level at which it cannot win, but the range of ability on the All-weather is quite narrow and ability to act on the surface is paramount.

When All-weather racing began, it was designed solely for moderate horses. Over time, better races have been established and better horses now compete during the winter season, but the bulk of the racing is still centred on the 70-rated horse. Other providers of speed figures use either a Group class horse as their standard base, or a horse rated 100 on the BHB scale. This produces an effect similar to a football fan trying to assess all the teams in the Vauxhall Conference by reference to the standard set by Manchester United. I felt then that it made more sense to set a standard within the realistic scale of All-weather racing and I've encountered nothing to make me change that view.

## The theory

The first requirement for any set of speed figures is a standard time for each distance at each track, against which all future performances can be measured. Lacking any computer power at the time, I produced these by the laborious process of ploughing through the formbook, writing down the final time for every race, subdivided by distance and by class of race. I then eliminated the fastest and slowest times and produced an average based on the remainder.

Since the majority of races on the All-weather are 0-70 grade, or similar (0-65, 0-75 and claiming races), that was the class for which I had the most data and that reinforced my decision to base my figures around a BHB 70 rating.

Once the standard time for each distance was calculated, I reduced each one to a figure showing the number of seconds for each furlong. Logically, the longer the race, the slower the horses should cover each furlong. These secs/furlong figures confirmed that the standard times for each distance had a correct relationship to each other. For example, my figures for **Lingfield** are:

| | | |
|---|---|---|
| 5f | 59.4s | 11.88 seconds/furlong |
| 6f | 1m 12.5s | 12.08 seconds/furlong |

| 7f | 1m 25.4s | 12.20 seconds/furlong |
|---|---|---|
| 8f | 1m 39.0s | 12.37 seconds/furlong |
| 10f | 2m 6.7s | 12.67 seconds/furlong |

To take one example which demonstrates the difference between my approach and that used by others, consider the standard time for the one-mile distance. In *Mordin On Time*, Nick Mordin defines a standard time of 1m 32.73s for eight furlongs on the Lingfield All-weather. The *Racing Post* use a time of 1m 36s and *The Sporting Life* 1m 36.1s. I have no doubt that all of these figures provide a correct balance for their users, who are concerned with equating their All-weather speed figures with figures produced by much better horses on the turf. But all three look bizarre as standard times, when you realise that the course record for eight furlongs on the Lingfield All-weather track is 1m 36.32s, set by Vanroy back in November 1989. Since I'm only concerned with the three All-weather tracks and the horses who run on them, I can take what I regard as a more realistic approach.

For the record, here are my standard times at Southwell and Wolverhampton:

**Southwell**

| 6f | 1m 18.0s | 13.00 seconds/furlong |
|---|---|---|
| 7f | 1m 32.2s | 13.17 seconds/furlong |
| 8f | 1m 46.0s | 13.22 seconds/furlong |

**Wolverhampton**

| 5f | 1m 03.0s | 12.60 seconds/furlong |
|---|---|---|
| 6f | 1m 15.8s | 12.63 seconds/furlong |
| 7f | 1m 30.7s | 12.95 seconds/furlong |
| 8.4f | 1m 51.7s | 13.20 seconds/furlong |
| 9.3f | 2m 04.0s | 13.25 seconds/furlong |

I don't produce figures for the five-furlong races at Southwell for two reasons. Firstly, there are very few of them, which makes it hard to produce a reasonable standard time; and secondly, they are run on a part of the track not used for other races (the stand side of the finishing straight), which could have the effect of upsetting the calculation of the daily variant.

The big difference between the seconds/furlong figures for the six and seven-furlong trips at Wolverhampton, is explained by the seven-furlong start being on a bend, which I suspect prevents the horses hitting top speed until they have covered almost a furlong.

The standard times for Southwell will have to be recalculated before the 1998/99 winter season, as the track is riding much faster since it was re-laid in the autumn of 1997.

Having established my standard times, the next step was to set the scale for the eventual speed figures. I decided I would use a figure of 100 for a time that matched my standard for a 70-rated horse. Adjustments to this base would be made at a rate of one point per tenth of a second, and two points per length. That might sound a little arbitrary, but it makes approximate sense if you calculate on the basis of one length equals ten feet. That gives a total of 66 lengths in a furlong, which equates to 132 points. Using the times above, the average is approximately 13 seconds for each furlong covered, which equates to 130 points. As we'll see later, I'm not too bothered about producing accurate figures for beaten horses anyway, so this level of crude mathematics is quite adequate.

We're now ready to calculate the speed figures for a typical meeting, but first I must introduce the idea of 'projected times'. In simple terms this involves predicting, before racing, the probable finishing time for each race for which I plan to calculate figures. It would be possible just to compare every race with the standard time for that course and distance, but that would take no account of the obvious differences between various classes of race. So the first method of projecting times is to decide a standard time for each grade of race, based obviously on the standard times quoted earlier.

My work to establish standard times showed that for each move up or down the scale from the basic 0-70, there was a difference of two-tenths of a second, or two points on my scale.

So the projected times chart, which I apply for all distances at all tracks, is as follows:

|  | Projected Speed Figure |
|---|---|
| 0-70 Hcps | 100 |
| 0-75 Hcps | 102 |
| 0-80 Hcps | 104 |
| 0-85 Hcps | 106 |
| 0-90 Hcps | 108 |
| 0-60 Hcps | 96 |
| 0-65 Hcps | 98 |
| Claimers | 100 |
| Sellers | 95 |
| Maidens | 100 |

Further adjustments can be made to allow for the slower times run by two-year-olds and by three-year-olds in the first two months of the year, but I haven't any formal figures. If in doubt, the times on two-year-old races are ignored when calculating the speed figures.

The second method of producing projected times is generally more accurate and should be used whenever possible. If the runners in any All-weather race have previous All-weather speed figures, then it is possible to use those past performances to generate the projection. For example, look at this six-furlong handicap at Lingfield on Dec 19. The runners are listed along with their last two speed figures:

| 1 | APOLLO RED | 0 | 100 |
|---|---|---|---|
| 2 | PALACEGATE TOUCH | 100 | 99 |
| 3 | THAT MAN AGAIN | | No Figures |
| 4 | ROBO MAGIC | 94 | 96 |
| 5 | RAMSEY HOPE | 90 | 86 |
| 6 | SCISSOR RIDGE | 96 | 98 |
| 7 | PLEIN GAZ | | No Figures |
| 8 | HALF TONE | 88 | |
| 9 | JOHNNY STACCATO | | No Figures |
| 10 | CHIPSTEAD BAY | 102 | 102 |

This was a 0-85 grade handicap, for which the default speed figure is 106. But as you can see, none of the runners here have shown the ability to run that sort of figure in their recent races. So it makes more sense to project a figure of 102 for this race, and to be prepared to modify that if the actual times point to the winner having improved. You see – I told you we wouldn't all generate the same answers using this method!

As an example, this is my chart for the Lingfield All-weather meeting on Thursday November 6, the first of the 1997/8 winter season. All the projected figures for this meeting were the basic figures of method one, since there had been little All-weather racing in the weeks prior to this.

## Nov 6 Lingfield

|  | Proj Figure | Time | Raw Figure | Diff | Variant = +3 | Adj Fig |
|---|---|---|---|---|---|---|
| 5f 0-75 Nrsy | 97 | 1 0.0 | 94 | -3 | | 91 |
| 5f 0-70 Hcp | 100 | 59.1 | 103 | +3 | | 100 |
| 7f Mdn | 100 | 1 25.2 | 102 | +2 | | 99 |
| 7f 0-80 Hcp | 104 | 1 24.3 | 109 | +5 | | 106 |
| 10f 0-80 Amtr | 100 | 2 7.4 | 93 | -7 | | 90 |

The projected figure of 97 for the first race reflects the fact that these horses are still two-year-olds and therefore naturally slower than the older horses. The projection represents a mixture of guesswork and experience, but as we'll see, it isn't a problem if I'm wrong. The projected 100 for the maiden race is automatic, although depending on the strength of the horses, anything from 80 to 120 might be more accurate – but there is no way of knowing the quality of horses that have mostly never run on the All-weather before. The projected 104 for the 0-80 handicap is, again, a normal figure for that class of race. The projected figure for the amateur riders' event is reduced by two grades based on past experience. I suspect these are the only races on the All-weather tracks where the weight carried does have a small impact on the final times.

The next column shows the actual final time for each race, using the times supplied by Timeform in their *Perspective* formbook, although the trade papers' times would do just as well. This time is then turned into the 'raw figure' by comparing the time with my standard for that distance and adding or deducting one point for each tenth of a second. Thus, for the first race, my standard is 59.4 seconds (see earlier lists) and the actual time is six-tenths slower than that standard. Deducting six points from the base figure of 100 gives the raw figure of 94. The second race was run three-tenths faster than standard, so the raw figure is 103.

The next column records the difference between the projected figure and the raw figure, in effect showing whether the race was faster or slower than I predicted. For the first race, I predicted a figure of 97: the actual figure was 94, so the difference is recorded as –3. The second race was a little faster than predicted, so the difference this time is +3.

Now comes the key part of the process, the calculation of the daily variant. This sounds like a fairly perverted hobby, but it is simply a numerical statement of how much faster or slower than normal the track is riding during a particular meeting. A purely objective calculation would add all the difference figures and divide by the number of races – thus:

$$\textbf{-3 + 3 + 2 + 5 + -7} \quad = \quad \textbf{0}$$

which would indicate that the track was riding absolutely normally and that all the final times were a fair representation of the merit of the winners. However, this is where the subjective takes over from the objective and I place my own interpretation on the figures. In this case I decided to ignore the amateur riders' race entirely, leaving me with an answer of +2 (-3 + 3 + 2 + 5 = + 7 ÷ 4 = +2). Still unhappy with that, I settled on +3 as the variant for this day, downgrading the nursery as a weak contest for which I probably set too high a projected figure. So the decision is that the raw figures have to be reduced by three points to reflect the fast state of the track, thus producing the final adjusted speed figures.

This is quite a simple example, as at plenty of meetings the range of differences is much greater, making the decision on the daily variant much more a matter of opinion. If in doubt I go with my gut feel – they're my bloody figures, and I decide them, which of course is one of the strengths of doing this work yourself, rather than relying on others. If subsequent results indicate that one or more of the figures looks out of line, I can go back and recalculate the variant, something that the formbooks find harder to do, because their figures are already published.

On this occasion, I was given a fairly quick confirmation of the figures. The winner of the seven-furlong handicap was Twin Creeks, with a speed figure of 106. On the basis of that performance, I backed him when he reappeared under a penalty in another 0-80 the following Tuesday. He finished second, but the winner of that race produced a figure of 110, so that Twin Creeks, beaten one and half lengths, was awarded a 107, thus reproducing his form, or as good as.

Here's an example of a card with somewhat wider variations in the class of horse running, and in the variations between the projected and actual times. This is my chart for Wolverhampton on 6 December 1997:

| | Proj Figure | Time | Raw Figure | Diff | Variant = -2 | Adj Fig |
|---|---|---|---|---|---|---|
| 9f 0-65 Hcp | 98 | 2 3.8 | 102 | +4 | | 104 |
| 6f 2-y-o Mdn | 96 | 1 16.9 | 89 | -7 | | 91 |
| 6f 2-y-o Sell | 90 | 1 17.8 | 80 | -10 | | 82 |
| 9f 0-65 Hcp | 98 | 2 4.6 | 94 | -4 | | 96 |
| 7f 0-100 Hcp | 110 | 1 30.6 | 101 | -9 | | 103 |
| 9f Listed | 120 | 2 0.7 | 133 | +13 | | 135 |

The difficulty here is a familiar one for those who calculate figures on turf, but not at All-weather meetings – how to project correctly a figure for a Listed race and a seller on the same card. Since top class races are a rarity on the All-weather, my projected figure of 120 for the Listed contest has to be considered a guess. And, as you can see, the 'difference' of 13 points for that race is bound to have a marked impact on the calculation of the daily variant. On this occasion, I've opted to ignore the two two-year-old races, where there was little previous information on which to base a projection. With the two divisions of the 0-65 handicap cancelling each other out, I've concluded that the time for the seven-furlong handicap looks the strongest indicator of a slightly slow surface and settled on a variant of –2. Given that the first two home in that seven-furlong handicap, Chewit and State Of Caution, had both record figures of around 108 in recent races, I could have chosen a variant of –7, which would give Chewit another 108. But that would put the first race winner on 109, and unless he was a ringer, I prefer to assume that a figure of 103 for Chewit indicates a strong early pace, leading to an ordinary final time for that class of race. If the first race winner, Mazeed, subsequently produces another fast time, I could return to this chart and adjust the variant accordingly.

To give an indication of the extent to which conditions can alter on the All-weather tracks, at the previous meeting, on November 29, the winner of a seven-furlong 0-65 handicap recorded a time of 1m 28.4s, over two seconds faster than Chewit. Does that mean that Girl Of My Dreams, a 35-rated filly, is faster than Chewit. No, it doesn't – it just means that for some reason the track was riding substantially faster on November 29 than it was on December 6. The variant for November 29 was +3.5 points per furlong, or +25 points for the seven-furlong trip – which means I calculate that a horse running at both meetings, would have covered the seven furlongs 2.7 seconds faster at the earlier meeting.

## The Practice

I produced my first All-weather speed figures, using the methods described above, during the winter of 1995/6. Initially I had no clear idea what to expect. But the one thing I had learnt from my American reading was that the big mistake many punters make is to regard speed figures as a form of Holy Grail. Speed figures are an excellent tool, and because I was making my own calculations, they were giving me pointers that weren't available to other punters. But I knew that to treat them as the way, the truth and the light would be a quick route to disillusionment. So, for the first three months, I simply looked at the figures and compared their predictions with the actual results.

It soon became clear that speed figures were a powerful technique and an accurate method of spotting those horses who came to the All-weather and proved to be well handicapped, because they were better on sand than they had been on turf. In February 1996, I started to make bets based on my own speed figures for the first time. I opted for the simple system of backing any previous winner who had recorded a speed figure of 102 or more. I reasoned that this figure identified a fast All-weather horse, who had won a truly run race and probably had enough in hand to go in again. With hindsight, it's a pretty crude system, but then again, so is my method of calculating the figures I was using. The results were astonishing – these are the details for every All-weather bet I placed during February 1996:

| | | | | Latest SF | Result | |
|---|---|---|---|---|---|---|
| Feb 3 | RAKIS | 7f Hcp | Lingfield | 107 | WON | 11-8 |
| Feb 16 | TATIKA | 8f Hcp | Southwell | 104 | WON | 9-4 |
| Feb 17 | DANCING SIOUX | 7f Hcp | Lingfield | 111 | WON | 6-4 |
| Feb 17 | KRYSTAL MAX | 7f Clm | Lingfield | 106 | WON | 11-8 |
| Feb 23 | PINE RIDGE LAD | 7f Hcp | Southwell | 112 | 2nd | 5-2 |
| Feb 24 | CHEWIT | 6f Hcp | Lingfield | 111 | WON | 6-4 |
| Feb 24 | SUPER BENZ | 7f Ltd | Lingfield | 110 | WON | 85-40 |

At that point, the power went to my head, and I started backing horses who hadn't won last time out, but had the best figure anyway. The next five bets all lost and I received a sharp reminder about the folly of thinking that my simple speed figures had provided the answer to life, the universe and everything. As you can see from that list above, the prices weren't spectacular, but given the strike-rate, they didn't need to be. What the speed figures seemed to do very well, was identify those winners who could follow up. Winners who hadn't reached the magic number of 102, didn't do so well next time out.

I stopped betting after the five straight losers, continued to create the figures up to the end of the winter season, and then went back to the drawing board. The first thing I realised was that the programme of All-weather racing on a daily basis during January and February provided an almost perfect environment for the use of speed figures. I was producing figures for a small group of exposed horses, running on just three tracks, over a small range of distances.

By February, I had sufficient data for all the runners to be able to calculate accurate projected times for most races. That in turn made it easier to trust the daily variant – I knew what these horses could do in terms of speed, and in most cases they proved entirely predictable. The second plus factor was that the horses running during that period came from a narrow range of ability. Because of a lack of suitable races, a horse rated over 80 on the BHB scale was more or less excluded, and the safety limits which restricted the number of runners in each race, also prevented those rated below 50 from getting into the races. Basically, if speed figures couldn't produce a profit under these circumstances, then they never would.

My post-season research also suggested that it was unwise to trust a good figure unless the horse was running in the same type of race. In other words, it didn't pay to back a horse in a handicap, if his speed figure had been earned in a maiden or claiming race. Time and again these horses simply failed to produce the goods when moved into handicaps. Consider the record of Rambo Waltzer:

| Jan 5 | 8f Clm | Southwell | Won by 8l | SF 112 | SP 11-8 |
| Jan 10 | 9f Hcp | Wolverhampton | 6th btn 6l | SF 100 | SP 6-1 |
| Jan 24 | 7f Clm | Wolverhampton | Won by Nk | SF 111 | SP 5-1 |
| Feb 5 | 8f Hcp | Southwell | 6th btn 15l | SF 82 | SP 11-2 |

I'm not sure I fully understand this phenomenon even now, but my working theory is that the level of competition is simply greater in the handicaps, probably resulting in a marginally quicker early pace. In the claiming races, Rambo Waltzer never seemed to come off the bridle. The final time would be the same, but the sectional times (if we had them) would look quite different. This would certainly tie in with American ideas on early pace being crucial in competitive races, with horses who look comfortable when making all in lower grade being beaten out of sight when put under pressure through the first quarter-mile. One thing in favour of Rambo's defeats in handicaps – they ensured he was a backable price when he was returned to claiming company!

I observed a similar situation with the winners of maiden races. No matter how fast the speed figure they achieved in the maiden race, they couldn't be relied upon to reproduce it, or anything close, on their first venture into handicaps. The second run in a handicap, though, could see a return to something nearer the maiden race figure. A prime example of this pattern was Ocean Park:

| Jan 17 | 8f Mdn | Wolverhampton | Won by 2l | SF 107 | SP 5-6 |
| Jan 31 | 9f Hcp | Wolverhampton | 5th btn 6l | SF 81 | SP 7-2 |
| Feb 20 | 10f Hcp | Lingfield | Won by 1l | SF 106 | SP 10-1! |

However, as long as a horse remained in the same type of race, I found encouraging evidence that he would produce consistent speed figures over a sequence of races. When that wasn't the case, I could usually find an explanation that tied in with the experiences reported by the American writers. For example, one multiple winner during the January/February season in 1997 was Sense Of Priority, who recorded five successes:

| Jan 6 | 7f | Hcp | Southwell | 7th btn 10l | SF | 83 | SP | 20-1 |
|-------|-----|------|-----------|-------------|-----|-----|-----|------|
| Jan 10 | 7f | Sell | Southwell | Won by ½l | SF | 105 | SP | 5-1 |
| Jan 20 | 6f | Sell | Southwell | Won by 3l | SF | 99 | SP | 6-4 |
| Jan 27 | 6f | Clm | Southwell | Won by 2l | SF | 100 | SP | 4-6 |
| Feb 3 | 6f | Sell | Southwell | 3rd btn 4½l | SF | 77 | SP | 6-4 |
| Feb 17 | 6f | Sell | Southwell | Won by Nk | SF | 91 | SP | 3-1 |
| Feb 26 | 7f | Clm | Wolverhampton | Won by Hd | SF | 89 | SP | Evs F |

Following the fairly obvious warm-up in a handicap, he produced three consistent speed figures, before the poor run on February 3. He probably didn't look right that day, as he drifted from 8-11 to the returned 6-4. Two subsequent wins were again consistent, although well below the figures he was producing in January. But basically, so long as Sense Of Priority remained in selling or claiming races, he could be relied upon to perform consistently.

At a much higher level of competition, Cim Bom Bom showed remarkable speed on his All-weather debut in November 1996, and sustained that level of performance throughout the winter:

| Nov 25 | 6f | 0-70 Hcp | Wolverhampton | Won by 7l | SF | 110 | SP | 10-1 |
|--------|-----|----------|---------------|-----------|-----|-----|-----|------|
| Dec 7 | 7f | 0-95 Hcp | Wolverhampton | Won by 1½l | SF | 107 | SP | 11-2 |
| Feb 12 | 7f | 0-90 Hcp | Wolverhampton | 2nd btn Nk | SF | 105 | SP | 10-3 |
| Feb 26 | 7f | Cond | Wolverhampton | Won by Nk | SF | 104 | SP | 8-15 |

If every All-weather runner were as consistent as that, speed figures would be the only thing a punter would need. The figure of 110 on his All-weather debut was astonishing, and provided a strong pointer to his ability to handle the step up in class that followed. His only defeat was by a neck, conceding in the final stride to the seven-furlong All-weather specialist Rakis.

As if to demonstrate that racing always retains the ability to surprise even the best informed of punters, the biggest debut figure in my entire experience was recorded by New Century. When winning a nine-furlong handicap at Wolverhampton on February 26, he clocked a figure of 118. When he returned on March 8 for the Lincoln Trial Stakes, a £20,000 added eight-furlong handicap, I thought defeat was out of the question. He was backed from 5-1 down to 11-4 favourite, but could only manage second behind his stable companion, the consistent claiming winner Rambo Waltzer – the horse who could never produce his form in a handicap. Oh well – if they all won, the bookmakers would disappear!

The figures also give me the confidence to oppose a winner who records a poor speed figure. When Aspecto Lad won a selling race at Southwell on January 6, his figure of 61 suggested he might be the slowest winner of the winter. He was beaten on each of five subsequent All-weather runs, twice going off favourite, including a defeat at 4-6 when ridden by one L Dettori.

I now have three years' experience of creating and using All-weather speed figures, using the methods I've described. The guidelines I've now settled on are as follows:

- Remember that a speed figure tells you what the horse did last time. It doesn't automatically predict what he'll do this time.

- Don't expect a horse to reproduce a fast figure in one type of race (i.e. handicap, claimer, maiden) when he runs in a different type of race.

- Most horses can produce a similar speed figure at more than one distance

- Any speed figure that is three points or more above the par for the class indicates a horse worth following.

- Most horses can produce similar figures at each of the three tracks.

- The fastest horse can't win if he's badly drawn, or if the likely pace of the race won't suit.

- Slow winners can produce good bets – oppose them. (This sounds ridiculously obvious, but a last-time-out winner invariably attracts market support).

I can guarantee that if you start using speed figures for the All-weather, there will be days when winner-finding looks amazingly easy.

# All-weather track bias

The title for this discussion uses the American term 'bias', and I think it is the best and most appropriate. When considering a race on the All-weather, there are two factors to consider that come under this heading. The first is track position – is it best to be on the inside rail, or on the outside and how is this influenced by the starting stall positions and the draw? The second is the question of whether the track is favouring front-runners or strong finishers. In my experience, as the All-weather tracks have bedded down and the owners have improved their maintenance programmes, there are no longer any clear-cut answers to those questions.

The most startling changes have taken place at Wolverhampton. When that track opened in December 1993, it soon became obvious that a front-runner with an inside draw might as well stay at home, as it had no chance in the race. The bias became so important, that jockeys were fighting to get to the outside rail in the finishing straight. If three or four horses were upsides with two-furlongs to run, in 90 per cent of races, it was the one running nearest to the outside rail who produced the strongest finish and went on to win. Jockeys with an inside draw were willing to give ground at the start in order to switch outside and improve their prospects of success. Those who saw the useful Cretan Gift win over six-furlongs on 22 June 1996, were given a perfect demonstration of this tactic. Running from stall two in a field of 13, the formbook reported 'slow to stride, but recovering to lead inside the last-furlong'. Those low drawn horses that stayed on the inside were beaten out of sight.

This remained the trend at Wolverhampton until the beginning of 1997. Around the Christmas and New Year period, there was a sustained spell of very cold weather. I attended an extra meeting staged to compensate for the loss of the NH racing on Saturday 4 January. The staff had worked long hours to keep the track raceable, but the meeting was still put in doubt after the second race. The jockeys complained that the surface was dangerous, with frozen lumps of Fibresand being thrown up. A delay to the third race allowed for some more work with the harrow, and the meeting continued. But it wasn't like any meeting I'd previously seen at the track. In the fourth race, Leigh Crofter made all in a seven-furlong handicap, starting from stall two of eight. Half an hour later, the 25-1 shot Amy Leigh made all in a five-furlong claiming race. In the final race, again over seven-furlongs, Elite Hope was in front before they had covered two-furlongs and made the rest of the running. And all of those winners came around the inside on the final turn, not the more normal route straight to the outside rail.

The change in the style of racing continued throughout the next few weeks; and, in fact, Wolverhampton has never returned to the come-from-behind and run-wide track it was prior to this year. Throughout 1997, there has been no clear pattern that I can identify, either in the importance of the draw, or in the running style required. Once again, the most likely explanation of these changes comes from the American experience. The American professional Joe Takach reports: "We have a phenomenon that happens every winter without fail. We call it the first freeze. It occurs after rain and the temperature plummets into the teens and the inside freezes. Horses breaking from the one, two and three holes dominate the finish line. It doesn't matter if they've ever shown a lick of speed. They more or less slide to the front and never back up."

Well, I wouldn't have put it just like that, but, once translated, the description matches what happened at Wolverhampton. Why only in 1997? I guess that was the first time we had a sufficiently severe spell of weather cold enough to affect the Fibresand that makes up the surface. What might be an annual event in the climate of Philadelphia is much rarer here. The major flaw in this argument is the lack of supporting evidence from the track at Southwell, which also uses Fibresand, but that has never shown the same bias to wide-running, fast finishers. Perhaps it doesn't really matter why the bias at Wolverhampton changed, but it was certainly important to be aware that a change had taken place. The lesson for punters is to recognise that the weather can have a marked impact on the way the All-weather tracks behave.

The cold spell also seemed to affect the surface at Lingfield. For much of their winter season during the early months of 1997, the inside rail was riding much slower than the ground four or five horses wide of the rail. In race after race, the leader into the home straight would flounder and be caught by something finishing wide. The bias was easy to spot, but not so easy to use to betting advantage, as plenty of the jockeys still seemed to be convinced that the inside rail was the place to be! To identify a bias of this sort, and to assess its importance, there is no substitute for watching the races. The formbooks make little or no effort to inform on the track position of the runners – it isn't considered important on turf and they have made no concession so far to the different requirements of All-weather information.

I have developed a simple, but reasonably effective method of keeping myself alert to the best draw positions on each track. As with the speed figures, I only bother about races at up to ten-furlongs. I record the draw positions of the first six finishers in handicaps, awarding six points to the winning stall, five points for second and so on. I limit the records to races with a full field of runners, or those within two of the safety limit. For example, the maximum number of runners over six-furlongs at Wolverhampton is 13 so only races with 11, 12 or 13, runners are included. I omit maiden, claiming and selling races from the analysis, as the differing abilities of the runners should be more important than the draw in such contests.

Here are some sample figures for Wolverhampton, which relate to the period in 1995 immediately after the introduction of the rule requiring jockeys to run straight after leaving the stalls. These are the results of nine six-furlong handicaps with a full field, showing each occasion on which points were scored:

| Stall | Points | Total |
|---|---|---|
| 1 | 4,3 | 7 |
| 2 | 3,1 | 4 |
| 3 | 2,4 | 6 |
| 4 | 4,6,1,1,3 | 15 |
| 5 | 6,1,4,6 | 16 |
| 6 | 4,2,2 | 8 |
| 7 | 6,3,4 | 13 |

| 8 | 2,5,5,2,2,1 | 17 |
|---|---|---|
| 9 | 1,2,5 | 8 |
| 10 | 1,1,2,3,3,5,5 | 20 |
| 11 | 5,3,3,5,6,6,5 | 33 |
| 12 | 3,2,6,4,4 | 19 |
| 13 | 6,6,4,5 | 21 |
| Stalls  1-3 | 17 pts | 0/9 winners | 0/9 seconds |
| Stalls  4-6 | 39 pts | 3/9 winners | 0/9 seconds |
| Stalls  7-9 | 38 pts | 1/9 winners | 3/9 seconds |
| Stalls 10-13 | 93 pts | 5/9 winners | 6/9 seconds |

Faced with figures like these, it would be a brave or foolhardy punter who decided to back a horse drawn one, two or three in a six-furlong handicap at Wolverhampton. I think this method is slightly better than just considering the stall positions of the winners. Once I have data covering ten races, I would eliminate the oldest race each time I added a new one. In that way, I'm only considering the most recent evidence, and a change in the trend can be spotted quickly. I could give you details of the current state of my statistics for all three tracks, but it would be out of date by the time this is published. You have to do some of the work yourselves!

By the way, I haven't employed the same method on turf, simply because the number of runners varies so greatly at most courses from race to race. One of the advantages of any sort of analysis of All-weather racing is that most races attract a full field of runners. This is particularly true at Wolverhampton, where the maximum number of runners for any race is 13.

# Pace in All-weather races

One of the attractions of All-weather racing over turf is that the great majority of the races are run at a true pace. That is especially true of the races on which I concentrate my efforts, those over distances from five to ten-furlongs. Indeed, on the sand it is more important to consider whether the pace might be too fast, as the jockeys all know the importance of a good early position in All-weather races. The American experience is that a lone front-runner is the best bet of all in a dirt track race, remembering of course that 99 per cent of their races are run over trips between six and nine-furlongs. Over there, the bias to early speed is so well understood that any horse who looks likely to get an unopposed run in front, will be heavily backed on their Tote system. But since pace is much less understood in this country, it is still possible to find standout bets by looking for front-runners.

The advantage of early pace hasn't always been apparent on our three All-weather tracks. During 1995/6, I would have opposed a front-runner at Southwell and Wolverhampton, both of which strongly favoured the strong finisher. But the tracks have changed and so, I suspect, have the attitudes of the jockeys. They have come to realise that the best way to ride on sand is the exact reverse of the ideal for turf. It's hardly surprising that this change has taken time – every rider knows that to go off at top speed on turf is to make defeat certain, as discussed earlier in the Turf section. But on the sand, the front-runner doesn't get swamped, because the horses in behind can't produce the same sort of acceleration that they do on turf. In addition, the front-runner avoids the kickback that deters those in behind. Anybody watching the All-weather meetings staged during November and December 1997 would have seen that the majority of the winners were either in front throughout, or running within two lengths of the pace from the start.

Unexpectedly, the races that were least likely to match this pattern were the five-furlong races at Lingfield. Having watched a number of these races several times on video, my guess is that the front-runner is beaten by the turn into the short straight. At a point in the race where he would achieve top speed on a straight five-furlongs, he has to slow to negotiate the turn. It probably only increases his time for the all-important penultimate-furlong by a fraction of a second, but the front-runner also loses momentum. That sets him up to be swamped close home by a horse who has approached the turn at the optimum speed and has sustained that speed all the way to the line. I could be completely wrong, but that theory would explain why the five-furlong races so often change dramatically in the last 100 yards, when the six-furlong+ races are run to a different pattern.

The biggest barrier to making bets on the basis of pace analysis, is the total lack of any official sectional timing. Horses who habitually front-run can be identified from the formbook, or by watching the races, but there is no easy way to distinguish a horse that runs the first two furlongs in 26 seconds, from one that takes 27 seconds. To the naked eye, if both were leading by two lengths after covering two-furlongs, it would be impossible to tell the difference. I could, of course, attempt to produce my own sectional times from the SIS films. But with a hand-held stopwatch, a lack of clear markers on the track and the frequent use of head-on shots by SIS, the results would be nowhere near accurate enough to be used for betting purposes.

As a result, the decisions on who the front-runners will be have to be made on the basis of personal observation, combined with the information available in the formbook. For an example of a pace-inspired bet, let's look at the first race at Lingfield on December 4, a six-furlong handicap, class 0-60. There were four leading contenders in the field of nine:

**SHARP IMP**     **7-10-0**          **Drawn 4**          **2-1  fav**
*No early pace, but usually running on at finish. Poor win-to-run career record. Fourth of 13 over 7f here two days ago.*

**TIME TO FLY**     **4-9-6**          **Drawn 5**          **4-1**
*Committed front-runner, better on All-weather than turf. Fifth of 16 over 6f at Southwell on Nov 24 after a three month break. Taken on for lead early by eventual winner.*

**TACHYCARDIA    5-8-10          Drawn 8          6-1**
*One time front-runner, now ridden from behind after two course wins in January using that method. No recent form.*

**RIVER ENSIGN    4-8-8          Drawn 3          5-1**
*Front runner on two recent starts at Wolverhampton, latest over seven-furlongs when headed halfway, but keeping on for third.*

The other five runners were all 10-1 or more, and their records suggested that the use of the term 'racehorse' could lead to a prosecution under the Trade Descriptions Act. This simple example could be quickly reduced to two front-runners, taking on two strong finishers. I was in no doubt that the current profile of races at Lingfield would see the front-runners successful, unless they took each other on at a suicidal pace. I thought that very unlikely for two reasons. Firstly, both had been beaten by early pace battles in recent races, and connections would surely have a Plan B if that happened again. Secondly, and more importantly, I felt that Time To Fly would simply be too fast for River Ensign. At the opening show of 5-1, he was tremendous value if I was right.

Time To Fly showed much the best early pace and was soon well clear of River Ensign and the other two, and ran on well to beat Sharp Imp by eight lengths, with Tachycardia and River Ensign close up in the next two positions. Mark up a gold star for pace analysis – well, almost. The four contenders had run exactly as predicted, but the race went to the 16-1 shot Chipstead Bay, trained by Ken Ivory and making his debut in Britain (and therefore his All-weather debut), having been bought from Ireland just a few weeks earlier. Clearly suited by the sand, Chipstead Bay was able to sit just off the pace set by Time To Fly and swallowed him whole before the final-furlong. Comparing the times for this race and Division II staged later the same day, showed that Time To Fly would have won the other race by at least six lengths!

Chipstead Bay went on to confirm that his performance was no fluke, rewarding support in his next two starts at Lingfield. Those two races showed the value of early pace, as he first won over seven-furlongs, disputing the lead throughout and drawing clear at the two-furlong pole. He was then dropped into a five-furlong race to take a last chance off his old handicap mark, and still had sufficient speed to keep in touch for the first three furlongs, whereafter he came back onto the bridle and won cosily. By comparison, the beaten favourite in the race analysed above, Sharp Imp, has no early speed whatever the trip. He is only able to win on the All-weather when the race is set up for him by several front-runners beating each other by going too fast – and even then he has to get a clear run and hit the front in the final fifty yards. Not easy!

Currently, all three tracks appear to be favouring early pace and I'll be concentrating on pace when analysing races. It has taken a few years, but All-weather racing in this country now shares many of the characteristics of dirt track racing in the USA. Things might change, but I don't expect to return to the situation in which strong finishers were the dominant force on the All-weather tracks. Punters who look for the speed to point to winners should hold the upper hand, until the rest of the mob catch on to the trend.

# All-weather workshop

This section provides the background to ten bets I made on the AW tracks during November and December 1997. Since I was generally attending NH meetings during that period, all of these bets were placed with tax paid on, as the racecourse shops and Tote Credit were no longer permitted to accept bets at board prices. Hopefully this ludicrous restriction will have been lifted by the time you read this, as part of the reforms due to be introduced to the on-course market in 1998.

I haven't accounted for the tax element in the figures in these pages. On-course, I still have the option to bet tax free at starting price, but as you'll see that wouldn't have been a very good idea in most cases. The market at the AW meetings isn't strong, even at Lingfield, which is by far the best. Most of these bets were also horses that I recommended on my phone service, with predictable impact on the prices.

**10/11  Ling  8f 0-80 Hcp  TWIN CREEKS  2nd  SP 2-1**
**£1250/500**

*Twin Creeks was running in a 0-80 handicap under a 6lb penalty for his win the previous Thursday. His speed figure of 106 in that race qualified him as strong contender to repeat his win, running in the same class. I was confident the weight increase wouldn't stop him, and the only doubt was the trip. His win had been over seven furlongs and this was a mile. I'm also of the opinion that the distance of the race, within reason, makes little difference to a decent AW performer. The ability to act on the surface and go the early pace are paramount. The horses are generally restricted to running over a narrow range of trips, but that is more due to trainers carrying over ideas from turf racing than from any evidence that it makes any difference. I backed him at early price 5-2, and he was returned 2-1 favourite.*

*He was in front before halfway on the inside rail, but always looked vulnerable once the winner, Puzzlement, came alongside. The pair finished clear of the rest, and I don't think the extra-furlong beat Twin Creeks. When I calculated the speed figures, that view was confirmed as he recorded a figure of 107, consistent with his previous run, with the winner on 110 and a horse to follow.*

**17/11 South 6f Hcp**      **PHOENIX PRINCESS**     **1st**    **SP 4-1**
                                                    **£2400/400**

*Since the new surface had been in use at Southwell, it had been clear that over the six- and seven-furlong trips, early pace and a low draw gave a horse a marked advantage. Because the track was now riding faster, it appeared to be more difficult to make up ground in the final stages.*

*The track also seemed to be more even across its entire width, so that the inside position on the long home turn was now favoured, since that was obviously the shortest route. This bias pointed me strongly to Phoenix Princess in the six-furlong fillies handicap. She was drawn in stall one in a field of 16, and had much better AW form than any other runner drawn in single figures. She had been running regularly at AW meetings during the summer, generally running in front or prominently over a mile. I knew that dropping down to six furlongs for the first time in her career would put off punters, but I felt that if she could go the pace for the first furlong, she would be in front on the turn and wouldn't be stopping at the finish. She opened 7-1 and rapidly dropped to 4-1 favourite - I managed to get on at 6-1.*

*Driven along early, she got in front after a furlong, was clear at halfway and ran on to win by two lengths. The speed figure was an amazingly slow 85, so it was no surprise to see her beaten at Wolverhampton four days later, when she was sent off at odds of 9-2.*

**18/11 Ling**    **5f 0-70 Hcp**    **PALACEGATE JACK**    **1st**    **SP 2-1**
                                                    **£1500/500**

*In the early part of the year, I had considerable success in five-furlong handicaps at Lingfield, backing horses who would ignore the usual furious early pace. So the two divisions of a five-furlong 0-70 handicap were the races I concentrated on at this meeting. Palacegate Jack had run here on November 6, finishing second over the trip, behind Anokato. That day, ridden by a 5lb claimer, he led at halfway and was headed inside the final furlong.*

*Going back to the previous AW season, he had several speed figures suggesting he could outclass this very ordinary field. I anticipated that today, ridden by the top-notch apprentice Carl Lowther, he would have his run delayed until the final furlong. I expected a price of around 9-4, so the opening show of 3-1 was compelling and I stepped in immediately. He briefly touched 100-30, before being backed down to 2-1 favourite.*

*Tucked in behind three front-runners, the only doubt came when* he clipped the heels of a horse in front on the final turn, and almost fell. He recovered his balance quickly, challenged 100 yards from home and got up to win by a head. He had produced a speed figure of 96 when second to Anokato, and ran a 97 here, confirmation that no improvement was needed to beat slow rivals.

**21/11  Wolv  7f 0-60 Hcp   TROJAN HERO          1st   SP 4-1**
                                                       **£1750/500**

Trojan Hero had come to Britain from South Africa as galloping companion for the top class London News, who ran behind Bosra Sham at Royal Ascot. Barry Hills ran him in a turf claiming race at Leicester, which he won, and he then moved to his current trainer, Mary Reveley.

He'd been disappointing on turf, but as a result had dropped to a handicap mark of 56. He made his AW debut in a 16-runner seven-furlong handicap at Southwell and caught my eye running on well to take third from an almost impossible draw in stall 14. The first two home in that race were drawn six and three, and the fourth came out of stall two, which emphasised the problem Trojan Hero had faced.

Dropped into a weak 0-60 handicap today, I expected him to be around 7-4 favourite, and when I phoned Tote Credit from the Reading motorway service area (on the way home from Ascot), I was very happy to take 7-2. He ended up at 4-1 in the face of support for the favourite Concer Arall – 5-1 down to 2-1.

Trojan Hero hacked up, exceeding even my expectations, winning eased down by six lengths. Despite that margin of victory, his speed figure was only 96, exactly the par for a 0-60 race. As a result, I wasn't interested in following up a week later when he reappeared in a 0-70 handicap at Lingfield and finished second, starting the 3-1 favourite.

**25/11  Ling  8f 0-70 Hcp   PUZZLEMENT           1st   SP 3-1**
                                                       **£1600/400**

Puzzlement's win over Twin Creeks, with a speed figure of 110, made him looked nailed on in this lower grade handicap, even with a 7lb rise in his official rating. His win had come off a mark of 63 in a 0-80 contest, and this was a 0-70 race, in which he carried top weight. My figure for his win had been supported by an excellent 'plus 14' from Timeform.

He won OK, but was probably a shade fortunate, as the runner-up, White Plains, failed to get a clear run and was only beaten a head. The speed figure for this win was only 100, equivalent to a *performance five lengths inferior to his earlier win, but a par figure for a 0-70 handicap and certainly good enough to win most races of that class.*

**28/11 Ling 5f Nursery CLASSY CLEO 1st SP 4-1**
**£1600/400**

*Classy Cleo had overcome her lack of AW experience to win a six-furlong nursery at Southwell last time, recording a speed figure of 102. That is a very good figure for a two-year-old, since I make no allowance for the slower times that younger horses produce due to their immaturity. She had shown plenty of speed on that occasion, and I didn't expect that the drop to five furlongs here would be a problem. She also had an apprentice called Adrian McCarthy riding and claiming 7lbs. He'd impressed me on two previous rides that I'd seen on the Racing Channel and I was confident he'd be good enough.*

*Given a confident and competent ride by a jockey who I expect to be a star of the 1998 season, Classy Cleo ran on to lead inside the final furlong, winning by just over a length. She recorded a speed figure of 103 this time, and went on to finish second in a seven-furlong conditions event at Wolverhampton, where she was disadvantaged by running widest into the straight. The handicapper raised her to a mark of 100 after the Lingfield win, which effectively disqualified her from running again on the AW.*

**6/12 Wolv 7f Hcp CHEWIT 1st SP 4-1**
**£1800/200**

*This was the Wolverhampton meeting that was shown live on Channel 4 on a Saturday afternoon. Chewit was top weight for the sponsored seven-furlong handicap, running from a mark of 99. His consistent record on the AW tracks included several wins at Lingfield, and he'd been placed in this same race the previous season. On his latest start, he'd finished two and half lengths third behind Farmost, over the extended mile at Wolverhampton. The winner's speed figure was 112, so Chewit recorded a 107 (minus 2 points per length).*

*In this field of twelve, only State Of Caution could match that on recent running, but I was confident that Chewit would be better suited by the drop to seven furlongs, as he'd looked the likely winner with a furlong to run last time. State Of Caution was likely to be taken on for the lead in a race with plenty of pace. Chewit looked ideally drawn in stall four, with the track favouring the inside at recent meetings. I took the early 9-1 with Corals to the small stake noted above, planning a top-up later.*

*Working from home that day, I waited for the opening show to appear on Text, only to realise too late that the computer system had failed and the text display was frozen. By the time Channel 4 gave a show for the race, Chewit was already down to 4-1. This was my first week trying to manage without the Tote Credit account that I'd used for many years past. The run of winners on the AW documented above had finally persuaded them that I couldn't be beaten, and I'd been restricted to Tote odds only – about as much use to me as an Arsenal season ticket.*

*Chewit missed a beat at the start, settled in just behind the leader, State Of Caution, on the inside, and cheekily challenged between that horse and Primo Lara in the straight. When that gap closed, he still had enough in hand to switch inside and quicken past them close home to win by almost two lengths. A high class performance, and very few horses can actually produce that sort of change of speed on the AW surfaces. I suspect that Chewit would be Group class on the sand, if he were only given the chance to demonstrate his ability in that grade.*

**6/12   Wolv   9f Lstd      RUNNING STAG      2nd   SP 9-2**
                                                    **£1350/300**

*This was the other TV race from Wolverhampton, the Listed contest over nine furlongs. The favourite, Centre Stalls, has been discussed earlier in this section of the book, and at around even-money he had to be opposed. Running Stag had finished a close second in a one-mile conditions race at Lingfield, recording a speed figure of 128. I had some reservations about the validity of that figure, but even if it were ten points too high, it would still have been the best AW performance by any of the runners in this race.*

*For most of the race, this looked a good bet. The favourite Centre Stalls never threatened to take a hand, and Running Stag looked likely to overhaul the all-the-way leader Farmost as they entered the straight. Inside the final furlong, he hung fire and Farmost galloped on to win by half a length, with the third horse seven lengths further behind.*

*First impression was that Running Stag hadn't tried very hard when he came under pressure, a view supported by his turf record of being placed, but rarely winning. But when I produced the speed figures for the meeting, I gave the winner Farmost a rating of 135, so Running Stag had improved on his Lingfield run and was probably flat out when he appeared to be shirking the issue in the final furlong. Farmost improved markedly on his 112 last time (when Chewit was third) and Puzzlement finished third, earning a figure of 120, also confirming the improvement he'd shown in recent races.*

**10/12  Ling   7f 0-70 Hcp   CHIPSTEAD BAY        1st   SP 5-2**
                                                    **£1400/400**

*Chipstead Bay had arrived from Ireland with no previous AW experience and a low handicap mark based on his turf form. He'd shown that to be all wrong with an easy win first time out at Lingfield, taking a six-furlong 0-60 handicap by two and a half lengths – speed figure 104. That figure suggested he could hold his own in any race up to 0-80 class, so he looked a good thing in this 0-70 contest, even over an extra furlong. As a bonus, he had a useful looking draw in stall 4, which should enable to hold a good early position close to the inside rail. I took the early 7-2, and he was backed from 3-1 to 5-2 on-course.*

*Never out of the first two, he led two furlongs out and ran on for a comfortable success, beating Salty Jack, who'd produced a 101 speed figure over course and distance last time, with those two clear of a well-spread field. The winner's figure this time was 102. Chipstead Bay went on to win a 0-60 handicap over five furlongs before the handicapper caught up with him, and he was a beaten favourite in a 0-85 handicap when trying for a four-timer, just as his speed figures suggested.*

**12/12  Ling   8f 0-85 Hcp   NORTHERN ANGEL       PU   SP 3-1**
                                                    **£2250/700**

*Northern Angel had split Farmost and Chewit (see above) in a 0-100 handicap on his previous start, yet he wasn't even going to be favourite in this 0-85 contest. That honour went to White Plains, who had followed his second to Puzzlement with two very easy wins over ten furlongs. Despite those victories, I felt he was well worth opposing on the basis of the drop back to a mile (he'd never won over this trip) and the rise in class. Having expressed the view that AW horses can perform over any distance, I should explain that I'm always happier to see them moving up in trip, rather than down. A horse like White Plains, who can handle the pace over ten furlongs, is likely to find himself under pressure to hold a position over a mile – it's simply a question of handling the early pace. If the horse is racing in a class below the level of ability his speed figures say he can handle, then he should be able to manage at any trip. But once the handicapper forces a horse to race in a class which is close to his limit, then I do feel that aptitude at the trip becomes more important. White Plains had already shown that he had difficulty going the pace in a 0-70 race at this trip, when beaten by Puzzlement. At the early price offer of 11-10, he was no bargain in a 0-85 race. Northern Angel looked well able to handle the pace and his speed figures gave him the edge over the rest of the field, with Twin Creeks the only other runner likely to feature on recent form.*

*White Plains did indeed fail to handle the pace and finished third, sent off 11-8 favourite. Twin Creeks confirmed his recent good figure by taking second at a generous 12-1 to repay each-way backers, but the race was won by Banzhaf. He improved on a figure of 100 on his last run to put in a 108 here – the sort of figure needed to win a race this competitive. Northern Angel was never going the pace, and was pulled up lame inside the final furlong. I made this bet from Cheltenham, where I was watching the NH card – you expect to back the odd 'PU' over fences, but on the AW?*

## Summary

Most of those selected bets come from the purple patch at the start of the 1997/98 winter AW season. I concentrate on the winter period when the horses are running only on the AW tracks. During the summer the meetings are less frequent and horses are switching from turf to dirt, which makes form less consistent.

| Month | Winners/Bets | Profit/Loss | Overall Total |
|---|---|---|---|
| January | 2/5 | +2,500 | + 2,500 |
| February | 0/4 | - 2,000 | + 500 |
| March | 3/8 | +2,250 | + 2,750 |
| April | 0/1 | - 400 | + 2,350 |
| June | 1/1 | +3,500 | + 5,850 |
| November | 5/9 | +7,250 | +13,100 |
| December | 3/7 | +1,850 | +14,950 |
| **Total** | **14/35** | | **Profit £14,950** |

# PART 3

## NATIONAL HUNT

I'm often asked whether I prefer jumping or Flat racing – and I usually reply that it depends on what the questioner means. If we are talking about the racing as a sport or a spectacle, then I go for jump racing every time. I could never feel about any Flat horse the way I felt about Desert Orchid during the eighties, when going racing was still just a profitable hobby. And given the choice between an ordinary Flat card at Salisbury or a midweek jumping meeting at Wincanton, there could only be one decision. Quite simply, any day at a NH meeting can produce a new star, quite unexpectedly – what I call the 'Wow' factor, which I only see five or ten times each year.

But if we are talking about betting, and specifically about profitable betting, then the answer has to be that Flat racing is the choice. There are a number of reasons for this, but the most significant is the number of other professional punters operating at the NH meetings. On a winter Monday afternoon at Fontwell or Plumpton, there will up to a dozen professionals, several of whom concentrate on NH racing and either never go Flat racing, or only when there is no jumping scheduled. Their presence means that the majority of the money bet on a race at Fontwell is placed by shrewd, dedicated and successful punters, who make few mistakes when pricing up a race. That represents stiff competition for any punter, and it's quite common that a horse I've identified as a plausible bet over fences will open at much less than the price I had hoped for, simply because the others have seen the race in the same way.

Even at meetings where the proportion of 'mug' money might be expected to be higher, the same problem arises. For example, at Ascot on Saturday 1 November, my overnight work on the Bagshot

Handicap Chase had identified God Speed You as excellent value at the early morning price of 14-1. Thanks to the availability of early prices, I was able to get on at that price, but the best offer seen in the ring prior to the race was 8-1 (there was a non-runner priced at 6-1 in the early market). That was no surprise, as every conversation I'd had with other professionals at Ascot had included a mention of God Speed You and a comment on the price of 14-1. Quite simply, everybody had reached the same conclusion that the price was too big, and several were still happy to back the horse at 8-1.

A fall at the first fence left us all none the wiser as to the value, but the example shows how the level of competition makes life harder on the jumping circuit.

When I go to a Flat meeting, I'm unlikely to find more than four or five other professionals in attendance, and our money is absorbed in a bigger market, thanks to the presence of more racegoers, coach parties, etc. The 14-1 shot at a Flat meeting is more likely to be offered at that price on-course and I don't face a race to get on, before some of the younger and quicker men step in and take the price.

Another factor is that it is harder to find an alternative approach to jumping, something that would enable me to assess the races in a different light from other professionals. As we've seen, on the Flat, I can look at the draw, the pace, speed figures and the shape of the race. Some of those ideas can be applied, at least partially, to NH racing, but not to the extent that they make a significant difference.

As a result of these pressures, I've reduced my level of involvement with NH betting, with the better meetings now attracting most interest. I used to specialise almost entirely in handicap chases, and they still provided most of my winners in 1997, but I now utilise the full range of races looking for opportunities. Well almost the full range – I still draw the line at NH Flat races, or bumpers, as they are more commonly known.

Before moving on to discuss hurdling and chasing separately, let's look at whether the methods I use on the Flat have any relevance to NH races:

## • The Draw

Obviously not, because there is no draw for places at the start in NH races. The only thing likely to happen at the start that might affect the way the race is run, is the fact that the inside positions on the rail are traditionally taken by the senior jockeys. If you back a horse ridden by an amateur, or a conditional, expect to be on the outside. It won't often matter, but it can make a difference on a sharp track like Fontwell or Taunton.

## • Pace

A few years ago, slowly run races were fairly common on the southern jumping circuit, but as in many other ways, the methods of Martin Pipe have changed habits. A few of the horses he trains are held up, but the majority still set off in front and ensure a good pace. Over fences it's almost impossible to get a really slow pace, as that would make it difficult to jump the obstacles. Not surprisingly, it happens most often with small fields but, even with that knowledge, it isn't easy to identify which runner might be suited by a slow pace. I'm more inclined to believe that most chasers are equally unsuited by slowly run races, and although such races can produce false results, they are not predictable results.

## • Speed Figures

Even if I had the time and the will to create NH speed figures, I'm unconvinced of their value when set against what I can see when I watch a race. With only two or three chases run at each meeting, I cannot see how it's possible to calculate accurately the all-important variant. Certainly the figure for chases and hurdles would have to be different, as many tracks offer totally different going on the two tracks. For example, at Leicester, the hurdle races are run on the Flat track, which is watered all year long, whereas the chase course has to rely on nature for irrigation. It can be heavy over hurdles and good over fences on the same day. Add in the variations in distance caused by movement of rails on the bends to provide fresh ground, omitted or bypassed fences, and wide variations in the ability of the horses on a single card, and the numbers must involve more guesswork than a lottery ticket.

### • Shape of the race

I always like to see a chaser I've backed set off in front, so long as it isn't at an obviously suicidal pace. It's the best place to be in any chase, providing a clear view of the fences and a guarantee that the horse can't be brought down or hampered by other's mistakes. It's interesting to note how often the horses who lead over the first fence produce the winner of a chase – if you watch the 1997 Grand National, Lord Gyllene and Suny Bay were first and second over the first fence and continued in echelon all the way to the finish. So the shape I look for is a race with a single front-runner, who is likely to meet every fence unpressured by his opponents. But I don't believe there are any other patterns that warrant consideration when looking for a bet.

# Hurdle racing

If during the 1996 Flat season it had been possible to stage a two-mile race featuring Theatreworld, I'm Supposin, Sanmartino and Make A Stand, only one thing about the result would have been certain. Under whatever conditions the contest had been staged, Make A Stand would have been a 33-1 shot and he would have finished last. Whereas the other three are at least top class handicappers, Make A Stand had changed hands for just £8,000 after winning a claiming race at Leicester.

From that unpromising start, Make A Stand progressed so far and so fast that in the 1997 Champion Hurdle, he comprehensively outpaced those three rivals, who would have left him for dead on the level. Whilst the remarkable talent of champion trainer Martin Pipe must be given a share of the credit, the most important factor in Make A Stand's success was his jumping. He is quite simply, the fastest and most fluent jumper of hurdles I've seen since the early days of Desert Orchid. Whereas the vast majority of horses slow down, shorten their stride and lose momentum at each hurdle, Make A Stand visibly accelerates and attacks the obstacle with naked enthusiasm, and yet retains his balance sufficiently well that he lands running with no loss of speed whatsoever. Combine that with the front-running style that epitomises horses trained by Martin Pipe and you have a formidable weapon.

When he won a novice hurdle at Ascot on the pre-Christmas card in December 1996, a leading professional punter remarked to me that his opening price of 11-10 had been the best bet of the season. As someone who rarely bets any horse at less than 2-1, I thought this smacked of the overstatement that comes naturally after a successful wager. I was wrong, and so was he – the 11-10 about Make A Stand that day was probably the safest odds-against bet of the decade. By the time he ran in the Tote Gold Trophy at Newbury in February 1997, he had already dominated the Lanzarote Handicap Hurdle at Kempton, in what was now becoming familiar style. As each race he ran during the season represented a further step up in class, so punters were convinced that he had reached the ceiling of his ability and that he would be unable to dominate this time.

At Newbury, we were once again proved wrong as he routed his field, taking lengths off his rivals at each of the early hurdles and setting a . pace that nothing else could sustain, whether the opposing riders wanted to or not. After the race a small group of professionals gathered by the pre-parade ring as usual to view the field for the next. But very unusually, on this occasion, it was the previous race that still held our attention. There was good deal of head shaking, a few 'how does he do it' questions and general disbelief that a horse of such unprepossessing appearance and obvious lack of scope could go on producing an ever-improving level of form.

Make A Stand looks what he is – a Flat-bred horse of limited ability. He is not small, but certainly less than medium size for a hurdler, carries no physical condition such as one would expect on an improving type, and certainly looks as if two or three races close together would exhaust his resources. As punters, we have learned that Martin Pipe can run up a sequence of wins with horses of this type, but normally only at the lower levels of competition that prevail at the 'gaff' tracks. With Make A Stand it all comes back to the jumping ability, which can be helped, but which has to be principally the horse's natural ability and courage.

When Make A Stand sets off in front, he does so at a pace that would exhaust any normal hurdler. But his jumping enables him to relax on the flat between obstacles, and because he doesn't slow at each hurdle, he doesn't have to use his resources to accelerate back to cruising speed after each jump. So not only is he gaining ground by his quick jumping, he is also saving energy by sustaining a level speed throughout the race, and it is this that transforms the moderate Flat horse into a star over hurdles. Whilst the natural fluency of Make A Stand made his success possible, credit has to be given to his trainer, Martin Pipe, for recognising the potential of his charge, and his placing of the horse to take advantage. It is hard to think of many other current trainers who would have got the horse from a minor race at Stratford to the Champion Hurdle in the space of seven months. Most would have opted for easier races, perhaps ending up in the Cheltenham novice championship, because they would never have been able to forget his humble origins.

When considering a horse transferring from the Flat to hurdling, always remember Make A Stand, as highlighting the impossibility of setting hard and fast rules about what type of horse will do best over hurdles. In recent seasons, quite a few high class horses have tried their luck, with the likes of Alderbrook and Royal Gait demonstrating what can be achieved. But I've seen plenty more that balance that picture of success, with horses of Group race ability unable to win a novice hurdle – River North, where are you now? In the closing months of 1997 we saw two more top-notch recruits apparently flatter to deceive, only to disappoint as soon as they stepped up in class – Zaralaska and Grey Shot. After a facile and impressive win at Ascot, featuring some fluent jumping, Zaralaska was turned over at 1-5 in a novice hurdle at Leicester, and ended 1997 with a total flop at Kempton on Boxing Day, this time at 4-6. He may well return and show that form to be all wrong, but it appears he can't cope with two miles except on good or fast ground. Grey Shot has fared rather better, but was beaten in the Tolworth Hurdle, having been backed at some pretty short prices for the Champion Hurdle on the strength of a win at Taunton against rivals whose only chance of appearing at Cheltenham is to join the police force.

Compare their record with that of the juvenile Sound Appeal. Her best form on the Flat was a fourth of 15 in a ten-furlong maiden handicap at Salisbury and she ended an unsuccessful season by finishing 14th in a 0-60 Limited Stakes at Leicester. She first appeared over hurdles at Kempton in mid-October – I could report the views of a couple of paddock experts on her appearance, but I have to bear in mind the libel laws, as well as the sensibilities of readers. Suffice it to say that she didn't catch anyone's eye as an obvious candidate for NH fame. She won that race at 33-1 and has gone on to record two further wins at the time of writing, establishing herself near the top of the juvenile rating lists. She isn't a brilliant jumper, so the most likely explanation of her success is that two miles over hurdles has tapped reserves of stamina that neither her looks nor her pedigree would have suggested.

So my first rule of hurdle race selection is to totally ignore what a horse has done on the Flat, and analyse only its form over hurdles. This alone will provide plenty of opportunities during any season for opposing short-priced runners who are either unproven over obstacles, or have only modest form.

A second significant factor is the question of stamina shown on the Flat, and how that translates to hurdle races. The common assumption is that any horse who has shown its form at two miles on the Flat will inevitably prove best suited by farther than two miles over hurdles. But once again, the usefulness of evidence from the Flat is limited. Earlier I mentioned two champion hurdlers, Alderbrook and Royal Gait, both of whom had top class form on the Flat. But although both were at their best over two miles over hurdles, Alderbrook was a ten-furlong performer on the Flat, whilst Royal Gait won the Ascot Gold Cup over twice that distance. A simplistic view of stamina requirements would have persuaded the connections of Royal Gait that they would be wasting their time running in the Champion Hurdle. Perhaps he would have been even better at three miles over hurdles, but if so, he'd have been an awesome, once-in-a-lifetime winner of the Stayers Hurdle!

Once again I look to oppose Flat-bred horses in hurdle races at two and a half miles or farther, until they have proved that they stay the trip. It's at that distance horses specifically bred for NH racing, and who have begun their career in bumpers, begin to come into their own. On soft ground in mid-winter, it isn't just stamina that's needed, but strength, and not many Flat racers can demonstrate both qualities.

## Novice hurdles

No type of race run in Britain has changed more in the past ten or fifteen years than the novice hurdle. I'm old enough to remember times when a track like Leicester or Warwick would run four divisions of a novice hurdle on a single card and have more than 20 runners in each race. Even the major tracks had no problem pulling in maximum fields at their major meetings, with Newbury always having two divisions on Hennessey Day at the end of November, with at least forty horses turning out for the novice hurdles. The first horse I ever owned, Comrie, ran in a novice hurdle at Cheltenham in January 1980, finishing seventh in a field of 25, and the same number contested the opening race on the card. At Windsor on the same afternoon, 40 four-year-olds ran in two divisions of the juvenile novice hurdle, and another 90 novices turned out at the two day meeting at Nottingham the following Monday and Tuesday.

What happened? Well mostly, AW racing happened and NH Flat races happened. But there was also recognition by the authorities that endless novice hurdles weren't attractive to the viewing or betting public, which led to a reduction in opportunities for dividing races. At Newbury in 1997, the novice hurdle on Hennessey Day attracted just 14 runners, the same as the feature chase. What this means for the punter, I'm not sure I'm best placed to say but, clearly, novice hurdles are less competitive than used to be the case and I tend not to bet in them as much as I used to when I was younger.

Another factor that has cut the fields since the eighties is the introduction of novice handicaps, which didn't exist at all in those days. If there is one category of race, after bumpers, that I reckon should be at the bottom of any punter's list, it's novice handicap hurdles. To qualify for one of these lotteries, a horse usually has to fail three times in novice hurdles. It's hardly surprising that these races don't respond to analysis. I've no doubt there are punters reading this who swear by novice handicaps as the source of their pension contributions, but count me out.

I normally prefer to watch novice hurdles rather than bet on them, looking for future opportunities in handicaps. When I do bet it will usually be on the basis already discussed, opposing a Flat-bred horse who's backed to short price on the strength of Flat form, especially over an extended trip. I participated in a couple of Cheltenham Festival previews in 1997, so I felt compelled to offer a view on the two-mile novice hurdle. It would have sounded a bit weak to accept an invitation and then say "no comment" for the first race on the card. The choice wasn't difficult, as I'd seen Shadow Leader win at Newbury and been deeply impressed. Having no knowledge of the Irish contenders, I didn't claim he would win, but I was confident he'd be the best of the local runners. He'd won both his starts over hurdles before Cheltenham, so by that stage his Flat form no longer mattered. He'd shown what he could do over hurdles and went on to confirm that he was top class.

In that race at Newbury, another Flat horse made his debut over hurdles. That was Polydamas, once with Michael Stoute and now in the care of Kim Bailey. Polydamas finished third, beaten 11 lengths. He later ran eighth behind Shadow Leader at Cheltenham, his final race of the season. He reappeared at Stratford in October, in a maiden hurdle over two miles, six furlongs. Although he was forecast as the odds-on favourite in both trade papers, and universally tipped to win, I felt he was worth opposing over that distance. As the only other horse to start at less than 11-1, the second-favourite, China Gem, was the obvious choice. His stamina was proven, as he'd been placed over three miles at Towcester. Polydamas started at 4-9, but could only manage third, beaten 21 lengths by the winner, Danger Flynn at 33-1. I'd mislaid the telephone number of Mystic Meg's tipping service, so I can't claim to have backed the winner. But taking on favourites at that sort of price only has to work once every three or four tries to produce a profit.

## Handicap hurdles

As always, I'm happier looking at races in which the runners have sufficient form for patterns to be apparent. In recent years, I've avoided two-mile handicaps, which I find to be closely related to sprint handicaps in their nature, with the horses apparently taking turns to win. I admit this prejudice may be illogical and that a rational analysis of such races would show my view to be incorrect, but no punter can keep on top of all the races run in this country and I'm prepared to ignore the two-mile events.

Over distances of two and a half miles or farther, I do bet on handicap hurdles and have had some success by the very simple strategy of supporting winners to do the same again. My theory is that long distance hurdle racing is a tough physical test for a horse, and only those who are one hundred per cent fit and sound can cope. The best way for a hurdler to demonstrate the qualities I'm looking for is to win a similar race. There aren't many qualifiers, but that suits me, as I'm not looking for a handicap hurdle bet every day, and I tend to concentrate on the better class races anyway. Two examples from 1997 will show that it's worth the wait.

The first was at Warwick on February 15, in a two-and-a-half-mile handicap, grade 0-115, about the lowest I'd normally consider. There were 13 runners, but only one of them, Lets Be Frank, had won a race during the current season. Two had pulled up last time and three others were returning after long periods out of action. Lets Be Frank had actually won three races already, all over this sort of trip, and had patently failed to stay when put over farther at Uttoxeter on his latest start. That had been in a much better race, grade 0-145, so it was hardly surprising that he'd been found out. Despite his successful record, Lets Be Frank was overlooked by plenty of the media pundits, who made cases for various rivals who might win if they returned to form. They didn't, and Lets Be Frank clocked up his fourth win of the season, at the generous SP of 3-1 joint-favourite, having touched 7-2.

It was a similar story at Ascot on March 26, a three-mile handicap, grade 0-135. The winner here was Tribune, who had won all four previous starts during the season, the last two over this trip, but was still sent off at 100-30 in a field of seven. Presumably in this case, the price stemmed from the fact that Tribune was trained in the north, and was unfamiliar to Ascot punters. But I never let prejudice get in the way of a 7-2 winning bet!

# Chasing

## Novice chases

I only made six bets in novice chases, including novice handicaps, during the whole of 1997, so you may feel that this chapter will be less useful than a Terry Venables guide to good business practice. Actually, three of those six bets were winners, so perhaps I do have a workable method. It's very simple and has just three rules:

- I only back a novice chaser who has already shown solid form, either a win or finished close-up

- I concentrate on the better class novice chases

- I ignore hurdle form

The first means that I know the horse has shown the ability to jump round, and is definitely preferable to backing a hurdler making his debut over fences. Those chasers who go on to reach the top level, almost always win one of their first two races, and that's what I'm looking for.

The second is an inevitable result of the first rule, since a previous winner in an ordinary novice chase isn't likely to be on offer at the sort of price I'm prepared to bet. The third rule is an obvious continuation of the idea of ignoring Flat form in hurdle races. Jumping fences requires a totally different technique and the best hurdlers are the one least likely to adapt.

I'm not concerned that these rules lead to a small number of bets, as I prefer to watch novice chases closely and form my own opinions about the future prospects of the runners when they move into better races or into handicaps. I am willing to bet occasionally in a novice handicap chase, although most are as unappetising as their hurdling equivalent. There are some better class novice handicaps that attract previous winners, and they can provide decent bets. It's going back a few years, but Monsieur Le Cure won a novice handicap at Cheltenham just seven weeks before his success in the Sun Alliance Chase. I don't think that any festival winner has emerged from novice handicap hurdles!

There is no substitute for actually going racing when it comes to learning the maximum amount about a chase. No television or formbook can equal seeing the horses in the paddock with your own eyes, and neither can they enable you to see the race like an experienced watcher.

This is especially true of NH racing, when much of what happens is out of view of the camera, and the formbooks cannot report at the required level of detail. I also find that the two-dimensional view of the TV screen distorts the impression of horses jumping, making it much harder to identify the fluent jumpers.

When I watch a chase through binoculars, I hold my head still as they cross each fence, so that the horses are jumping through my field of vision. The TV camera is either constantly on the move, or else providing a too distant long-shot – or, worst of all, is mounted on a car running alongside the horses, a device which produces dramatic television of absolutely no use whatsoever to a punter!

Let's look at an example of the detail that can be obtained by watching a chase in the flesh. This is the official formbook report on the Parliament Novices Chase at Kempton on Wednesday November 5:

1 **SHEKELS** - *made all, pecked 2 out, pushed out*

2 **SPRING GALE** - *steady headway 12th, chased winner approaching 3 out, every chance 2 out, unable to quicken*

3 **LETS BE FRANK** - *held up, chased winner 11 until approaching 3 out, close 3 when mistake 2 out, soon weakened*

4 **WHO AM I** - *mistakes, chased winner 10 to 11, 4th when mistake 3 out, soon weakened*

As far as that goes, it's all accurate, but it omits at least one key fact about each of the four horses. I don't actually keep written notes, but like most professional punters I have total recall of any race I've seen (it's part of what makes us so boring!). My version would look like this;

**SHEKELS** – *looked well, jumped well in front and produced a great leap at the last when asked. Had things his own way here and could be hard to place, but his jumping will win him races. Should stay three miles and goes well on a right-hand track.*

**SPRING GALE** – *fit enough for seasonal debut, but lacks size for these big fences. Jumped safely but ponderously and in last place passing post looking unlikely winner. Moved up smoothly to challenge three out, but outjumped at last and earlier exertions told. Still moving freely on run-in and nailed on for a novice chase over softer fences.*

**LETS BE FRANK** – *looked fit enough beforehand, jumped safely throughout, but tiring when clouted two out and very leg-weary on run-in. Probably needed race, but may also have lacked stamina for this trip with 17 fences. Could do better held up over two miles, but unlikely to be tried at that trip. One to oppose over a stiff two and a half miles or farther.*

**WHO AM I** – *looked outclassed on previous form, but close up when hitting four out and kept on encouragingly in straight. Would be interesting in a handicap off his current mark of 94 on an easier track.*

Of course, simply having a more detailed summary of the event doesn't necessarily mean that my opinion is better than that of others, but it is my own and I'm happier to trust it when it comes to making future betting decisions. In fact I backed Spring Gale next time, when he ran in an open handicap over the same trip at Uttoxeter, and he won narrowly at 5-2. To emphasise the erratic nature of novice chasing, he was then turned over at 1-3 at Doncaster, before winning at Stratford. Those results would seem to support my view that the lesser tracks are likely to be his natural home, due to his lack of inches.

Shekels, on the other hand, has twice failed to get round in better company, Lets Be Frank failed again over two and half miles at Huntingdon and reverted to hurdles, and at the time of writing, I'm still waiting for Who Am I to run in a handicap.

The specifics from that one race aren't important, but I hope you can see how it helps to have a firm opinion about the horses you've seen. That applies to all types of racing but in my view especially to chasing given the difficulty of translating second hand information about chases. I certainly find it very useful to make those sort of assessments after any novice chase I've seen, even if most of them are good deal more negative than the examples shown above.

## Handicap chases

For the past ten years, handicap chases have been my main specialisation in NH racing. I've always liked the fact that all the runners have sufficient previous form to provide information on their preferred pattern, and I was confident that seeing races live provided me with greater insight into past performances than those punters that relied on TV or formbooks. In eight of those ten years I've made a profit on these races, so I must have been doing something right. Inevitably over a period of ten seasons, my methods and ideas have changed, but the key remains 'keeping it simple'. The general principles can be reduced to four statements:

- Weight doesn't matter
- Young chasers are the best bets
- Suited to track and trip
- Good jumpers in form

*Let's look at each of those points in more detail.*

### Weight

I take no account whatsoever of the actual weight a horse is carrying in a handicap chase. The current weight range in most handicaps is 24lbs. That would represent 24 lengths, maybe more, in the calculations of most pundits who like to analyse races in that way. I take the view, based on my experience, that the issues of jumping, fitness and suitability to the track and distance are far more significant in any handicap chase, than a difference of a few pounds on a horse's back. I believe that weight is most significant when a horse is trying to change speed – quicken or accelerate – at the deciding stage of a race. Hence my view that weight is relevant in a turf Flat race. But in a chase, the horse gallops at a steady pace throughout, with only very slight changes of speed at any stage of the race.

When you watch handicap chases regularly, it is clear that the most usual pattern is one in which the entire field set off at a uniform pace, with the beaten horses dropping off that pace one by one as they make mistakes, tire or simply find themselves outclassed. In the great majority of these races, the winner will have been leading or sitting close to the pace throughout the race. It's quite unusual for a horse that is deliberately held up more than ten lengths behind the pace to win a handicap chase, although it does occur in some long distance chases. When watching for this pattern, you have to ignore a solo front-runner, and concentrate on the chasing group. The only time the pace changes in most chases is starting out on the final circuit, but it's a gradual process, not a sharp change of speed, and I don't believe that carrying 10st or 11st 10lbs makes any difference.

One reason why chases are run at a uniform pace is the fences. There is a maximum speed at which a chaser can safely negotiate a fence and any attempt to jump at a faster speed usually invites disaster. We've all seen the dash to the last fence over two miles on firm ground, and the inevitable result of a fall or a serious blunder that follows. In the heat of a finish the jockey will try to ignore the natural speed limit and sometimes he'll get away with it, but not often.

Watch any chase from close to the action over the last few fences, and you'll see the jockeys taking steps to slow their mounts down as they approach the fences. They are not acting out of self-preservation, just common sense allied to experience. They know that an accurate jump at 30 mph is more likely to win the race than an attempt at the spectacular at 35 mph.

The weight carried may not matter, but the official BHB handicap rating certainly does make a difference to a chaser's prospects. If a rating of 124 means that a horse carries 10st 4lbs, why should a rating of 127 (10st 7lbs) be a problem? The answer is that the rating decides in which races the chaser can run, and more importantly, on which courses.

As a successful chaser climbs the ratings, he reaches a level at which he no longer qualifies for races on the lesser tracks. At any point over a mark of 135, he will have to run at the major tracks in good class races. Not only will he be meeting better opponents, he'll be facing stiffer fences. Plenty of horses are capable of winning over the smaller, softer, more forgiving fences at tracks like Hereford, Worcester, Huntingdon or Towcester. But faced with the fences at Sandown, Newbury or Cheltenham, they find that it's a different game altogether.

So it's the jump in class (excuse the pun) that I watch out for, not the weight carried. Good jumping allied to galloping ability can take a chaser a long way, but every horse has a class limit and once they reach that level, it becomes very hard for them to win. That is one reason why successful chasers run up a sequence of wins at the beginning of their handicap career and then come to a dead stop.

## Age

Of all the types of racing in this country, the one that takes the greatest toll of the horses is steeplechasing. If you've never walked away from the stands and down to one of the fences at a jump meeting, I advise you to do so at the next opportunity. Watching a race on television, or from the top of the stands, makes chasing look a controlled and fairly safe sport. From a few yards away, the noise, the bumping and the sheer physical exertion of both horse and jockey become all too clear. It's no wonder that the average chaser falls victim to the wear and tear at least once during his career.

Desert Orchid is remembered for his great races, but the truly remarkable feature of his career was the fact that he raced over hurdles and fences for eight seasons without a single layoff for injury. The worst affliction he suffered was corns, but apart from that he retained his soundness and enthusiasm throughout. Most of his fellow chasers follow a more predictable path, as age takes effect. They accumulate knocks that make them harder to train, they lose their basic speed and their enthusiasm declines. In punting terms they become much harder to win with.

I have concentrated my betting on younger chasers for many years. The simple fact is that young chasers win more often than old ones. They have more natural speed and if they can jump well, will inevitably outpace older horses. The shorter the distance of the race, the more certain this equation is to rule. The exceptions to the rule are either horses at the very highest class, in the mould of Desert Orchid and Viking Flagship, or horses who have had one or more seasons off the track. The older horses also fall foul of the problem stated in the previous paragraphs: they rise through the handicap, if successful when young, and reach a level at which it is hard to win. Their loss of speed simply exacerbates the problem. The only way in which the older horse can overcome the problem is to improve its jumping technique to a level of real efficiency, or to step up in trip so that speed is less of an issue.

Desert Orchid epitomised both these remedies. His jumping improved from flamboyant but risky when a novice, to a style that was supremely efficient and quick as he developed. He also changed from success at two miles in his early career to winning over the longer trips at Sandown in the Whitbread and in the Irish National. Few horses are capable of such adaptability. Viking Flagship has also become one of the most consistent and economical jumpers of a fence, but is hard pushed now to win over two miles in the top class, although still very effective at two and half miles.

The first thing I do when analysing any handicap chase is to eliminate the older horses and concentrate my efforts on those of the ideal age. The annual equine birthday, on January 1, coming in the middle of the season, complicates the issue slightly, but in general terms I like to see the horses within a two-year band, depending on the race distance:

- Two miles                     6- and 7-year-olds
- Two and a half miles          7- and 8-year-olds
- Three miles                   7- and 8-year-olds
- Three and half miles plus     8- and 9-year-olds

I add one year to those categories for the period from January to April, after the equine birthday, so that, for example, nine-year-olds would be acceptable over two and a half and three miles. As with any 'rule', there may be exceptions, and I would consider an older horse if he had shown winning form during the current season. That would persuade me that the horse was currently free of problems and had retained sufficient speed.

One other point to note is that the French-bred horses who are appearing in chases in this country, generally seem to be more mature than their local rivals. They can often handle three miles over fences at five or six years of age, but they also seem to decline sooner as well, so that a French-bred eight-year-old might be less attractive than the figures above would suggest.

In recent years, I noticed that the young horses doing well at the top level had often started their chasing careers very young, usually as five-year-olds. This seemed to give them a useful balance of jumping experience and speed by the time they reached maturity at seven and eight.

The field for the 1997 King George VI Chase at Kempton provides an interesting demonstration of this pattern. The eight runners, in finishing order, were:

| Name | Age Now | *Age First Chase |
| --- | --- | --- |
| See More Business | 7 | 6 |
| Challenger Du Luc | 7 | 5 |
| Rough Quest | 11 | 5 |
| Suny Bay | 8 | 5 |
| One Man | 9 | 5 |
| Barton Bank | 11 | 6 |
| Djeddah | 6 | ? |
| Senor El Betrutti | 8 | 6 |

I don't have access to the full record for the French-trained runner, Djeddah, but he must have raced over fences in France at five, and quite possibly at four. See More Business had one season over hurdles in novice company, but had already run in point-to-point races in this country before that. Apart from this early start, they share two other features in their NH careers:

- All were successful immediately in novice chases, winning either their first or second start
- So far as I can trace, Challenger Du Luc is the only one of the eight to have run in a handicap hurdle

This is probably an extreme example, and plenty of successful chasers have had careers over hurdles before switching at seven or eight years of age, but they are the exceptions rather than the rule. I could produce a long list of top class chasers in the nineties who fitted the pattern described above, and starting chasing young must avoid the horse picking up bad habits over hurdles which then have to be eradicated. Certainly, whenever I hear a trainer say that he'll give a horse one more year over hurdles, I mark that as one to oppose over fences. The natural optimism of NH followers tends to remember the horses who make the switch successfully, such as Dawn Run and Desert Orchid. They forget the likes of Morley Street, Large Action, King Credo, who switched after success over hurdles and took to chasing like ducks to a Peking restaurant.

## Track and trip

The career of Desert Orchid was the first to bring most punters' attention to the idea that chasers might have a preference for a right-hand or left-hand track. I've always been aware that it made a difference to some horses, but it was only when I was watching an explanation of the techniques involved in human 400m hurdle races that I realised what might cause the preference.

An athlete sets out to cover the distance between each of the hurdles in an odd number of strides, so that he always takes off with same lead leg. Try it yourself – just attempt to step over some obstacle on your living room carpet – you'll instinctively lead off from your right or left leg. If you force yourself to lead with the 'wrong' leg, you're odds-on to fall over. Hence the athlete's desire to take 13 strides for the first eight hurdles and then 15 strides for the last two. When they get tired and miss that pattern, hurdles get hit and momentum is lost.

It must be the same for a horse. He has a natural lead leg for the take-off at each fence, and a natural lead leg for galloping between the fences. A chaser who leads with his left leg (off fore I think, but I'm a punter not a horseman), is never going to be entirely happy on a right-hand track.

There are horses who seem able to cope equally well with both directions, and they are presumably the equine equivalent of an ambidextrous human. But most horses do have a preference, and the problem for punters is deciding what it is, based on the strength of their early runs. For example, it could be argued that the 1997/98 novice chaser Chief's Song is better going right-handed, based on his wins at Kempton and Ascot, and a defeat at Cheltenham. But the fact is that Chief's Song has spent most of his career running at the London tracks, because he is trained at Epsom, so it is not surprising he appears suited by right-handed courses. When he ran at Cheltenham over fences, he met a top class rival in Mandy's Mantino, and he has hurdle wins on his record over that course. So all that can be said for sure is that he does act on a right-handed track and probably acts on a left-handed track.

The same problem in assessment can arise with chasers who run mainly on the northern tracks. Once you go north of Leicester, there are only three right-hand tracks, those at Carlisle, Musselburgh and Perth. Any chaser who is officially rated above 125 is going to be totally restricted to running on the major tracks at Haydock, Newcastle, Wetherby, etc – all left-hand tracks. So I'm always a bit wary of a chaser that looks well suited by going left-handed, if he's only run in the north.

The media seem to identify a chaser's preference by watching which way he adjusts on the approach to a fence in order to meet the obstacle in his stride. This leads to the simple line that a horse who jumps out to the right on a left-handed track will be better suited by a right-handed track. That ignores the possibility that he may just be a rotten jumper! I've certainly seen horses who veer away from the inside rail whichever way round they are running. I prefer to concentrate on the actual jumping. A horse who is happy on the track will jump in his stride at most fences, but if they prefer going the other way, they tend to put in a short stride on take-off and pop the fence, rather than clear it fluently. The performance of Suny Bay in the King George provided a good example, with half a dozen fluent jumps interspersed with some really scratchy efforts, totally unlike his earlier running at Haydock and Newbury.

Any owner with a horse who prefers a right-handed track and needs long distances is also going to have a problem. Every Grand National run in this country (Aintree, Midland, Scottish and Welsh) is run on a left-handed track, leaving only the Irish National for the right-handed horse. In Britain, Sandown is the only right-hand track regularly staging races over more than three and a quarter miles for good class chasers.

Having decided whether a horse prefers one direction, the next question concerns the nature of the track. I divide them into two groups – flat and undulating. I don't worry about slopes or even hills on a track if the fences are on the flat parts, so Warwick counts as a flat track, despite the big hill on the far side. I'd also count Sandown as a flat track, although it does have one downhill fence on the run away from the stands. Chepstow could also be argued as having its fences on the flat parts of the track, but that doesn't hold water if you've walked down to the third last, from which point the fifth last is still invisible in the dip on the home turn. So that goes on the list as undulating, along with the obvious candidates like Cheltenham and Towcester.

Another categorisation that some pundits use is to separate tracks as sharp and stiff, or galloping. I think this has less relevance, as with few exceptions, the top grade tracks are stiff and the gaff tracks are sharp. Thus an apparent preference for sharp tracks is inevitable for any chaser who wins a few races round the gaffs, and vice versa for one who wins at Newbury and Cheltenham. One course that always seems to me to be wrongly assigned by the media is Kempton, which for some reason is usually called sharp. As the circuit is the same length as, for example, Haydock and Wetherby, I find this hard to accept and I think it probably stems from the fact that the ground is rarely very soft at Kempton. As a result, tired horses of the sort seen at the finish elsewhere, are not a common sight at the track. The short run-in from the last fence is another factor in this, but a check on the number of tired falls at the last at Kempton might produce a different view of the track. If somebody insists that Kempton is a sharp track, try asking how the Racing Post Chase managed to be won by successful stayers, such as Rhyme N' Reason, Bonanza Boy, Docklands Express and Mudahim.

Moving on to consideration of the ideal trip, in most cases the chaser will soon find his best distance and his form will clearly show what suits. Personally I'm always prepared to give a chaser a chance when stepping up in trip, until it proves to be a mistake. I never forget that most pundits were convinced Desert Orchid (he keeps coming up, doesn't he?) wouldn't stay a yard beyond two miles before he won his first King George. That was in the forefront of my mind when I backed another two-mile tearaway, Antonin, when he stepped up to three miles plus, and he justified the support. As long as a horse adapts to the slower pace and doesn't ruin his chance by pulling too hard, then good jumping can compensate for any lack of stamina in the pedigree.

I've always liked the races over extreme distances, those at more than three and a half miles. Find a chaser who is genuinely suited by that sort of trip, and you've probably found a moneymaker. These long distance races often fall to a previous winner of a similar contest in the same season. The form of Lord Gyllene in his Grand National season is a prime example of a horse who could go almost any distance, because he seemed to use an absolute minimum of energy in his jumping.

## Good jumpers in form

As a professional, I have plenty of time for race analysis, obviously much more than a punter with a full-time job. Whilst that has advantages, it can lead me to forget that the simple ideas are the best. Some basic research into the results of good class chases in the months immediately prior to the writing of this chapter provided a timely reminder. This isn't the sort of detailed scientific study that would satisfy my esteemed colleague Nick Mordin, but I think it's worth giving in detail. These are all the Class A and B races at the major tracks (Ascot, Cheltenham, Haydock, Kempton, Newbury, Sandown and Wetherby) in the period from the Murphys Gold Cup to the end of the year:

| Winner | Track | Age | Last Run This Season |
|---|---|---|---|
| Senor El Betrutti | C | 8 | Second |
| Banjo | C | 7 | Debut |
| Cumbrian Challenge | W | 8 | Winner |
| Suny Bay | H | 8 | Debut |
| Super Tactics | K | 9 | Winner |
| Leotard | A | 10 | Second |
| Cool Dawn | A | 9 | Unplaced |
| Simply Dashing | A | 6 | Winner |
| Callisoe Bay | N | 8 | Winner |
| Him Of Praise | H | 7 | Winner |
| Native Mission | N | 10 | Third |
| Suny Bay | N | 8 | Winner |
| Oatis Regrets | S | 9 | Debut |
| Samlee | S | 8 | Winner |
| Ask Tom | S | 8 | Pulled Up |
| Strath Royal | W | 11 | Winner |
| Cumbrian Challenge | W | 8 | Winner |
| Senor El Betrutti | C | 8 | Winner |
| The Grey Monk | H | 9 | Debut |
| Cool Dawn | A | 9 | Winner |
| Celibate | A | 6 | Unplaced |
| Him Of Praise | H | 7 | Winner |
| See More Business | K | 7 | Winner |
| Strath Royal | W | 11 | Winner |
| Cumbrian Challenge | W | 8 | Winner |
| Edredon Bleu | K | 5 | Winner |
| Arfer Mole | K | 9 | Fell |

The key fact to be drawn from that list is that a last-time-out winner won 16 of the 27 races. You can also see that several horses appear twice in this list, but despite their good previous form, they didn't necessarily go off at short prices. It also emphasises that it is not a good idea to make excuses for a poor run last time out, with only two winners having failed to complete on their last start.

Given the trend shown in these races, I went back to the same set of races for the previous season. I'll spare you the entire list, but the results were similar, except that more of the winners were making their seasonal debut, reflecting the drier autumn in 1996. The number of wins for chasers who failed to make the first three on their previous start that season was just one. The winners on their debut are also worth a mention as a potentially valuable source of profit. Training methods have changed enormously over the past ten years, thanks to the influence of Martin Pipe. The traditional comment that a chaser first time out will "need the race", or is "bound to improve", is no longer worthy of consideration when betting in chases. If the horse showed the necessary level of ability last season, then assume it will be fit first time, and you'll be rewarded with some nice priced winners. Equally, don't fall for the common view that a chaser will do better on its second start than it did first time out. As you can see from the statistics above, failure isn't often followed by success.

Those trends are based entirely on top class chasers, and I don't think that the same patterns apply so clearly as you drop down the scale. To be successful in those Class A and B chases inevitably requires a sound jumper. The chasers whose careers are confined to the bottom grade of handicap are there because they have never become fluent jumpers, and, as such, the results are less predictable. There is no way of knowing which of half a dozen clumsy individuals is most likely to put in a clear(ish) round today. These horses are meat and drink to the platoon of professionals who follow the jumping circuit all year around, and comment will mostly concentrate on their defects, whether it be their jumping, their breathing, their stamina, or their courage. Or even a combination of all four! If the owners could hear the ritual of disparagement by the paddock before most midweek NH races, writs for slander would be a daily occurrence.

# National Hunt workshop

Once again a selection of NH bets taken from my records for 1997. In line with what I've written earlier, most of these were in handicap chases, but I've included other races in proportion to the actual bets placed during the year.

**17/01  Kemp  3m Hcp Ch    DEXTRA DOVE         1st   SP 11-4**
**£1200/400**

*I couldn't resist including this bet on a horse who I had followed with great success. He had a remarkable record over fences, having won more than half his races, most of them in handicaps. Consistently rubbished by the trade press for winning round the gaff tracks, he had provided me with two successes at Cheltenham the previous season, at 9-4 and then 9-2. Once again here, he found himself in a small field against some dubious characters, including Philip's Woody, Grey Smoke and Le Meille. The first named had displayed a passion for finishing second (Timeform politely phrased it as "consistent but beatable"), and the other two had seen promising careers affected by illness and injury. Dextra Dove was the only one in the field sure to run his race, and his fifth in the Hennessey suggested he wasn't finished yet.*

*Grey Smoke might have won, but fell three out. Le Meille clouted the same fence and folded up in a few strides. That left Dextra Dove and Philip's Woody to contest the finish and there was never any doubt as to which would show the greater desire from the final fence. Dextra Dove won by three lengths. Throughout his career he was a perfect example of the profit to be made by backing chasers with the winning attitude. He was as tough as old boots, often looked to be going badly through a race, but invariably kept going when others had had enough. I'm embarrassed to recall that after a successful £2700/600 at Cheltenham, I declared to anyone within hearing distance on the Members Lawn that I loved him, and would sleep with him if it weren't illegal. Fortunately Dextra Dove had been gelded years earlier and didn't share my passion!*

**25/01  Chelt  2m 5f Hcp Ch  CHALLENGER DU LUC   Unpl  SP 11-4**
**£2200/800**

*This was a bet inspired by the age of the three main contenders. Challenger Du Luc, a seven-year-old, appealed far more than Addington Boy did at nine and Dublin Flyer at 11. He'd also won over the course and distance in the Cathcart Chase and again in the 1996 Murphys Gold Cup. I gave Dublin Flyer no chance, not only because of his age, but also the fact that he was running off a mark of 168. Regardless of age, very few horses can win a handicap chase off that sort of mark. I haven't carried out a detailed study, but I think that only Burrough Hill Lad and Desert Orchid had won off higher marks in the previous fifteen years. Having stated earlier that weight carried doesn't matter, this statistic shouldn't bother me, but there does seem to be a levelling-off of ability at the top level of chasing, and perhaps the extra weight does have some effect. I think it's more likely that by the time most chasers have reached that sort of handicap mark, they are already starting to decline due to increasing age and injury, and hence the rarity of such wins.*

*Challenger Du Luc was never going a yard in this race, and all credit to Dublin Flyer, who shrugged off his years with an exhilarating display. I thought that the betting on this race was fuelled entirely by sentiment, with Dublin Flyer backed from 5-2 in to 15-8, and the younger horses both drifting. I expressed this view to anyone who cared to listen before the race, and to several people who later wished they hadn't listened! It was humble pie and chips for supper.*

**8/02   Newb   3m 2f Hcp Ch   CALL IT A DAY        1st    SP 11-4**
                                                    **£2775/1100**

*I'd been following Call It A Day since he passed what I call the 'Towcester Test'. That is simply a plus mark for any chaser that climbs the stiff hill at Towcester and is able to draw away from his rivals over the last two fences. Most horses who run at Towcester are legless by that stage, so anything on the bridle probably has reserves to spare. Call It A Day had passed the test when running second in a novice chase, beaten by the ill-fated Major Summit. That pair had both galloped strongly up the hill and Call It A Day had confirmed since that the form was solid. He'd run twice this season, winning a 2m 5f race at Uttoxeter when odds-on in a field of three, then finishing third over an inadequate 2m 3f in Ireland. This step up in trip looked ideal, and, as a seven-year-old meeting older rivals, and with a win this season, he looked a great bet to me. I'd anticipated a price of around 2-1, so when Tote Credit offered 9-4, I took that to £500 for starters when I arrived at Newbury. When he drifted in the market, I upped my bet with a further £600 at 11-4 in the ring. The total stake was actually £100 more than my planned maximum in the 1997 staking plan, but three or four times each year you are offered a price that looks massive value and you have to bet according to your faith.*

*Call It A Day wasn't impressive, but won by one and a half lengths, and you get paid on the result, not the style. I subsequently backed him in the Racing Post Chase and at Aintree, giving back 60 per cent of the profit on this bet, but they were, with hindsight, much better races than this.*

## 17/02  Font   3m 2f Hcp Ch   WOODLANDS BOY     2nd   SP 9-2
£3200/400

*The official distance for staying chases at Fontwell is one of several that I regard with suspicion. The published trip is 3m 2f 110yds, but based on times, I reckon it's at least three and a half miles, and thus a greater test of stamina than most punters realise. Woodlands Boy had won over course and distance on similar soft ground, and despite some in-and-out form this season, I felt he was overpriced at the morning 8-1, given that record. The short-priced favourite Flaked Oats had also recorded a win here, but that had been in a poor novice chase on better ground, and having fallen last time, he looked worth taking on at 5-4. The morning 8-1 didn't last long, and Woodlands Boy never beat 11-2 on-course.*

*Woodlands Boy justified support with a prominent run ending with him beaten just over a length by Flaked Oats.*

## 11/03  Chelt   2m Nov Ch      OR ROYAL          1st   SP 11-2
£3000/600

*A statistic I've discussed at Cheltenham previews as well as in Odds On magazine, is the terrible record of short-priced favourites at the festival meeting. In the five years from 1993–1997, only four of the 22 horses priced at 2-1 or less have obliged. One of those beaten horses in 1997 was Mulligan in the Arkle Chase. Given those figures, I'm always keen to oppose the favourites, and Or Royal fitted the bill perfectly. He was a dual winner at Chepstow, one of the best trial grounds for Cheltenham, being another undulating left-hand track. He jumped well when beaten subsequently at Ascot in December, and had then been rested and aimed specifically at this race. Mulligan had done nothing wrong, but he'd had plenty of racing and all his wins had been on flat tracks. I stepped in when Or Royal reached 5-1 and was surprised to see him drift further to 11-2. I'm not sure why, but the market at Cheltenham is one of the most difficult to predict, with significant variations from ante-post and morning prices being quite common. I remember The Fellow winning the Gold Cup at 7-1, having been nearer half that price in the morning.*

*Mulligan fell four out, so we'll never know how he would have fared. Or Royal survived a mistake two out to catch Squire Silk close home. This was one of only three races during the 1997 festival meeting in which the leader at the last didn't win the race. The other two were the ultra-competitive handicap hurdles, the Coral Cup and the County Hurdle. Given the generally large fields and tight races, the fact that 17 winners led at the last suggests that the 'fearsome final hill' isn't quite the influence on results that romantics would have you believe.*

## 12/03   Chelt   2m Champ Ch   STRONG PROMISE          Unpl   SP 5-2
£2800/800

*Six runners for the Champion Chase, and in this two-mile race I'm always looking to back the young pretenders against the older established horses. So I eliminated Martha's Son and Viking Flagship, both ten-year-olds, and Lord Dorcet as being outclassed. The eight-year-old Ask Tom, I had always felt, was best suited to a flat track, although his trainer believed there were different reasons for his defeat in the Arkle last season. That left Klairon Davis and Strong Promise, and I plumped for the latter as the younger horse by two years and in my view the better jumper. His second in the Murphys had confirmed his ability to act on the track. I took the early price 7-2, a correct decision this time, but I would have stepped in again if he'd shown longer in the afternoon.*

*He looked to be in the box seat at the top of the hill, but made a serious mistake at the third last, which is usually the most important fence in this race, and had no chance of getting back after that. Martha's Son provided a rare winner at ten years of age, probably due to his year off the track, which kept his mileage down to reasonable levels for his age.*

## 9/05   Strat   2m 6f Nov Hd   GOWER SLAVE          1st   SP 9-2
£2000/400

*I haven't discussed the subject of the going anywhere earlier in this chapter. It's such a basic issue that it didn't seem to warrant any detailed investigation, but suffice it to say it has a primary impact on NH races. Unusually for May, this meeting was run on soft ground and I thought it likely that it might provide some opportunities to oppose horses who had run well recently on fast ground. I bet against the favourite in the first division of this novice hurdle, but she scrambled home at 10-11. This time I felt pretty confident about taking on Sharp Command. A Flat-bred four-year-old, he'd won* twice on fast ground, and although he'd proven his stamina at this trip, he didn't look to have the strength to cope with soft conditions. Gower Slave hadn't run on soft ground either, but paddock inspection showed him to be a chasing type, with no lack of size or strength. He'd shown improved form last time when stepped up to three miles at Bangor, finishing third to two useful novices. The only other runner at less than 11-1 was Sioux To Speak, and he had been pulled up at Hereford the only time he'd encountered soft ground. I didn't especially 'fancy' Gower Slave, but he was clearly the most likely winner if the favourite failed. Backing him was very much a means of laying the favourite, and I felt that 5-1 was real value.

The outcome was somewhat confusing. Sharp Command went clear from some way out, with Gower Slave looking one-paced (well, dead slow if I'm honest) in a distant second. I was watching from a position close to the last hurdle and, as Sharp Command turned for home, it was obvious that he was out on his feet. He didn't so much fall at the second last, as topple over it exhausted. Gower Slave plodded on to win in a time almost seven seconds slower than the first division. Sharp Command lay down for five minutes and then recovered and walked back okay. It was a perfect demonstration of what can happen to a Flat-bred horse under genuine NH conditions. I took some ribbing from the bookmakers as I collected, especially as I claimed that Gower Slave would have caught the leader even if he hadn't fallen. Confucius he say, "Tongue in cheek more fun with cash in pocket".

### 18/10  Kemp  2m Hcp Ch    CELIBATE              1st   SP 7-4
                                                     £1000/500

This was almost a perfect bet, epitomising everything I've written about handicap chases. Celibate was a six-year-old making his seasonal debut. He'd won his first chase as a five-year-old and was proven at this trip and on a right-hand track. He was high on my list of chasers to follow for the 1997/8 season. He had only one significant rival, another six-year-old, Amancio, who met most of the same criteria, except that he'd shown temperament in the past and was on the list of chasers to oppose. The other four runners were all older and I wouldn't have wanted to lay Celibate at more than 6-4 if I'd been making a book. Given that eulogy, you might reasonably ask why I only bet £500. In a nutshell, the 2-1 ran out before I could get any more money down and although he was returned at 7-4, most boards were showing 13-8 or 6-4 as they lined up.

*He won okay, but not quite in the style I'd expected, looking in trouble three out, before staying on to catch Amancio on the run-in. He reappeared just two weeks later in a £20,000 contest at Ascot and was sent off the 5-2 favourite but I suspected that he would need a longer break after a fairly hard race here, and ducked him. He justified that decision by finishing fifth and it wasn't until December that he recovered his form, winning at Ascot. But I'd lost faith by then!*

**8/11   Winc   3m 1f Hcp Ch   CAROLES CRUSADER   Unpl   SP 6-1**
**£4100/680**

*I had followed up the win on Celibate with a £3600/540 on Caroles Crusader when she got up in the final strides to win the Charisma Chase. She offered all the same virtues here, as a six-year-old meeting older rivals, with her current form and fitness in no doubt. Favourite here was James Pigg, a ten-year-old who had won an uncompetitive amateur's race at Cheltenham on his first start after returning to Martin Pipe from Paul Nicholls. Most of his recent form was dire and his price was a tribute to the magical powers of his trainer. He had to be opposed. Second-favourite was Cherrynut, beaten a short-head by Caroles Crusader at Kempton and now equipped with first-time blinkers. In my experience, the worst thing any trainer can do with a dodgy jumper is put the blinkers on – how can restricting the vision help a horse to measure his fences? I could see no logic in this one being half the price of a horse who had beaten it last time, especially as Caroles Crusader was likely to benefit from the extra furlong and a half at Wincanton. I bet with enthusiasm at 11-2 and then 6-1 when I failed to make an impact on the market.*

*James Pigg and Tony McCoy set a suicidal pace and Caroles Crusader was well in arrears until moving up as they passed the stands with a circuit to run. She then made a bad mistake at the water running along the side of the course, and Bradley accepted defeat from that point. That mistake wasn't visible on the TV coverage, and the journalists present from the main form guides also missed it. I was confident I was almost alone in knowing that Caroles Crusader had run better than the result would suggest. On the strength of that, I backed her next time at Towcester, nine days later, taking £1,800/600 in a four-runner race. She was beaten by the outsider of four, Him Of Praise, and as he went on to run up a sequence in better company, I think I can regard that loss as a shade unlucky. She returned to Towcester on December 6, but I was distracted by the AW racing at Wolverhampton (see Chewit in*

*AW workshop) and failed to consider a bet. She won at 100-30. You can only shrug and accept this sort of thing as an inevitable result of the mass of racing thrown at punters every Saturday nowadays – if it can happen to me, it can certainly happen to you, and probably will. The thing is that punters only remember the winners they miss through this sort of mishap, never the number of losing bets that would result from following every meeting, every day.*

**22/11  Ascot  2m Nov Ch     CHIEF'S SONG          1st    SP 7-2**
                                                     **£2000/500**

*My second novice chase bet of the new season (the first was Direct Route at Cheltenham six days earlier). This one fitted all the criteria, being a previous winner taking on two highly-touted hurdlers making their chase debut. The favourite at even-money was Boardroom Shuffle, who was unbeaten in five starts. He obviously had a decent chance, but if you have a strategy to bet against this sort, it doesn't matter if half of them win, because you'll be taking much better odds yourself. Certainly, Ascot wouldn't be every trainer's choice as the best course for a novice chaser first time. The other hype horse was Wade Road, who looked to be beating himself in the paddock, sweating and fighting his handlers. He was also fitted with a cross-noseband, the sign of a hard puller, and hardly ideal on a course with a lengthy downhill stretch early on in the race. Chief's Song had always impressed me as a solid professional over hurdles, with a good winning record, and he'd jumped really well over the stiff fences at Kempton on his chase debut. He was the one runner who looked sure to show his form and to get round.*

*Chief's Song always looked the likely winner after Boardroom Shuffle fell at the fourth, and Wade Road lost his chance by taking control at the downhill fences. Although the winning margin was only one and a half lengths, I thought he'd idled in front and could have produced more if necessary. When he met the runner-up, Ground Nut, again back at Ascot on December 20, I was amazed to find Ground Nut on offer at 11-10 and Chief's Song at 2-1. That betting was explained by a 7lb penalty for Chief's Song, and the fact that the race was over a longer trip. Since I don't think either of those things matter very much, I bet Chief's Song again, and collected again, although it was made easy as Ground Nut fell.*

**22/11  Ascot  3m Hcp H     COUCHANT          Fell   SP 11-4**
                                                 **£1500/450**
*Couchant had already won four races this season, although most*

had been during the summer jumping. This was an apparent step up in class, but it looked a pretty weak contest by Ascot standards, with only six runners, and only three real contenders. Name Of Our Father hadn't impressed me with his attitude when winning a four-runner event at Wincanton last time. He'd been on the bridle two out, but as soon as he hit the front, his ears went back, his head went up and he looked less than keen on the run-in. Haile Derring had run well the previous season, but his stable were in terrible form and he hadn't achieved much on his debut at Cheltenham. I was happy to oppose both of those, and the only other possible was Clifton Set who was returning from a 14-month layoff and didn't look fully fit in the paddock beforehand. Couchant drifted in the ring and that was what persuaded me to bet, taking 100-30 before he was cut back in to 11-4.

He was still hacking along on the bridle at the back of the field when he fell four out. This is fairly unusual in a handicap hurdle, but backing fallers is part of betting on NH racing. It's another area in which punters often delude themselves, remembering the fallers who cost them money, but forgetting the winners who might have benefited from the falls of others.

### 25/11  Hunt  3m Hcp Ch    HIGH LEARIE      1st    SP 10-1
£4000/400

I'd backed this horse on his debut at Kempton but he'd fallen early. He'd followed that with defeat over two and a half miles here, but he'd jumped well enough in front for a long way and was sure to do better back at three miles. The track clearly suited him, as he'd run his best race here as a novice last season, when second to Teinein. As a seven-year-old, he looked to have only two serious rivals in this moderate race. The favourite was Coole Hill, a mare from the in-form Nicholson stable. She'd won a similar race at Market Rasen, but only four of the nine starters finished that race, and she hadn't impressed me with her jumping. Mister Blake had won a poor handicap at Bangor but had needed all of the three miles there to win, and looked almost certain to be outpaced on this flat track on good ground. I had not arrived at Huntingdon with the fixed intention of backing High Learie, having anticipated a price of around 5-1 to 6-1. However, punters had piled into Coole Hill and made her 11-10, so the 10-1 I on offer was too good to resist. The market at Huntingdon is not noted for its ability to absorb large bets, but with a sizeable crowd present for the Peterborough Chase (One Man, Viking Flagship and Martha's Son), I was able to place four bets of £1,000/100 without causing any stir.

*I watch races at Huntingdon from an earth bank set back from the last fence, which provides a much better view than from anywhere in the main stand. High Learie set out to make all and it looked like being close before Coole Hill made a mistake at the last, and he held on by one and a half lengths. I had been joined at Huntingdon by a young lady anthropologist from Cambridge University, who was observing my work as part of an academic study into the behaviour patterns of people working in racing (and people think I've got a cushy job!). Having watched me betting, she'd detoured to the Tote and put £5 of her grant on High Learie. When he jumped the last in front, I maintained my usual calm pose – no shouting or jumping up and down – but Rebecca had no such qualms. She collected £57 from the Tote and left Huntingdon with a revised opinion of professional gamblers, having greeted me three hours earlier with the news that all the punters she'd met were dull and miserable!*

## Summary

Those selected bets give the impression of a very successful year of NH betting, but I've chosen them to make specific points and winners obviously do that better than losers. The accounts for 1997 show a total of 27 winners from 110 bets, with the monthly profit and loss as follows:

| Month | Winners/Bets | Profit/Loss | Overall Total |
|-------|-------------|-------------|---------------|
| January | 1/4 | - 500 | - 500 |
| February | 3/14 | - 445 | - 945 |
| March | 5/15 | + 3,890 | + 2,945 |
| April | 1/18 | - 6,100 | - 3,155 |
| May | 2/14 | - 830 | - 3,985 |
| October | 4/9 | + 6,350 | + 2,335 |
| November | 9/26 | + 4,660 | + 6,995 |
| December | 2/10 | - 1,870 | + 5,125 |
| **Total** | **27/110** | | **Profit £5,125** |

A perfectly satisfactory figure, but it's worth noting that the short-head win of Caroles Crusader at Kempton on October 15 made a difference of £4,140. On such slim margins are profit and loss decided, even over an entire year.

# PART 4

## SPREAD BETTING

## A beginners guide

Spread betting has a great deal in common with cricket and sex, in that written explanations of the procedure make it sound far more complicated than it really is. I have read a number of attempts to persuade the uninitiated that spread betting is simple, but I rarely reached halfway before I got lost in a maze of numbers. Most writers use football or golf as the medium for introducing the novice, but as this volume is solely concerned with horse racing all my examples will come from that sphere. Undeterred by the failure of others, here is my own definition:

A spread bet is a statement of your opinion about the outcome of an event.

- If your opinion is right, you win.

- If your opinion is wrong, you lose.

- The more right you are, the more you win.

- The more wrong you are, the more you lose.

From a punters' point of view, much the most important of those is the last. If I achieve nothing else in this section, I must persuade you that the number one rule of betting on horse racing spreads is:

- **Always calculate your maximum possible loss before you bet.**

I emphasise this point, because the main difference between spread betting and fixed odds betting is that your losses are not fixed before the event. The spread betting firms go out of their way to stress this to new clients, and all their advertising contains wealth warnings. My personal favourite is the phrase 'Spread betting can be very volatile'. My dictionary gives several definitions for volatile, but the relevant ones must be 'dangerously unstable, explosive, characterised by rapid change'. To combine those into one phrase that will stick in the memory, I suggest you concentrate on the idea that a spread bet can blow up in your face at any time.

One of the firms publicised a cautionary tale a couple of years ago highlighting how things can go wrong. In the market for the Monaco Grand Prix, the backmarkers on the grid were lumped together under the heading of 'The Field', and given a derisory quote of 0.5-2 in a market in which first place was worth 50 points, second 25 points and third ten points. One client sold the field at 0.5 for £250 per point. Since we all know that overtaking is impossible at Monaco, this looked a secure way to bank £125 with no risk. The race was run in torrential rain, the favourites all dropped out in accidents or with mechanical problems, and Olivier Panis scored a miracle win from something like 16 on the grid. Another backmarker inherited third place in a race with just three finishers, and 'The Field' made up at 60 points. Instead of winning £125, the client lost £14,875. If the punter in question is reading this, I apologise for revisiting his agony, but there is no better way of making the point.

Apart from that, most of the common-sense rules that apply to any form of betting apply equally well to spreads. We'll consider strategy for specific spreads in more detail later, but first an introduction to the terminology and the available markets, using the results from the Flat meeting at Kempton on September 21, 1997 to show how each is calculated.

## Spread Betting Glossary

I'm sure that one of the most off-putting features of spread betting is the jargon, so it makes sense to start by clarifying exactly what I mean by the terms that will appear in this book.

**Market**    the type of bet, as detailed below.

**Quote**    the high and low figures for each market;
e.g. the opening quote for the market on favourites
might be 66-70.

**Spread**    the difference between the high and low figures of the quote, e.g. if the quote is 66-70, the spread is four. The term spread is more commonly used (mis-used in my view) to describe the quote.

**Make-Up**    the final result of a market. If the points scored by the favourites at a meeting total 60, then that is the make-up. Your profit or loss is calculated as the difference between the opening quote and the make-up.

**Buy**    to bet that the make-up will be greater than the high figure of the opening quote.

**Sell**    to bet that the make-up will be less than the low figure of the opening quote.

**Long**    to go long is the same as to buy.

**Short**    to go short is the same as to sell.

**Position**    if you have sold, you have a short position.

**Trade**    a single bet in a spread market.

**Stop Loss**    a limit set by the spread firm on the maximum amount of points that can be won or lost in a specific market on a single trade.

**Close**    to terminate a bet before the market reaches its natural conclusion. If you have sold favourites before race one, you can close that position by buying at the revised quote at any time prior to the last race.

**Tenth**    also called a 'tick'. Some markets are traded in tenths of a point, for example the total SP market.

## Horse Racing Markets

### 1 Starting prices

The total of the winner's starting price for all races at a meeting. The results of the Kempton meeting were:

| 5-1 | 9-4 | 12-1 | 12-1 | 5-4 | 3-1 | **Total** | **35.6** |
|-----|-----|------|------|-----|-----|-----------|----------|

The total is calculated as $5 + 2.3 + 12 + 12 + 1.3 + 3$ – all prices are rounded up to the nearest tenth (0.1), thus 9-4 becomes 2.3 and 5-4 becomes 1.3. The same rounding is used for prices such as 15-8 (1.9), 100-30 (3.3), and for any odds-on winner. When you trade in this market, the dealer will record the bet as, for example, £20 per point, £2 per tenth (or tick).

The dealer sets an initial quote, in this example it was 34-37, and the punter decides whether to bet lower than 34, or higher than 37. On this day, all punters lose as the dealer has got the quote spot on, but that is quite rare, and nobody loses very much.

If you'd bet low (sold) at 34, you lose 1.6 x your stake. If you'd bet high (bought) at 37, you lose 1.4 x your stake.

One important rule to remember here is that there is no provision for an adjustment of the starting prices after the late withdrawal of a fancied runner, i.e. no equivalent of the fixed odds Rule 4. If an odds-on favourite refuses to enter the stalls, and the race goes to a 10-1 shot, that still counts as ten points on the SP market, even though fixed odds punters would only collect about 5-1.

All the firms operate a 50-point maximum per race, so that a 66-1 or 100-1 winner counts just 50 points, and some also operate a 50 point stop loss on the meeting total, which reduces the need for suicidal thoughts if you've sold at 34 and there are three 33-1 winners on the card.

## 2 Favourites

The starting price favourite for each race scores 25 points for a win, ten points for finishing second, and five points for third.

At our example meeting the finishing positions of the favourites were:

| 4th - 0 pts | 2nd - 10 pts | 2nd - 10 pts | |
|-------------|--------------|--------------|-------------|
| 4th - 0 pts | 1st - 25 pts | 1st - 25 pts | **Total 70 pts** |

Where there are joint- or co-favourites, the one with the lowest racecard number is the only that counts for points in this market. If the favourite is a late withdrawal, and no new market is formed, then points are awarded on a scale based on the official price at the time of the withdrawal:

| | |
|---|---|
| Evens or odds-on | 15 points |
| Under 5-1 | 10 points |
| 5-1 & over | 5 points |

If no SP is returned, then it's the favourite in the trade paper betting forecast that counts.

## 3 Winning distances

The total of the distances between the first and second finishers in all races at a meeting. The distance is that announced by the racecourse judge. At Kempton the distances for the six races were:

1.25l + Neck (0.3) + 1.75l + Neck (0.3) + 1.25l + 6l =

**Total 10.85 Lengths**

For Flat racing there is a maximum of 12 lengths for a single race, and for NH racing that is increased to a maximum of 30 lengths. Those maximums also apply if the winner finishes alone. Distances of less than one length are settled as follows:

| | | |
|---|---|---|
| Short-head – 0.1 | Head – 0.2 | Neck – 0.3 |
| Half-length – 0.5 | Threequarters of a length – 0.75 | |

## 4 Double racecard numbers

I think this market is the one that edges closest to the National Lottery, but as the name implies, it is calculated by multiplying the racecard number of the winner by two, and then adding together the resulting figure for all the races on the card.

At a normal six race meeting, the minimum make-up on this market is always 12, i.e. 1 x 2 x 6, if the top horse wins every race. The maximum depends on the number of runners.

## 5 Single race index

This market is only offered on major races, and is the nearest equivalent that the spread firms offer to the standard fixed odds market on a race. The make-up is 50 points for the winner, 25 points for the second and ten points for the third, although the combination of 25-10-5 is also used.

The market offers a quote for each runner, which will broadly equate to an equivalent each way bet at fixed odds.

For example, in a 50-25-10 market for the King George at Ascot on July 26, the short-priced favourite Helissio was offered at 26-29 in early trading.

A buyer at 29 needs Helissio to win to show a 21pt profit and will be reassured by a potential loss of only four points if the horse finishes second, or 19 points if he finishes third. Only if Helissio is out of the first three is the full 29 points at risk.

A seller of Helissio, at 26, will lose 24 points if he wins, but makes increasingly large profits the worse the horse runs. The points for second and third make it quite difficult to make a direct comparison between the spread market offering and fixed odds, and personally I would prefer a straightforward win-only alternative. But the race index does provide the opportunity to play bookmaker and oppose a specific horse without having to back another runner, something that can be very attractive and which certainly isn't an option in your local betting shop.

## 6 Match bets

The match bet market selects a pair of horses from a race and sets a quote for the distance between them at the finish, regardless of their position within the race. The quote is made in lengths, and is usually something like:

### Horse A / Horse B   0.0-1.5

This means that the spread dealer is predicting that A will beat B by 1.5 lengths. It doesn't matter whether they finish first and second, or last and one from last. If you buy Horse A at 1.5, then he has to finish at least 1.5 lengths in front of B before you make a profit. If he beats B by four lengths, then you win 2.5 times your unit stake. If he finishes four lengths behind B, you lose 5.5 times your stake.

There is a general maximum make-up of 12 lengths for Flat

races, and 15 lengths for NH races. If either horse fails to finish the race, then the maximum make-up applies.

## 7 Performance index

Occasionally the spread firms offer a quote for all of a jockey's mounts at a particular meeting. The scoring system is the same 25-10-5 for first, second and third that is used for favourites. On the text pages this will be shown something like this:

**L Dettori (6)   35-38**

The figure 6 in brackets indicates the number of rides the jockey has booked. If any of his rides is a non-runner, then points are allocated on the same basis as for a withdrawn favourite (see two above), but using the average of the forecast SP from the trade papers as the deciding price.

## Spread betting strategies

I steered clear of spread betting for quite a while, for two reasons. Firstly, I felt that every spread bet was equivalent to a fixed odds bet at odds-on, since it seemed to me it was always possible to lose more than you could win. In fact that isn't entirely accurate, but experience hasn't convinced me that my caution was misplaced. Secondly, I recognised that in a sequence of spread bets, it was possible to make a profit on four or five consecutive trades, but lose the lot with one bad decision. That cannot happen in fixed odds betting, so long as the punter has any sort of staking discipline.

With my subsequent exposure to spread betting, it is clear that my second concern is the thing that makes this type of betting so seductive to the punter. For the spread player, success comes on a regular basis.

Betting on horse races at fixed odds, a professional punter might just achieve a 50 per cent strike-rate if he concentrated entirely on short priced favourites. In the spread market, an optimist armed with a pack of Tarot cards is likely to manage 40 per cent. With most of the firms operating weekly accounts, the cheques appear with disarming frequency. I certainly haven't carried out any sort of survey, but I'd be willing to lay 4-6 that a majority of the people who lose overall on their spread betting honestly believe that they win.

The continued existence of the pioneering companies, the rise of new ones, and the obvious size of their marketing budget, confirms that those punters are suffering a common delusion.

So the first strategy for any aspiring spread player is the same as it should be for a fixed odds punter – keep detailed accounts and records. Because I began with this discipline already second nature to me, I have a complete record of every trade, from the outrageous success of all six favourites at a Newmarket evening meeting, which netted me £2,580, to the painful buy of Pat Eddery's mounts at Windsor that produced a string of fourth places and just one miserable third for five points and a loss of £1,170. The great majority of my trades have been on the starting price markets, and my records look like this:

| Date | Course | Trade | Stake | Make-up | Result | Balance |
|------|--------|-------|-------|---------|--------|---------|
| 17/9 | Sandown | Sell @ 45 | 70 | 43 | +140 | 140 |
| 20/9 | Newbury | Sell @ 53 | 70 | 41/48.5 | +615 | 755 |

The stake is in pounds per point. The split make-up on the second line represents a partial close prior to the last race, of which more later. The records cover all the salient points of each trade, except that I don't try to keep track of my results with the different firms any more than I record the name of the bookmaker for my fixed odds bets.

Apart from keeping a clear profit/loss account, I can use these records to analyse the type of trade that produces profits, see whether my staking has been consistent, and also check on how the level of the opening quote affects the outcome.

One key area of difference from fixed odds is that the amount at risk isn't recorded. On a normal bet, that is simply the stake, and I refer to the total staked as my turnover on fixed odds, and set targets for a profit of at least ten per cent on turnover. I have attempted to define a similar figure for use with spread betting, but have concluded that it has to be different for each market and probably isn't all that useful anyway. For example, in the starting price market, I decided that a figure calculated as:

### Unit Stake  x  Spread on Opening Quote  x  2

was about as good as any other formula I could dream up. The spread on this market varies from two if the opening quote is low (say 20-22), to a maximum of four if it is very high. In both examples above, the initial spread was three, so the virtual turnover was 70 x 3 x 2 = 420. Since a unit stake of £70 per point can easily produce a profit of £2,500 or just as easily an equivalent loss, I'm unsure whether the figure of £420 has any relevance or usefulness, or whether any other formula would be better. For the present I've decided that turnover isn't a concept suited to spread betting.

Perhaps the other important point to raise now is that I've concentrated entirely on trading in the horseracing markets. I have very rarely dabbled with fixed odds sports betting, and I see no reason to modify that approach simply because this is a different type of business. It may sound depressingly dour, but my objective is to make a profit, or in more basic terms, a living. It would be ludicrous to work hard on racing in order to secure that living from fixed odds betting, only to fritter the money away trying to guess how many corners there will be in a football match. Horse racing is my specialist subject, and it doesn't appear to be as well understood by the spread firms – at least so far.

The essence of spread betting is that you, the punter, are testing your opinion against that of the dealer at the spread firm who sets the quote. In most of the sports markets, he has access to vast quantities of statistics that give him the edge, but racing isn't predictable in the same way. As I hope I can show you, as we look at each market in turn, the knowledgeable punter does have at least a chance of gaining the upper hand.

One of the advantages of spread betting is the ability to get in and out of a market at any time during the course of a race meeting. In all the markets that operate on the total for a meeting (SP, Favourites, Distances, Double Numbers), the player can open a bet at any time up to the start of the last race, or close at any time. There is a price to be paid for this option, but there are occasions when, in my view, it's worth paying. To take advantage of this, the player has to have access to the updated quotes provided by the spread firms after each race, usually through the text service on Channel 4, Sky Sports or The Racing Channel.

This emphasises the need for a serious player to be able to concentrate on the progress of the market during the meeting. It is perfectly possible to bet the spreads at lunchtime and then forget about the bet until you finish work, but that approach will certainly not produce the best chances of a profit in the long-term. If you are working nine to five, I would recommend limiting your bets on the meeting long markets to the evenings and weekends.

The possibilities for opening and closing bets early will be looked at in the following sections as we examine each market in turn. I should add that I take my own advice on this – I don't play the spreads on days when I'm actually on the racecourse. I don't believe I can cope with fixed odds betting and spread betting at the same time, or on the same card.

Playing the spreads is an attractive option for me when I'm at home, because of their favourable position with regard to betting tax. At present, the spread firms absorb the betting duty and levy payments within the spread of the opening quote. They can afford to do this as the duty charged is based on the unit stake per point, rather than on the total amount that can be won or lost on a single trade. Thus, if I trade at £100 per point in a market with a three-point initial spread, the firm pay £6.75 in betting duty and around £1.25 in levy, from their total nominal profit of £300. I say nominal profit advisedly, because actually to achieve that profit, the dealer must attract equal total stakes from buyers and sellers, and then maintain that equality throughout the meeting with his revised quotes. It has been interesting to watch the public stance of the spread companies with regard to their results, as reported in the trade press. When they are hit by a bad result, such as ten bookings and a sending off in a football match that looked potentially rough on paper, we are often given detailed figures on the amount lost. But when the world and his dog wanted to support West Ham to put six or seven goals past non-league Emley in the Third Round FA Cup match, little was heard beyond a modest 'good result' quote after the Hammers only managed a 2-1 victory.

If you ever reach the stage of thinking that beating the spreads is easy, just ask yourself one question:

*Have Sporting Index closed yet?*

Need I say more!

## Starting prices

One of the key skills for a professional punter is to be able to predict the likely shape of the betting market for a race – in effect preparing a 'tissue' which is then used in comparison with the actual prices on offer in order to identify value bets. There is no easy formula for this, but I have found that by looking at a race from the bookmakers' viewpoint, I can produce figures that are a close match to the actual market, whether early prices or the on-course market. Given this background, it is hardly surprising that the SP market was the one that most interested me when I started to study the spread firms offerings.

Their initial quote has to be based on the tissue prices available at a point about a couple of hours before racing. This means that they can take account of any moves in the early price market, but for other races they are limited to the betting forecasts available to the punter in the trade papers. Clearly if the punter has information not available to the spread dealer, he has an edge in this market. Once I had played these markets on paper for a couple of weeks, without hazarding any hard cash. I worked on a method of producing my own initial quote, to compare with the spread firms figures.

The procedure I developed involves completing a chart as follows:

| York | 1 | 2 | 3 | 4 | 5 | 6 | 7 | Total |
|---|---|---|---|---|---|---|---|---|
| Minimum | 5 | 4 | 6 | 2.5 | 2.5 | 4 | 2 | 26 |
| Estimate | 9 | 6 | 12 | 5 | 7 | 7 | 4 | 50 |
| Maximum | 16 | 16 | 25 | 12 | 16 | 14 | 10 | 109 |

Those are the actual figures I produced for the York seven-race card on 8 October 1997. For each race, I first predict the minimum possible SP, which is of course the price of the favourite. In addition to my own tissue, I use the trade paper forecasts, the selection charts showing the tips by the national newspapers and any early price information available for the main races. I also check for any non-runners already announced, as these can obviously have an effect on the likely SP.

The next step is to predict a maximum figure. I don't simply assess the odds of the biggest outsider in the race, but try to look for a realistic figure, omitting the longest-priced horses from the calculation. For example, in the opening race on this card, a 15-runner nursery handicap, only three horses actually started at a price longer than 16-1, and in fact all the others were priced between 11-2 and 14-1, so that a realistic maximum was 14. Obviously it is possible for every race to go to a 33-1 chance, but long-priced winners are actually less common than you might expect, as we'll see later.

The third figure is the most important, and is my estimate of the likely MEAN price of the winner. This is where the punters' own view of the outcome of the race can be incorporated into the figures. Again using the first race here as an example, my estimate of nine reflects my view that this is an open contest in which a 12-1 winner is just as likely as a 5-1 winner. It is also based on my belief that a majority of the runners will be priced up in the range 8-1 to 10-1. If I had felt that the fancied horses had a strong edge, then the estimate could have been as low as seven, but equally it could have been 11 if I'd favoured the longshots. In this example, the mean figure is much the same as the average, but they can be very different in a race with a short-price favourite and several horses at 33-1 or longer.

With the benefit of hindsight, the accurate figures for this race would have been a minimum of 5.5, a maximum of 14 and an estimate of eight, but hindsight makes every punter a winner. The one figure about which there can be no argument is the minimum, as that can be compared with the actual returned price of the favourite. In this example the comparison looks like this:

**5-5.5  4-4.5  6-6.5  2.5-3.3  2.5-1.6  4-4  2-2.5  Total 26-27.9**

which is an acceptable margin of error.

The actual results compared with my estimate looked like this:

**9-5.5  6-16  12-10  5-4  7-10  7-4  4-2.5  Total 50-52**

This set of results shows how the errors can balance each other out to produce a total close enough to the original estimate. I'm sure you're all thinking that I've picked my best prediction from months of attempts, but in fact this is another of those spread betting skills that is much easier to acquire than my laboured explanation would suggest.

I use the estimated total to compare with the initial quote from the spread firms, to decide whether there is sufficient margin between my figure and theirs to persuade me to trade. This is exactly the same as setting a price for a horse in a fixed odds bet and then only having a bet if that price or better is available. I rapidly found that, using this method, my estimate was always lower than the midpoint of the initial quote, and thus I always perceived a sell as the value bet in the SPs market.

In this example, the various firms offered initial quotes of 59-62, 60-63 and 61-64. Given a 10- or 11-point margin over my estimate of 50, I was happy to sell at 61 and 60, with the eventual outcome of 52 giving me an eight to nine point profit. In deciding whether to trade I also the use the minimum and maximum figures as pointers to the best and worst outcomes for the bet. If my figures are correct then a sell at 61 could produce a profit of 35 points if all seven favourites win, or a loss of 48 points if my maximum is reached.

As a consistent seller in the SPs market, I have made regular small profits and by treading carefully at meetings with big fields, soft ground, or both, I've avoided any major losses. In midsummer, with small fields the norm, and with form relatively consistent on fast ground, the initial quote can be very low.

For example, on June 27, I sold the Newmarket SPs at 26 for their afternoon meeting, and then sold Goodwood SPs at 27 in the evening. I suspect that most punters would find it psychologically difficult to make that sort of trade. Quite clearly the potential profit is limited and the losses if a 33-1 or 50-1 shot win would be very damaging. In fact both trades produced a profit, with results:

- **Newmarket**
  15-8 (1.9)   10-11 (0.9)   9-2 (4.5)   7-4 (1.8)   7-4 (1.8)   15-8 (1.9)
  **Total 12.8**

- **Goodwood**
  2-1 (2)    3-1 (3)    15-8 (1.9)   5-1 (5)   11-2 (5.5)   7-2 (3.5)
  **Total 20.9**

At Newmarket, with a total of just 38 runners, only 11 horses started at a price of 10-1 or longer, of which only four were at a price that could do real damage for a seller, 20-1 or more. It was a similar story at Goodwood, where only ten horses went off at more than 10-1. So far I haven't lost on any trade where I sold an opening quote of less than 30. On the only occasion I bought at that sort of figure, a buy at 28, the make-up was 17.1. I lost money and learnt my lesson. In total, during the summer period (June, July, August), 21 out of 31 sells in the SP markets were profitable.

Here is another sample chart, this time from the NH meeting at Bangor on December 17.

| Bangor | 1 | 2 | 3 | 4 | 5 | 6 | 7 | Total |
|---|---|---|---|---|---|---|---|---|
| Minimum | 2.5 | 1 | 1 | 2 | 3 | 2.5 | 1 | 13 |
| Estimate | 5 | 2 | 1 | 6 | 5 | 3 | 3 | 25 |
| Maximum | 8 | 7 | 10 | 14 | 12 | 5 | 10 | 66 |

The range of possible prices for this meeting is much lower than the example from York, a common factor with NH meetings. The races are generally less competitive, in terms of the number of possible winners, and most races feature hopeless (but for the seller, very dangerous) outsiders. The second-race favourite was predicted at around 1-3 and eventually was returned at 2-9. In this market, the difference between that and an even-money winner is so small, that I've chosen to use an estimate of one for all odds-on prices. The third race also requires explanation; it was a novice chase with predicted even-money joint-favourites, 10-1 bar the two, and 25-1 bar three. At about 1-20 the front two in the betting producing the winner, an estimate of one seemed reasonable.

The comparison of minimum forecast to actual price of favourite was:

2.5-2   1-0.2   1-0.7   2-1.4   3-2.5   2.5-1.4   1-1.5   **Total 13-9.7**

The actual results compared with the estimate were:

**5-9    2-0.2    1-0.7    6-9    5-5    3-1.4    3-2    Total 25-27.3**

The opening quote was generally 35-38, giving me a healthy ten-point margin over my estimate, and producing a 7.7 point profit.

The second and third races at this meeting highlight one of the key concerns for the player in this market. In the second race, Deano's Beeno was the 2-9 favourite. If he wins, then the seller is well placed, and the buyer is struggling. If he doesn't win, the positions are reversed, as all the other runners have a starting price well in excess of my estimated mean figure. It is the gulf between the price of the favourite and the prices of the remaining runners that makes this sort of race riskier than a handicap with four or five horses priced between 3-1 and 6-1. In the third race, the two fancied horses went off at 4-6 and 13-8. If they fail, and novice chasers have been known to fall, then a long-priced winner is inevitable. In the context of an opening quote of 35-38, a 33-1 winner is highly significant.

I sold SPs at a summer jumping meeting at Worcester on August 11. The opening quote was 26-28, and I was short for £100 per point. The second race was a three-mile novice chase, in which the seven runners were returned at the following prices:

> Evens Lady Of Mine; 2 My Guy; 7 Sigma Wireless; 16 Jobingo;
> 33 John Roger; 40 Taylors Highflyer; 50 Roaming Shadow

No apparent problem for a seller, with the front two in the betting at a combined 1-6. By halfway both those horses had been pulled up lame, and Sigma Wireless was left in front with a circuit to run, chased by John Roger and Roaming Shadow. He jumped hopelessly in front, but managed to clamber over each of the remaining fences and kept going to win by 19 lengths. The eventual make-up was 18.7, so it was a profitable trade, but the second circuit of that novice chase seemed the longest three minutes of my spread betting career to date. I avoided the SPs market at NH meetings until mid-November, by which time the runners were better quality, and hopefully more predictable!

The meeting at Uttoxeter on December 19 demonstrated what

can happen. The first race was a novice hurdle featuring Andanito as the 1-2 favourite, with a 4-1 shot as second-favourite. Everything else was sent off at a double figure price. The average opening quote for the SPs on a seven-race card was 32-35. Sellers knew their fate after Claudia Electric, returned at 66-1, won the first race. I would like to be able to claim that I gave this meeting the swerve because I instinctively knew that it would prove expensive. In fact, I was absorbed in writing the All-weather Workshop section of this book, and forgot that the novice hurdle had been divided, so that the first race was 30 minutes earlier than originally scheduled. With the first winner counting 50 points, the total make-up was 73.1. By December, I was regularly playing the SP market at £100 per point, so even before this book reached the publisher, it had already earned me over £4,000!

That example highlights the key factor in playing the SP market. Whether you are buying or selling, it is the long-priced winners that make the difference. As a seller, I know that a 25-1 shot or worse is almost certain to guarantee a losing trade, regardless of other results. As a buyer, it is just the sort of result that inspires the trade in the first place. Two questions therefore need to be asked:

- How many long priced winners are there in a season?

- Is it possible to predict when they are likely to happen?

To answer the first question, I carried out some research into all the results during the 1996 and 1997 Flat race seasons. The sample covered 6,600 races, which probably equates to about 1,000 meetings. Long-priced winners featured as follows:

- 50-1 or greater     20 winners
- 40-1     6 winners
- 33-1     74 winners
- 25-1     82 winners

There were two occasions when the same meeting had two x 33-1 winners, and three occasions when there were 2 x 25-1 winners. So, in broad terms, we can say that about one in every 5.5

meetings will produce a winner at 25-1 or more. That answers the first question, but I could find no pattern that would help with predicting when or where these longshots will occur.

They covered the entire spectrum of race type, with three of the 50-1 shots winning Group races, which one might expect to be the most predictable class of contest. I considered the possibility that soft ground might result in more upsets, but only 13 of the 182 winners came on ground described as soft or heavy. That compared with 58 on good ground, and 65 on good-to-firm. The number of runners in the races also had little influence, with 42 winners in fields of ten or less, compared with 28 in fields of more than 20. On this evidence a four-runner maiden is just as likely to produce a 50-1 winner as the Wokingham Stakes.

The conclusion is that sellers must be able to take a long-priced winner in their stride, accepting that they will happen unpredictably. The best advice I can offer is that the player shouldn't panic after a 50-1 shot wrecks his trade and look to get out of the bet immediately. I experienced this situation on a trade at Windsor on June 23. On a six-race card, I had sold SPs at 45 for £40 per point. After three races, the running total was just 11.6 and I was looking at a substantial profit. The fourth race was a two-year-old maiden auction with 25 runners, in which nine horses were sent off at a price equal to or less than my estimate of 12-1. The race went to the 50-1 shot Ben Rinnes, with Merlins Ring, at 20-1, in second. The quote immediately rose into the high seventies, but I opted to stay with the bet to the end. The remaining two races produced winners at 7-4 and 3-1, giving a total make-up of 66.4. I lost £856, but it would have been more if I had closed the bet after the fourth race.

That experience confirmed my view that taking a loss halfway through a meeting is essentially illogical. My initial bet was based on the assumption that the starting prices would be lower than the quote produced by the spread firms. Even after Ben Rinnes had won, that was still the position for the last two races. The dealers were now predicting a total of around 80, allowing approximately 19 points for the last two races. My initial estimate for those same races was much less than 19, so it made sense to sit tight. Just because I had been wrong about the maiden race, it didn't automatically follow that the last two races would make things worse. It follows of course, that a buyer should close his bet immediately after a long-priced winner, unless he still anticipates a higher make-up than the revised quote. Since that evening, I have always stayed with a losing bet and I have always ended up losing less then I would have if I had closed after the longshot winner.

Of course, for every rule, there is an exception. One meeting during 1997 provided a chilling example of what can happen if you stick to your guns. The card at Newmarket on Thursday October 16 offered seven races, with the first six all competitive contests with big fields – a typical autumn Flat race meeting. The opening quotes recognised the nature of the card and were in the region of 76-80, the highest I have ever seen in the SPs market. Daunted by the number of plausible outsiders, I dodged the Newmarket card and traded on the meeting at Catterick. The winning SPs at Newmarket were:

**20-1   16-1   20-1   20-1   16-1   33-1   6-1   Make-up 131**

For any punter who had sold at 76, it would have been better to get out early (actually it would have been best to go out early – to the pub). The longer they stayed in, the worse it got! But that is an extreme example, and the card should have sounded warning bells to any punter. I was happy to take a small loss at Catterick!

Although I don't believe in taking a loss, there are occasions when it is worthwhile at least considering whether to take a profit on an SP trade. The opportunity will not arise very often for the seller in this market, since the profits are generally small anyway. But it can happen, as these two examples demonstrate. The first came at Newmarket on May 31, where I sold at the opening quote of 41. This was the day when Cape Verdi made her debut and won at 8-13, having been 5-2 in the trade papers. And two races later, the heavily backed steamer, Blue Goblin, won at 11-10, having been much longer in the morning. When The Prince took the sixth race at 4-7, the running total was just 13.6, with only a seven-runner staying maiden to come.

In that maiden, the favourite went off at evens, with fancied runners at 100-30 and 9-2, outsiders at 9-1, 14-1 and 16-1 and a rag at 66-1. The revised quote after the sixth race was 17.5 – 18.5, so I could have bought at 18.5, for a profit of 22.5 points. But I reasoned that I would be no worse off if any of the first three in the betting obliged, with a profit of 26.4 points if the favourite won. I let the bet run and the 16-1 shot Three Cheers won by seven lengths. Despite my 11.4 point profit, I felt I had lost! This was my first such experience, and I started to consider the options more carefully, and monitor the difference between letting the bet run, and closing with a profit. As you might guess, the best option in the long-term is to let the bet run to its natural conclusion.

Once again, however, there is one exception to that rule. Consider the card at Newbury on September 20. As usual, I was a seller of the SP market at 53, to £70 per point. After six races, the running total was 32.5. The seventh race was a two-year-old maiden with a field of 19 and a very short-priced favourite in Deep Space, who drifted from 4-5 to 5-4 at the off. Nothing else was returned at less than 8-1. The revised quote for the SPs was 40-41, which meant that only one of the 19 runners would show a better profit than closing before the race. In effect, if Deep Space failed to deliver, my paper profit could disappear. I bought at 41 for £40 per point, taking a £480 profit, and left the remaining £30 to run. The race went to a 16-1 shot, giving a final make-up of 48.5, leaving a profit of £135 on the rest of the trade. I ended up £300 better off than if I had let the entire bet run. If the favourite had won, the decision would have cost me £288. But with one runner in my favour, and 18 running for the spread firm, an early close looked the best tactic. I opted for a partial close, but I think now that I would terminate the entire stake in similar circumstances.

For the calendar year 1997, my accounts show 66 separate trades in this market, of which only two have been a buy. Of those 66, 43 have produced a profit. I began to relatively small stakes of around £40 per point – I mean small relative to my turnover in fixed odds betting. But having established that this isn't a volatile market, I increased my stakes as the profits mounted, and I now average around £100 per point. That does, of course, mean that I could lose £5,000 in a single trade, but past profits could absorb that and I fully understand the risk.

The most profitable single trade was at Newton Abbot on August 4, when a sell at 38 and 37 for £100 per point produced a profit of £2,060. The 38 and 37 reflects the differing initial quotes from different firms, as my stake is split. The biggest single loss was at Newmarket on August 9, when a sell at 45 for £100 per point produced a deficit of £1,830, principally due to a 25-1 winner in the two-year-old Listed race. The total profit from all 66 trades was £14,765. There is some evidence from those accounts that the dealers have tightened the opening quotes down a point or two in the last two months, although it could just be that NH racing is less profitable for sellers.

One other potentially significant point that emerges from my records is that several of the most profitable trades have been at courses with notably weak betting markets. High on that list would be Nottingham, where the bookmakers' overround is usually substantial. That is partly due to the weakness of the bookmakers present, but also to small crowds, little real money and large fields of maidens and moderate handicaps. For the spread player, this leads to shorter prices about most horses than would be the case is the same races were run at Ascot or York. I have no idea whether the dealers take this into account when setting their quotes, but I do know that four consecutive trades at Nottingham produced the following results:

| Sep 15 | Sell @ 78/76* | £80/pt | Make-up | 57.4 | +£1,548 |
| Sep 23 | Sell @ 59/58 | £80/pt | Make-up | 39.1 | +£1,532 |
| Oct 15 | Sell @ 65 | £60/pt | Make-up | 45.1 | +£1,194 |
| Nov 3 | Sell @ 58/57 | £80/pt | Make-up | 40.8 | +£1,326 |

*two figures indicate stake split between two firms offering different quotes*

The only other course to produce more than one four-figure return was Newton Abbot, but that had more to do with the number of winners produced by two gentlemen called Pipe and McCoy, than any weakness in the market!

# Favourites

My early involvement with this market wasn't, in any sense, scientific. Like most punters, I looked at the card and decided how many favourites I thought would win, then either bet high or low depending on the initial quote. My first trade using this hit and miss method was successful, but the next four were losers. I struck lucky with a buy of favourites at a Newmarket evening meeting when all six won, and I netted a profit of £2,580. I followed that with four more losing bets, and then decided I needed some sort of proper system if I was to continue playing in this market.

Three things were already clear from my early trades:

- This market was more volatile than the SP market, thanks to the 25 points awarded for a winning favourite. Successful favourites are more common than the 25-1 winner that would produce the same result in the SP market.

- The points for second and third places tended to confuse the issue and were hard to predict.

- It helped if you had a clear idea in advance which horse would be favourite.

As with the SP market, I looked for a method of preparing my own initial quote. It proved deceptively simple, and is almost certainly the method used by the spread firms as well. For each race, I award a number of points between one and 25 for the favourite, based on its prospects of success. If the market only awarded 25 points for a win, it would be easy enough to produce a table of points according to the probable starting price – i.e. if an even-money favourite has a 50 per cent chance of winning, then that would equate to 12.5 points, or 50 per cent of the maximum 25. The points for second and third make it trickier, but the basics are the same. The factors I take into account are:

- The probable starting price of the favourite.
- The number of runners.
- The balance of prices across the field.

The last of those points needs further explanation. If a 2-1 favourite is one of three short-priced runners in a race in which everything else is at least 20-1, then his prospects of being at least placed are greater than his odds would suggest. Another 2-1 favourite in a race in which five or six other horses are on offer between 5-1 and 10-1 probably has a slightly greater chance of winning, but a lesser chance of being placed. Let's look at an example:

| Towcester (Nov 6) | | | | | | | | |
|---|---|---|---|---|---|---|---|---|
| | 1 | 2 | 3 | 4 | 5 | 6 | 7 | Total |
| Estimate | 10 | 11 | 12 | 13 | 17 | 10 | 14 | 87 |

In practice I have a more or less fixed table of points according to the probable price of the favourite. I then adjust that one or two points either way to take into account the other two factors. And finally I might make a further, purely arbitrary adjustment, based on my assessment of the race. It is, after all, part of the job of a professional punter to find opposable favourites. That search also highlights races in which I don't think the favourite is worth taking on.

The first race at Towcester was a selling hurdle, with a 5-2 favourite, which would normally mean an allocation of eight points. Only nine runners, with several no-hopers, so I added one point for the extra chance of being placed. The favourite also had McCoy riding for a small stable, for which I added another point. The second race had a probable 9-4 favourite, normally scoring nine points, but I added two points as there were only six runners, increasing the chances of a place.

The third race had a probable odds-on favourite in Star Manager, and at a price around 4-6 he would count for 16 points, probably 17 in a small field of seven. But I was certain this one had been overrated and I would have wanted to oppose him had I been at the track – hence the cut to 13 points. The fifth race was a mares' novice hurdle with a likely even-money favourite, normally scoring 14 points. But this looked a very uncompetitive race, with four runners going off at 50-1 or more. Even if she was beaten, this favourite seemed almost sure to make the frame, so I added two points for that, and one more because she came from a red-hot inform stable.

Having generated my own estimated score of 87 for the card, I then, and only then, look on Text for the initial quotes. In this case two firms were offering 78-82, and I bought at 82 for £50 in total. This was my result chart for that trade:

| Race | 1 | 2 | 3 | 4 | 5 | 6 | 7 | Total |
|---|---|---|---|---|---|---|---|---|
| Fav finished | 1 | 3 | 4 | 2 | 1 | 3 | 1 | |
| Points | 25 | 5 | 0 | 10 | 25 | 5 | 25 | 95 |
| Running Total | 25 | 30 | 30 | 40 | 65 | 70 | 95 | |
| Updated Quote | 93 | 89 | 73 | 72 | 83 | 81.5 | | |

This chart enables me to keep track of the score and also records the figure at which I can close the bet – or in other words the revised figure quoted by the dealer for a sell bet after each result is known. From these quotes it is possible to calculate how many points the dealer estimated for each favourite during the afternoon. For example, after the first race favourite won, the score has risen by 25, and the quote has gone up from 78 to 93. From that we can deduce that the dealer was allowing ten points for the first favourite, hence the rise of 15 points after it scored 25 points.

Similarly, after the third race favourite was unplaced at 6-4 on, the quote drops by 16 points, so that was the dealers allowance for that race. With a final make-up of 95, I won 13 times my stake, a total of £650. Since the final favourite won, the decision to run with the bet through to the end was justified. I couldn't have made a greater profit by closing the bet at any point during the meeting. The issue of early closing is more significant in this market than it is with SPs, because of the greater volatility of the quote during the course of the meeting. Given an initial quote of 78-82, as in the example above, if the first two favourites win, then the quote will rise by 25–30 points. That offers buyers at 82 the chance to take a decent profit. I don't think it's worthwhile trying to set hard and fast rules to cover this aspect of the market – it's a matter of personal preference. My own choice is generally to let the bet run, and to accept the irritation that can arise if later results go the wrong way.

But I've no doubt that a policy of taking profits any time that they reach a certain level could also be made to pay in the long-term.

The volatility of this market also means that punters should look at the option of coming in late and running a trade over just one or two races. If you have a strong opinion for or against consecutive favourites, then a buy or sell can provide an opportunity to profit from that view, which isn't always an option with fixed odds betting. Some pundits will tell you that this sort of trade can't be profitable, because the punter is paying the spread twice, and that has to be taken into account. But the spread does reduce as the meeting progresses, and of course it disappears after the final race, when trades are settled on the final make-up.

Reverting to the Towcester meeting above, let's imagine that you strongly fancy the last three favourites. The starting prices of those three were 11-10, 7-2 and 7-4. As a fixed odds punter, your options are three singles, three doubles and one treble or any mix of those bets. If you take the professional option and stake three singles, then the return to a £100 level-stake is £485, a profit after tax paid on of £157. Now consider the spread bet alternative, which is to buy the favourites at 74 after the fourth race. If all three favourites were unplaced, you could lose 34 points, so a stake of £10 per point equates to the same potential risk as the three singles. In the event, with two winners and a third, the make-up is 95, and the profit is £210. If all three favourites had won, that would boost the fixed odds profit to £502, whilst the spread trade would return £410. So even with the best result for fixed odds punters, the difference isn't that great.

The real bonus of the spread bet comes from the points for second and third, which effectively give the spread punter an each-way bet. If all three favourites finish second, the fixed odds punter merely gets another lesson in the cruelty of betting and a sorry tale to tell in the pub that evening. The spread player picks up 30 points to add to the initial 40 and loses just four points on his trade, £40 instead of £327. The total number of permutations (256) is too many to cover in detail, but I think the advantage to the spread option is clear. Of course, much depends on the prices of the favourites, but the principle generally holds good.

It is also possible to play the favourites market for just one race, especially the last race on the card, when there is no spread to pay at the end of the meeting. As we've seen above, the buyer gets the advantage of an each-way bet on the favourite. The reward for a win will be less than an equivalent win single at fixed odds, but the points for second mean that placing will result in a break even or a small loss, Once again, look at the Towcester card as an example. Here it was possible to buy the last race favourite at 82.5. That means the four possible results of the spread bet are as follows, assuming a stake of £10 per point:

| Favourite wins | Make-up 95 | Profit £125 |
|---|---|---|
| Favourite 2nd | Make-up 80 | Loss £ 25 |
| Favourite 3rd | Make-up 75 | Loss £ 75 |
| Favourite Unpl | Make-up 70 | Loss £125 |

Compare the worst-case spread outcome with the result of £100 win single (£109 inc tax), and the risk is similar. The profit on that is £166 if the favourite wins – SP was 7-4 - but second or third mean the loss of the entire £109. Try multiplying the stakes by ten, and spread options look increasingly attractive. Placing a trade at £100 per point is much easier than trying to place £1,000 win singles with an off-course bookmaker, and the spread firms don't ban winners. And imagine the problems you would have persuading any bookmaker to accept £500 each-way on a 7-4 favourite in a nine-runner novice hurdle, in which five horses went off at 14-1 or more.

It is harder to make a case for selling favourites over a small number of races, or just one race. In fixed odds betting, getting the favourite beaten only involves him not winning. If it finishes second, the objective has been achieved. In this market, with ten points for second and five for third, the real profits only accrue when you find a favourite who is out of the frame. However, if you can find one who looks vulnerable at a short price, selling the favourite can be a better bet than trying to profit by backing one or more of the opposition at fixed odds. At Stratford on December 29, the last race was a novice hurdle, in which Goodtime George opened up as

10-11 favourite. With the ground riding heavy, and with an earlier runner from the stable having finished well beaten, there seemed a chance that this one might stop quickly if it was beaten. The pre-race quote was 50-51.5 (current total 35), offering a possible profit of 15 points, with a maximum risk of ten points. This time a sell would have returned the full 15 points as Goodtime George faded rapidly from three out to finish fifth.

In all these trades, it's important to recognise that a small change in the quote makes a significant difference to the balance of the bet. For example, if the offer in that last race at Stratford had been 49-50.5, then the risk rises from 10 to 11, and the maximum profit drops from 15 to 14. That's about the same as a fixed odds change from 6-4 to 5-4 – and if you think you can make a profit backing 6-4 shots at 5-4, I've been wasting my time!

# Other markets

I'm going to lump together all the other markets into this one chapter, for the simple reason that I don't have much to say about any of them. I could pretend to have extensive experience, but that would be untrue. I could simply assume that anything I have to say about, for example, match bets, must be worth passing on because the reader is certain to benefit from my unrivalled wisdom. If I ever aspire to such arrogance, I know that this game will undoubtedly bring me back to earth double-quick, not to mention the mickey-taking I would endure on the racecourse! The vast majority of my trading in the spread markets has concentrated on SPs and favourites, so I will limit myself to telling you why I don't generally play the other markets.

## 1 Winning distances

I've been watching races up and down the country for over thirty years and, based on that experience, I've no doubt whatsoever that betting on distances has had an impact on the way races are finishing. I have never seen so many horses eased down in the closing stages as I have in the last twelve months, especially in NH races. There is nothing illegal going on, nor is any official Rule of Racing being broken, but the common explanations about "giving a horse an easy race", or "protecting the handicap mark" simply won't wash.

Easing a horse in the final furlong of a two-mile race isn't going to make any difference to his condition, and the handicapper is more likely to punish a heavily eased horse than one driven all the way to the line. They have full access to the SIS pictures, and they weren't born yesterday. In view of the libel laws, I'm not going to offer any names, and anyway I don't have any evidence that would stand up in a court of law. However, I could give chapter and verse on at least one case of a jockey being paid a small fee to ease down an odds-on favourite to keep the winning margin to a minimum. The punters involved sold distances before the race, and were able to close with a 12-point profit before the next. The sum involved was at least twenty times the amount paid out to the rider. In my view it's probable that this market will have disappeared by the end of 1998, and quite possibly by the time you read this. If it survives, I cannot recommend anyone on the outside to get involved.

Apart from the problem of guessing riding plans, my own first experience of this market was also a deterrent. I drove to Goodwood on a day when rain throughout the morning had left the Sussex lanes awash, and soft ground looked a certainty. And, as everyone knows, soft ground means bigger winning distances – doesn't it? I bought at 13 lengths, and then watched in amazement as the first three races produced photo-finishes. The next two races were better, but the score going into the last was only 5.65. Still, surely the short-priced favourite in this small field should win by three or four lengths to cut my losses – no such luck as he scrambled home by a head. Final make-up 5.85, and one punter persuaded that the SP market was more fruitful.

## 2 Double racecard numbers

I have played this market just once, in the pursuit of experience. I managed a small profit, but never felt in any sense in control of my destiny. There must be punters who like it, otherwise the spread firms would withdraw, but I cannot see how it's possible to make a logical case for deciding whether to buy or sell. I suspect this appeals to the same sort of punter who enjoys trying to outwit the dealer on a football match by guessing how many times the trainer will come onto the pitch. In fixed odds terms, this is the equivalent of forecast doubles, traps five and six through the card at Monmore dogs.

## 3 Match bets

Clearly a more logical market, but I've not become involved so far, for four main reasons:

- Match bets are not offered daily, only on major races, which usually coincide with the days when I'm out racing.

- The dealer chooses the two horses involved in each bet, not the player. I may want to oppose horse A with horse B, but if the dealer only offers a quote on horse A against horse C, I'm scuppered. The risk I can see here is the temptation to play anyway, supporting horse C, even though that wasn't your number one choice.

- The spread on match bets on the Flat is generally 1.5 lengths, and I suspect that many of the results fall within or close to that range, making long-term profits hard to come by.

- The maximum make-up of 15 lengths in NH races, applies if one of the two horses fails to finish. I don't think I would ever get over supporting a horse in a match who fell at the last when well clear, leaving the other to finish tailed off and cost me 15 times my stake.

Boiling down those last two comments, I seem to be saying that in this market, Flat racing isn't volatile enough, but NH racing is too volatile. There's just no pleasing some people, is there?

## 4 Performance index

I've nothing specific to say against playing this sort of market, which does have the advantage that you know exactly which horses are involved. However, the fact that a market in, for example, Dettori's rides at Ascot, is going to be offered, only becomes clear when the spread firms post their initial quotes. That limits the time available for producing a personal quote, whereas the player knows for certain that the other markets will be offered every day at most meetings. But if you have a strong fancy for his rides, or an equally strong case for opposing them, then I've no doubt that this market can be made to pay.

# Final make-up

When I opened accounts with three spread firms early in 1997, I was approaching the whole thing as an interesting experiment, but something that might become more significant in future years. I had monitored the markets for a couple of months, playing mostly on paper, and making just a few small trades through the good offices of my partner, Mark Holder. I expected that I would have to pay a price for my tuition in early losses, and would have been perfectly happy to break even at the end of 1997. The actual results were startling by comparison with that modest ambition:

| | |
|---|---|
| May | + £940 |
| June | − £1460 |
| July | + £5795 |
| August | + £2025 |
| September | + £3595 |
| October | + £2920 |
| November | + £3220 |
| December | + £25 |
| **Total** | **+ £ 17,060** |

I suspect that I will find it difficult to match that figure in 1998! The results I was achieving in the SP market are likely to be difficult to duplicate if, as I suspect, the opening quotes are now a little lower than they were during the summer of 1997. I probably found an opening left by 'mug' players who preferred to go high and look for outsiders, but I can hope for their return. It's always worth remembering that spread betting is no different to fixed odds in one crucial way – you can only win what someone else is prepared to lose.

But although it can't be as easy as it often felt during the summer, I wouldn't hesitate to recommend spread betting on the racing markets to any punter. So long as you are fully alive to the risks, it is good fun, and getting a bet on is much easier than chasing early morning prices about a horse tipped by Pricewise! A spread bet can provide an interest throughout the card, and it enlivens a meeting that you might never consider for fixed odds betting – for me it's the only option for a Brighton meeting! And it's certainly a more serious punting proposition than that other through-the-card fun bet, the Placepot, of which more later!

# Spread betting workshop

Having discussed the strategies for the various horseracing markets, this chapter demonstrates how I operate those ideas in practice. What follows are the actual trades I placed over a period of one week in January 1998, along with the relevant charts I prepared in advance of the meetings. Much of this chapter was written in real time, as the meetings were being run, so the race by race decisions are discussed as they occurred.

## Saturday, January 24

The usual four meetings this afternoon. But I know that the spread firms will concentrate on the televised cards at Haydock and Kempton, and that quotes for the other two meetings at Catterick and Lingfield (AW) are likely to be restricted to favourites and distances only. The initial quotes will be shown on Teletext approximately one hour before the first race at 12.45. I start work at about 11.00, with Kempton as my first priority, as I know more about the horses and am therefore more likely to have an edge at that meeting. The betting forecasts for the seven races were taken from the trade papers and advertised early prices, where available:

**Race 1    2m 5f Novices Hurdle      15 runners            NR No. 12**
7-4 Bracey Run, 9-4 King On The Run, 6 Prospero, 10 Sunuvugun, 14 Moon Devil, Over The Glen 16 Endeavour, Super Saffron, 25 Bar

**Race 2    3m Novices Chase       4 runners**
Evens Northern Starlight, 9-4 Ebullient Equiname, 4 Occold, 10 Lottery Ticket

**Race 3    2m 5f Handicap Hurdle    15 runners       NR No. 4 & 12**
5-2 Three Farthings, 11-2 Toby Brown, 13-2 World Express, 8 Deymiar, 9 Robingo, 10 Big Strand, Eau De Cologne, Handy Lass, 12 Far Dawn, 16 Bar

**Race 4    2m Novices Chase       5 runners**
4-5 Kadastrof, 3 Morstock, 4 Stompin, 10 Bar

**Race 5    2m Handicap Hurdle      10 runners**
3 Alabang, 4 Nahrawali, Nipper Reed, Serenus, 9 New Inn, Shahrur, 14 Doctoor, 16 Bar

**Race 6    2m 4f Handicap Chase    10 runners**
7-2 Even Flow, 9-2 Prate Box, 6 Stately Home, Frazer Island, 7 Easthorpe, Monks Soham, 8 Greenback, 10 Aardwolf, 14 Bar

**Race 7    2m NH Flat         22 runners**
5-2 Dunbury Lad, 4 Matchless, 6 Durnford Bay, 8 In the Van, 10 Guard Of Honour, 12 Mr Music Man, 14 Bar

This was my prediction chart for Kempton:

| | 7 races | 1 | 2 | 3 | 4 | 5 | 6 | 7 | Total |
|---|---|---|---|---|---|---|---|---|---|
| | Minimum | 2 | 1 | 2.5 | 1 | 3 | 4 | 2.5 | 16 |
| SP | Estimate | 4 | 2 | 8 | 3 | 4 | 6 | 7 | 34 |
| | Maximum | 14 | 5 | 12 | 10 | 10 | 10 | 16 | 77 |
| | Favourite | 12 | 15 | 9 | 18 | 8 | 6 | 10 | 78 |

The estimates reflect confidence that one of the first three in the betting will take the opener, that the first handicap hurdle looks very open, and that it's around 1-4 that one of the first four in the betting will win the second handicap hurdle. I carried out the same process for Haydock, with the totals estimated as follows:

| Haydock | 7 races | | |
|---|---|---|---|
| SP Min 13 | Estimate 22 | Maximum 55 | Favourites 97 |

Those figures are typical of a card with several odds-on favourites, in this case Collier Bay, Paddy's Return, Sparkling Cone and Festive Teak in the closing bumper. This sort of card is hard to play on the spreads because the favourites take on an unbeatable look, and with small fields they earn points on the favourites index even if they do get beaten. The SPs are inevitably going to be low, even if the second- or third-favourites win these races, and as a result the spread on the initial quote represents a big percentage of the probable range of make-ups.

Based on my estimates, I set my own initial quote for each market, and then record the offers from the three firms with whom I have accounts. Throughout this chapter, I'll use the initials H = Hills, L = Ladbrokes, S = Sporting Index.

| Kempton | SP 35-37 | Offers | H 41-44 | L 42-45 | S 42-45 |
|---|---|---|---|---|---|
| | Fav 76-80 | Offers | H 75-79 | L 74-78 | S 73-77 |
| Haydock | SP 24-26 | Offers | H 28-30 | L 28-30 | S 28-30 |
| | Fav 95-99 | Offers | H 96-100 | L 94-98 | S 96-100 |

I had also prepared an estimate for favourites at Lingfield, but none of the firms opted to trade that market.

You will see that I set my own opening quote for SPs slightly higher than my actual estimate This provides me with a safety margin, but also takes account of the balance between possible maximum profit and loss. With my estimate at Haydock being 22, but the minimum only 13, the dealer knows that he'll have to set the quote higher in order to attract sellers. Otherwise the potential risk is too great compared with the maximum reward.

Looking at my four trading opportunities, it's clear I have no edge on either of the favourites markets. At both meetings, my estimate falls within the spread on every offer. I felt that the figure for Haydock was very high, but this was based on a gut feeling that the odds-on shots weren't going to find things that easy and might well be opposed in the market. That would mean that their eventual SP would be longer than the forecast on which the spread firms would be basing their calculations. But with a substantial upside risk if the good things all obliged, I wasn't sufficiently confident to want to trade. This is the point at which instinct has to be applied to the figures, and instinct said it was too risky.

On the SP markets, the potential profit at Haydock was insufficient to warrant a trade, especially given my doubts about the favourites. But at Kempton, there was a healthy seven-point difference between my low figure and that offered by Sporting and Ladbrokes. That represents a 20 per cent margin in my favour, and I traded in that market:

Sold Kempton SPs @ 42 for £60 per point with Sporting
Sold Kempton SPs @ 42 for £30 per point with Ladbrokes

The two separate trades provide me with two different quotes if I want to take a partial profit during the meeting, but they also represent the limitations of my credit with each firm. Having bet, I then maintain a result chart during the meeting:

| | | 1 | 2 | 3 | 4 | 5 | 6 | 7 | Total |
|---|---|---|---|---|---|---|---|---|---|
| SP | Estimate | 4 | 2 | 8 | 3 | 4 | 6 | 7 | 34 |
| | Actual | 1.9 | 4 | 2.3 | 0.8 | 8 | 3.5 | 12 | 32.5 |
| Running total | | 1.9 | 5.9 | 8.2 | 9 | 17 | 20.5 | 32.5 | |
| Revised quote | | 39 | 41 | 35 | 33 | 33.5 | 30.5 | | |

The revised quote is the figure at which I can close the position, i.e. buy the SPs to balance the sell I made before the first race. If I had wanted, I could have closed after race four with a nine-point profit – 42-33. I let the trade run to completion and hoped for a short-priced winner in the final race to produce a substantial profit. The 12-1 winner meant that I finished slightly worse than if I'd closed before the last, but the difference was only two points. It could have been a lot worse, as the second and third in that race were 25-1 and 50-1. As you can see, the final make-up was very close to my original estimate of 34, although as usual that resulted from several wrongs conspiring to make one right.

That was a pretty typical example of a profitable sell in the SP market, with the profit not large but the risk of a big loss also fairly small. The dangerous races were the opening novice hurdle and the bumper, and with hindsight it probably would have been smarter to close at 30.5 before the final race.

The make-ups in the other markets I worked on were:

| Kempton Favs 100 | Haydock SPs 28.8 | Haydock Favs 50 |
| --- | --- | --- |

The Haydock SPs were inside the initial quote, so no player could win in that market. The Haydock favourites lived down to my worst fears with all the so-called good things being beaten. With the favourite winning the opening novice hurdle, it would have been possible to sell at 110 after that race, giving an eventual profit of 60 points. But it would have been a brave man who sold to high stakes with 25 points already on the board and four odds-on favourites still to come!

**My profit on the Kempton SP trade was £855 – 9.5 points at £90 per point.**

## Monday, January 26

Two meetings this afternoon, at Windsor over jumps, and Southwell on the AW. As usual on a Monday, the quality was poor, especially at Southwell, with one dire maiden offering seven runners with a career record of zero wins from eighty-five starts. One of the better races featured a six-year-old maiden filly as a short-price favourite at an early even-money! My estimates for the SP and Favourite markets, along with the initial quotes were:

| Windsor | SP | 46 | Offers | H 44-47 | L 43-46 | S 42–45 |
|---|---|---|---|---|---|---|
| | Fav | 72 | Offers | H 74–78 | L 74–78 | S 74–78 |
| Southwell | SP | 44 | Offers | H 43-46 | L 42-45 | S 42–45 |
| | Fav | 56 | Offers | H 65-69 | L 64-68 | S 64–68 |

Neither SP quote offered any edge, which is quite unusual, but reflects the fact that my estimates were generous, making allowance for the moderate quality of the racing, of the type which produces more surprises. The obvious trade is a sell of the Southwell favourites, with an eight- to nine-point advantage, but I wasn't keen on selling at such a low level on a seven-race card. Even if all the favourites were beaten, the place points could still add up to a substantial part of the 64 available, and it would only require two winners to make losses certain. In essence the risk is much greater than the likely reward. I opted to wait and see how each meeting developed, with the option of stepping in after one or two races. This was especially so at Windsor, where the second 'race' was a 23-runner selling handicap hurdle in which I'd allowed 14 points for the SP in my estimates. There would be no advantage in selling Windsor favourites before this race, as the quote would only allow four points – if the favourite was beaten, the quote would hardly change, but if it won, it would do considerable damage.

Avoiding Southwell was already looking a good decision after two races, with a winning favourite in the dire maiden taking the score to 30 points, and at that stage I decided to leave Southwell alone and concentrate on Windsor. The first race went to a joint-favourite, but as it had the lower racecard number, that counted 25 points. The second-favourite was unplaced, so after two races the quotes were:

| H 81–84 25-2 | L 82–85 25-2 | S 82–85 25-2 |
|---|---|---|

Allowing for the points already on the board, my estimate was now 80, so this was a narrow sell, reinforced by my instinct that the short-price favourites in the three chases were vulnerable.

Sold Windsor Favourites @ 82 for £25 per point with Sporting

Sold Windsor Favourites @ 82 for £25 per point with Ladbrokes

The next race produced a piece of good fortune, of the sort that can occur in this market. I had anticipated the favourite would be Storm Damage in this two-mile novice chase, and I was happy to oppose him, having been unimpressed with his jumping last time. He opened up as 6-4 favourite, but drifted to 2-1 joint with Clifton Beat at the off and as that was number one, Storm Damage's performance was no longer relevant. In fact, he didn't jump all that well but stayed on to win anyway, with Clifton Beat back in fourth, scoring zero points for my trade – a right result!

The following favourite was Prince Buck in a three-and-a-half-mile handicap chase, and he was another, for me, suspect jumper. He ploughed through the sixth from home, never looked likely to win after that and finished up a tired fourth. No extra points after two races, and I could now buy at 60, taking a 22-point profit. Tempting, and possibly a mistake, but I still felt that the next two favourites were worth opposing, so I opted to let the bet run. That didn't look too smart after the fifth, with original favourite General Assembly drifting alarmingly, leaving the winner Moonlight Air as the point scorer under an inspired ride from Tony McCoy. Now the quote was 73–75, so I could take a seven point profit, or hope that McCoy wouldn't double up on Capenwray in the handicap chase. Hope springs eternal!

Ten minutes later, it was clear that hope wasn't going to be paying the rent this week, with Capenwray overcoming a number of slow jumps to win narrowly. The quote moved up to 82.5–84, and having scorned a £1,100 profit, I was now looking at a possible £900 loss. The last race was a wide open 13-runner handicap hurdle, so I gritted my teeth and kept the bet going. The favourite, Storm Tiger, was well backed, never came off the bridle until leading and going clear at the last and galloped on to win easily. I could hardly have found a better demonstration of the ups and downs of playing this market if I'd reviewed a whole year's trading. It also highlights the need to be able to keep in touch with the results and the revised quotes, in order to consider the options available after each race.

This time it had all gone pear-shaped for me after a great start but I've followed the strategy of keeping a trade going throughout, and it has generally been more profitable than closing early. However, on this occasion, the account reads:

**My loss on the Windsor Favourites trade was £900 – 18 points at £50/point. Running Total: -£45**

The other markets made up as follows:

| Windsor SP 25.2 | Southwell SP 26.9 | Southwell Favs 65 |
|---|---|---|

So the Southwell favourites made-up exactly on the initial quote, and no profit would have been possible there. Both SP markets made up well below my estimate, thanks to the number of favourites going in at both meetings. A day of missed opportunities, but no serious damage done.

## Tuesday, January 27

Again two meetings, NH racing at Leicester and the usual AW meeting at Lingfield. I wasn't keen on Leicester as a betting option, because the card included four hurdle races on heavy ground. With short-price favourites down the card, the SP market offered limited scope and the initial quotes for favourites covered my estimate of 67. So I opted to concentrate on Lingfield, where the races shaped up as follows:

**Race 1     5f Handicap        7 runners**
All priced up between 7-2 and 8-1

**Race 2     1m Claimer        10 runners**
Anonym likely to be around 11-10 favourite, with only one realistic rival in Waikiki Beach

**Race 3     6f Handicap        14 runners**
A weak 0-65, with Chipstead Bay supported from 3-1 to 7-4 at early prices and I was keen on his chances of victory.

**Race 4     10f Maiden        9 runners**
The Cole-trained newcomer the key to the race. As a $95,000 yearling, he could well be a short priced favourite if the subject of support.

**Race 5     10f Handicap        9 runners**
ten runners originally, but forecast favourite Nisaba was an early non-runner, leaving Mystagogue at 7-4 in the early price market.

**Race 6     7f Limited        5 runners**
This looks a lay down for the favourite Philistar, with Digpast always slowly away,

Blue Flyer looking totally out of form, and the other two outclassed in this 0-70 event.

As at Leicester, the SP market looked likely to produce a low quote and limited potential profit for sellers. However, I felt that this could be a good day for the favourites, and my estimate and the opening quotes were:

| Estimate  79 | H  67-71 | L  66-70 | S  65-69 |
|---|---|---|---|

That looked an excellent buy, with the difference probably stemming from my greater confidence in Anonym, Chipstead Bay and Philistar than their forecast prices would justify. My trades were:

Bought Lingfield Favourites @ 69 for £30 per point with Sporting
Bought Lingfield Favourites @ 70 for £20 per point with Ladbrokes
Bought Lingfield Favourites @ 71 for £20 per point with Hills

The quote had moved up to 68–72 with all three firms before the first, with Digpast declared a non-runner in the last race, which should see Philistar priced at around 1-2. Any points from the first race would have been a welcome bonus. The early-price favourite was Half Tone, who ran on to finish second (as usual), but punters in their wisdom opted to support Palacegate Jack down to 100-30, and he could only manage fourth, so zero points after one race.

That was followed by a temperamental performance from Anonym, but he did run on close home to take second a long way behind the 20-1 winner Hawaii Storm, so ten points after two. The revised quote was now 59–62, but I'd budgeted for 24 points at this stage, so I'd be happy to escape with any make-up over 65. A lot now rested on Chipstead Bay in the sprint handicap, but he didn't run anywhere near his previous form, seeming to resent the kickback when in behind the leaders from halfway. With just ten points scored after three races, the quote has now dropped to 49–51 and this punter is left hoping for something to keep losses to a minimum – thoughts of profit have now disappeared. At this stage, I could take a 20/22 point loss, but as usual I prefer to stick with the trade. This policy has produced the profits I recorded during 1997, and halfway through a meeting is no time to be adopting a new strategy.

In the following maiden race, the newcomer New Yorker drifted from 7-4 to 6-1 and ran worse than that suggests. You sometimes hear a trainer say that a horse needs a race to wake him up – in this case it would have needed more than that, as New Yorker appeared to be comatose! The exposed three-year-old Younico was sent off favourite at 11-8, but could only manage third place for five points. A look at my record cards confirmed that my current biggest loss on a single favourites trade stands at £1,725. Ominously, that was also at a Lingfield AW meeting.

The fifth race favourite, Mystagogue, won at 11-8 and I relaxed, expecting Philistar to win easily, as did punters who sent him off at 4-9. That would have reduced the loss to 5–7 points, but he could only manage third, producing a final make-up of 45.

**My loss on the Lingfield Favourites trade was £1,740 – an average of 25 points at £70 per point.**
**Running Total : -£1,785**

I was very confident prior to racing and that's reflected in the stake of £70 per point, but in the end I'm relieved to have got out with a loss that is bad enough, but which could have been a real disaster. When I started this diary, I obviously had no idea how things would work out, but I'm certainly providing a valuable lesson on the risks inherent in this game.

## Wednesday, January 28

I went racing at Wolverhampton today, and fortunately stuck to my policy of not trading on the spreads when I'm on the racecourse. I did consider a sell of the favourites, as conditions at all the AW tracks appear to be changing during the current dry spell and the form isn't always working out. But the initial quote of 72–76 didn't appeal. Even if the favourites were beaten here, it was hard not to see them picking up points for second and third. In fact the first four all won, and although the last two could only manage a third place between them, it would have cost me over 30 points with no chance to get out early better placed. The quote for starting prices was 29–31, and I also felt that offered limited profit to a seller, as I was expecting one or two upsets on the surface. The eventual make-up was 6.2, probably the lowest total for SPs since I first played this market!

Going racing cost me £780 lost on fixed odds bets at Wolverhampton, but that looked a bargain compared to what I might have lost if I'd stayed home.

## Thursday, January 29

Three meetings today, with Huntingdon and Wincanton staging competitive NH cards, plus the usual AW racing at Lingfield. The SP market is only likely to be offered at the two NH meetings, with the favourites available at all three.

The Wincanton card poses a particular problem, as the first two races on the card both feature long odds-on favourites. Both are highly likely to win, but they offer the player little margin as a buyer of favourites or a seller of SPs. The dealer will set the quote on the assumption that they'll win, and with four very open races to follow, my first inclination is to give this card a miss. However, I prepared the estimates as usual, but I would want a sizeable margin to persuade me to trade before the third race:

| Wincanton | 6 races | | |
|---|---|---|---|
| SP Min 18 | Estimate 31 | Maximum 88 | Favourites 67 |

The Huntingdon card has a better balance, but also has a couple of tricky contests over fences. In the novice chase, Potters Gale will be around 11-10 favourite, but has been slowly away on occasions and is making her chasing debut, both factors that make it difficult to produce a confident point estimate for the race. In the later two-mile handicap chase, the 5-4 favourite is Sierra Bay, who ran out at Warwick two races ago, and only just lasted home when winning at Folkestone last time, looking a weak finisher. In both these races, I've dropped the favourite estimate a couple of points and made the SP estimate higher than would be usual with such a short-priced runner.

| Huntingdon | 7 races | | |
|---|---|---|---|
| SP Min 19 | Estimate 46 | Maximum 96 | Favourites 62 |

The Lingfield AW card has a couple of favourites that look nailed on to finish second even if they don't win, and I've estimated 40 points for those two races. Given my experience on Tuesday, I'll be looking for a good margin of error before I trade here. The track is riding very slow at present due to the prolonged dry, cold spell, and times on Tuesday were the slowest of the winter so far.

| Lingfield | Favourites 86 |
|---|---|

Taking those estimates and using them to set my opening quotes, this is how they match up with the initial offers from the spread firms:

| Wincanton | SP 32-34 | Offers | H 39-42 | L 38-41 | S 39-42 |
|---|---|---|---|---|---|
| | Fav 65–69 | Offers | H 67–71 | L 68-72 | S 68-72 |
| Huntingdon | SP 45-48 | Offers | H 50–53 | L 48-51 | S 48-51 |
| | Fav 60-64 | Offers | H 67-71 | L 69-73 | S 70-74 |
| Lingfield | Fav 84-88 | Offers | H 84-88 | L 84-88 | S 84-88 |

The obvious candidates are the SPs at Wincanton and the favourites at Huntingdon, both as possible sells. With the question marks over those two chasers at Huntingdon, I opted to play the SP option, in the expectation that, if the first two odds-on shots oblige, there will be almost no upside risk. The margin of seven points looks sufficient to allow for one of those two to lose and still leave a chance of a profit.

Sold Wincanton SPs @ 39 for £60 per point with Sporting
Sold Wincanton SPs @ 39 for £30 per point with Hills

This diary chapter is certainly reinforcing the warning message I offered in my introduction to spread betting! The 2-5 favourite Miss Ondee led and fell at the first hurdle in the Wincanton opener, and with the second-favourite priced at 12-1, there were no good results available. But even then, the winner, at 12-1, was a better option than the runner-up, who was a 33-1 shot. That result also reduces any prospects of closing this trade at a profit before the final race, a wide open 21-runner handicap hurdle. Here's the result chart for the entire card:

|  |  | 1 | 2 | 3 | 4 | 5 | 6 | Total |
|---|---|---|---|---|---|---|---|---|
| SP | Estimate | 1 | 1 | 6 | 4 | 7 | 12 | 31 |
|  | Actual | 12 | 0.3 | 2 | 3.5 | 4.5 | 20 | 42.3 |
| Running total |  | 12 | 12.3 | 14.3 | 17.8 | 22.3 | 42.3 |  |
| Revised quote |  | 48 | 45 | 39 | 37.5 | 35 |  |  |

The only decision was prior to the last race, when I could have taken a four-point profit, but with anything at 16-1 or less on my side, I took my chances in the hopes of a winner at a single figure price. Much in line with all the trades this week, there were three longshots clear of the field jumping the last, and it was Walters Destiny who stayed on best to win at 20-1, thankfully holding off a 50-1 shot in second. A small loss, but it could have been a lot worse. As I'd anticipated, had Miss Ondee won the first, there would have been a useful profit.

**My loss on the Wincanton SP trade was £297 – 3.3 points at £90 per point. Running Total : -£2,082**

The two 'dodgy' chasing favourites at Huntingdon both won, with a final make-up of 90, so a sell at 67 or 68 would have been bad news. The Lingfield favourites scored 90, almost in line with my estimate of 84–88.

## Friday, January 30

The figures in this chapter so far show how volatile spread betting can be, so it's worth pointing out that it can work both ways. Earlier this month, I recorded a profit of £3,100 in a single trade on Southwell favourites. That was on a day when the inside draw was dominant, and there were four favourites drawn in stall one, all of whom won. There is a Southwell AW meeting today, but it doesn't look as promising at first glance. The NH meetings are at Doncaster and Folkestone, with plenty of runners, especially at the former.

The seven-race card at Doncaster looks very competitive, with no favourite likely to go off at less than 2-1. That means that most races have a group of horses priced between 3-1 and 8-1, so that the SP market is more predictable than it might seem. These races are in fact less volatile than the type we encountered at Wincanton yesterday, where the defeat of a 2-5 favourite means a big number, whatever wins. Folkestone looks less competitive, with only two or three contenders in most races, and the SP make-up could be very low if there are no shocks. My figures were:

| Doncaster | 7 races | | |
|---|---|---|---|
| SP Min 24 | Estimate 45 | Maximum 96 | Favourites 54 |
| Folkestone | 7 races | | |
| SP Min 14 | Estimate 31 | Maximum 72 | Favourites 78 |
| Southwell | 8 races | | |
| | | | Favourites 85 |

The initial quotes were:

| Doncaster | SP 45-49 | Offers | H 52-55 | L 52-55 | S 52-55 |
|---|---|---|---|---|---|
| | Fav 52-56 | Offers | H 59-63 | L 62-66 | S 59-63 |
| Folkestone | SP 31-33 | Offers | H 37-40 | L 37-40 | S 37-40 |
| | Fav 76-80 | Offers | H 84-88 | L 84-88 | S 84-88 |
| Southwell | Fav 83-87 | Offers | H 80-84 | L 82-86 | S 79-83 |

Given a choice of seven-point margin on Doncaster SPs and a six-point margin on Folkestone SPs, I had no problem deciding to opt to trade at Folkestone, where the risks look much lower. The favourites at both meetings were a possible sell, but in neither case did the potential profit look attractive, especially selling at Doncaster, where two winners from seven races would involve probable loss.

Sold Folkestone SPs @ 37 for £60 per point with Sporting
Sold Folkestone SPs @ 37 for £25 per point with Hills
Sold Folkestone SPs @ 36 for £25 per point with Ladbrokes

As you can see, the quote had already moved down by one point by the time I called Ladbrokes. Here is the result chart:

| | | 1 | 2 | 3 | 4 | 5 | 6 | 7 | Total |
|---|---|---|---|---|---|---|---|---|---|
| SP | Estimate | 4 | 3 | 6 | 4 | 2 | 5 | 7 | 31 |
| | Actual | 5 | 1.5 | 4 | 6 | 1.8 | 3 | 25 | 46.3 |
| Running total | | 5 | 6.5 | 10.5 | 16.5 | 8.3 | 21.3 | 46.3 | 46.3 |
| Revised quote | | 38 | 35 | 33 | 33 | 32 | 29 | | |

All progressed smoothly, with the first six races all falling to one of the first three horses in the betting. This time I decided to close part of the trade prior to the last race, securing an eight-point profit. A picture on the Racing Channel, showing the 6-4 favourite for the last race running loose, prompted this decision! I closed the £60 trade with Sporting, for a guaranteed profit of £480, and left the others open. This looked a good idea ten minutes later, when the favourite faded after leading and the race went to a 25-1 shot. It would have been an even better idea if I'd closed the entire trade, but the overall outcome was relatively neutral.

**My loss on the Folkestone SP trade was £10.**
**Running Total : -£2,092**

That brings this chapter to a close, not only because the week is over, but also because I can't afford to keep on losing at this rate! At least the figures should persuade even the most sceptical reader that I'm not massaging my results to make myself look good. There have been three key moments during the week (excluding the actual choice of trades) that have decided the outcome:

- Refusing the 22-point profit available on the Windsor favourites after the first two had been unplaced. That turned a potential £1,100 profit into a £900 loss, which as you can see would have transformed the account for the week.

- The unexpected demise of Philistar at Lingfield in the final race, only managing third of four as the 4-9 favourite. That made a 20-point difference and cost £1,400.

- The decision to close partially before the last race at Folkestone, which saved 17.3 points at £60 per point – a gain of £1,038.

The amounts look large, but I should put them into perspective by pointing out the obvious that you don't have to trade for such large stakes. I do so for two reasons – I can afford it, and I've made substantial profits from my trading to date. Spread betting is now part of my work and I'm betting at this level in an attempt to make a living, not as a hobby.

As so often, I've found the experience of writing about my betting has forced me to think more clearly about my methods, and I'd recommend anybody taking this form of betting seriously to adopt the same approach for a few days. The decision not to take the 22-point profit on Monday, at least to part of my total stake, was easy to justify to myself, but it doesn't look anywhere near as logical in black and white.

So I may well revisit my approach to that factor, especially when trading in the favourites market, which has the greatest volatility. Spread betting on horseracing requires the same flexibility of thinking as fixed odds. A willingness to continue questioning methods is essential, to avoid the dealers and the spread firms gaining the upper hand. My experience of these markets has convinced me that this is the best option for the off-course punter who wants to make the game pay. The removal of one more of the available outlets for fixed odds punters, with the take-over of Corals, leads me to anticipate a tightening of margins and increasing difficulty in getting bets accepted. So far, that hasn't been a problem with the spread firms, and long may it last.

# PART 5

## PUNTERS AND OTHER PEOPLE

## Who are they?

There is a moment in most Channel 4 racing broadcasts when John McCririck invokes the mysterious power of 'they'. He adopts that tone which suggests he shouldn't really be telling us this, but, after all, we're consenting adults and he knows his secret is safe with us – then he reveals that 'they' are backing horse X in the next race. In all the years I've been watching, the exact identity of 'they' has remained a secret, although McCririck sometimes extends the definition to include 'faces' and 'shrewdies'.

Personally I spend a lot of time in the betting rings of the South and Midlands, and I'm none the wiser – all the punters have a face and most look none too shrewd! Of course, he could be referring to professional punters, including me, but it's not easy to make the transition from 'I' to 'they'. At what point does a regular punter become a 'face'? Perhaps that question can be answered – it's probably at the point when you become sufficiently well known to the bookmakers that they no longer give you a ticket when you bet. In my case, the bets go into the ledger as 'down to Alan'. But I doubt if I'd fit Big Mac's definition of a 'shrewdie' – I don't take any notice of stable whispers and the only steamer I like is a stodgy pudding covered in golden syrup!

The implication in McCririck's reference is 'they' know something (or perhaps lots of things) that is not common knowledge amongst punters. There are times when the suggestion is more forceful, indicating that 'they' know exactly what the result of the race will be in advance. I've encountered the public belief in this mystical power quite a lot in recent years. Professional punters lay no claim to knowing for certain what will win any race. Discussion of a race will centre around chances, prices, shortlists, and which horses can be opposed. In conversation we are more likely to ask someone how he sees a race, rather than come right out and ask what will win. But if I tell a questioning member of the public that I've no opinion about a race, or that I might back so-and-so if the price is right, he's probably convinced I know the result but I'm just not willing to share my knowledge.

The power of 'they' spreads much further than just to Channel 4 viewers. 'They' are invoked with great regularity in betting shops and by Racing Channel presenters, in the time-honoured phrase "they're backing this one". Do the people who use this cliché ever stop to ask who exactly it is that is placing the money? Once again the implication is that if a horse shortens in price, it must be because the person making the bets has inside knowledge. I'm sorry to disillusion supporters of this theory, but it holds less water than a tea strainer. Much the most likely reason for a longshot to shorten in the betting is that one or more professional punters thought the initial price was too big. It has never been my chosen method of operation, but there are professionals who operate solely on price. They have a target price for every runner in a race, and back any horse who exceeds that target. If the difference is substantial, they will continue their support as the horse shortens.

To give an example from my own experience, let's look at a handicap chase staged at Towcester. I have no strong fancy for this race, but the field includes a horse previously successful over course and distance and now returning after a lay-off. I expect this animal to be priced up at around 6-1 to 7-1, so an opening show of 16-1 is a surprise, and when 20-1 is offered on some boards, I feel compelled to bet. Knowing the impact this decision is likely to have on the weak market at Towcester, I hand half my stake to a colleague, and we bet simultaneously, each taking £2,000/100. Meeting back in the centre of the ring, we watch the effect of those two bets ripple through the ring, and inside thirty seconds the price is rubbed off on most boards. The next SIS show is 10-1, although there are several boards showing only 7-1 or 8-1. In the back of my mind, I can hear five thousand betting shop pundits uttering the catch phrase – "they're backing that one at Towcester".

But in fact, they aren't – I am, and as it later transpires, one other punter who placed a bet at 16-1 on the rails. Just two of us, motivated by a price we considered too large. Not a stable-inspired gamble, not a coup, not inside information, not "my contact is having his biggest bet of the decade", not "thousands taken out of the ring at Towcester", nor even "we've been waiting all year for this one – today's the day". Not in fact any of the lurid phrases that are adopted to describe the simple application of the laws of supply and demand in an open market. The horse – his name doesn't matter – was pulled up!

So it can be just one punter, or it can be something equally irrelevant to the true chances of the horse apparently being backed. Consider a scenario in which Bookmaker A and Punter B join forces against Bookmaker C, who is noted as the strongest at the track. In an eight-runner race, A and B have identified a possible outsider to make the frame. B waits for C to offer 33-1 about the horse and then requests a very large each-way bet, half of which is accepted. Both A and B know that C will now seek to reduce his liabilities by backing the horse elsewhere in the ring. A is able to accept money for the horse at prices less than 33-1, comfortable in the knowledge that he makes a profit whatever the result. The effect of C's hedging activity is to shorten the horse from 33-1 to 16-1 quite quickly. The public spots this apparent 'gamble' and join in, providing A with further opportunities to take money at a price much less than 33-1. The horse was returned at 12-1 and finished tailed off. Once again the actions of just two people (A and B) have been sufficient to produce a sharp reduction in the price of an outsider.

Another apparent source of inspiration for those who like to follow the money is provided by the provision of information on Text services, concerning early-price support for races later in the day. Once again the theme is that such support is 'inspired' by inside knowledge. Wrong again! In the eighteen months I have now been working as an advisor, providing a daily telephone message to clients, I have had three or four spells of considerable success. The punters become flush with funds, the number of customers increases, and bookmakers soon take cover if they find that caller after caller wants to back the same horse, especially if their price is out of line with the opposition. Once again, it is far less likely that inside money will cause this effect. The owner may ring and back his horse, but even if he tells all his friends, it still won't equal the money that will follow from a well-supported advisory service.

I could quote any number of examples from my own experience, with prices cut by a point or two within fifteen minutes of my message going online. And I should add that I certainly don't see this as a reason to shout and complain. Nobody expects a racecourse bookmaker to lay a price beyond a certain level of liability and I can't see why the Big Three should be required to operate in a way that defies commercial sense. There have been occasions when friends have been able to tell me what I have recommended on a particular day without needing to listen to the telephone message – the market has provided the only message they needed. And if you doubt the scale of the impact, remember the massive cut in the ante-post price of The Grey Monk, when that horse was recommended by a rival service for the 1998 Cheltenham Gold Cup – down from 20-1 to around 7-1 in a single day.

Much of this faith in the power of 'they' is fuelled by the belief that inside information is the only possible way to make betting profitable. Your average Joe Punter needs to believe that the game is manipulated by trainers, jockeys and owners for their own ends. It relieves him of the responsibility of explaining his persistent betting losses – if the game is bent, then of course he's going to lose. I personally take the view that racing is generally straight, and that what chicanery does go on is at the bottom end of the game in sellers and maidens. If, like me, you concentrate your efforts on exposed horses and better class races, you won't find much villainy. Having said that, I can quote occasions when I did have knowledge about the likely outcome of a race, that wouldn't have been available to the general public.

The first goes way back to my days as an owner in the early eighties. I was living and working in Kuwait City in 1979/80, and the owner of 83 per cent of a gelding called Comrie, trained by David Elsworth. I had been present with the trainer at the Newmarket Sales in October 1979, when the horse was purchased for 1,900 guineas. The price seemed suspiciously cheap for a big, strong looking colt who had won a ten-furlong maiden at Windsor during the latest season. When we went to his box after settling the bill, we found the reason. Six sedate circuits of the sales ring had reduced Comrie to the breathless state more commonly associated with smoking sixty Gauloise per day. As a lifelong asthmatic, I could sympathise with the horse, but then again I wasn't planning to contest a series of two-mile hurdle races that winter. Within two months, poor old Comrie had suffered the double indignity of tubing at one end and gelding at the other.

He showed signs of ability over hurdles during a first season in novice company, with a seventh in a big field at Cheltenham in January being his best effort. The following autumn, he was given a quiet run at Newton Abbot in September, and then entered for a selling hurdle at Exeter. The morning of the race, I received a Telex from the trainer at my office in Kuwait, with the simple message:

```
COMRIE RUNS TOMORROW • DEVON • SHOULD WIN
• CONFIRM BY TELEPHONE MESSAGE RECEIVED •
```

That was easier said than done, the phone service in Kuwait being about as reliable as the British railway system after heavy snow. But I did make sure that I got through to my father and my flatmate back in London, with instructions to back the horse with the funds I had left for the purpose. The message from David Elsworth was spot on, and Comrie reportedly won very easily by five lengths after leading at the last flight. With the owner 3,000 miles away, and the trainer at Ascot watching stable star Heighlin, there was no support for Comrie at the track, and he drifted from 5-2 out to a very pleasing 4-1. He was my first ever winner, and the £400 I'd had on at SP was much more important than the prizemoney of £374. My subsequent experiences as an owner were never so predictable, nor so profitable, but I had seen that a trainer could find the right race on the right day. But as the betting shows, that information never went beyond a couple of close friends. That's always the case with the best information.

I had an experience of a different sort of 'inside information' as a result of the next horse I had with David Elsworth, a four-year-old gelding called Rising Fast. He won a couple of staying handicaps in the middle of 1981 and gave me a great deal of pleasure and taught me valuable lessons about horses. But in May, when he ran in a one-mile six-furlong handicap at Salisbury, he was still a maiden and carrying bottom weight of 7st 7lbs. Having left trainer and jockey talking in the paddock, I was walking across the lawn in front of the Members stand, when I was sent flying by a bloke charging down the steps from the bar. He picked me up, apologised, and explained that he'd met the owner of one of the runners in the bar and had been told his horse was bound to win. As compensation for knocking me over, he explained that I must back Rising Fast. I expressed my surprise at the source of his information, pointing out that I was the owner of Rising Fast, and I wasn't expecting a victory. He thought that very amusing, advised me to "pull the other one" and rushed off to have his bet. Rising Fast dropped from 20-1 to 8-1 in the market, and finished fifth.

My unfortunate punter had encountered one of racing's cast of characters – the con-merchant. Sit at the corner of the members bar, strike up conversation with any apparent novice with too much cash, explain that you can't bet yourself because the bookies all know you, and persuade the mug to put £50 on for you. If the horse wins, the con man is still at the bar, collects his winnings and buys a round of drinks. If the horse loses, he moves on to a different bar and starts again. He knows that the lure of 'inside information' will pull in the mugs as easy as shooting fish in a barrel. (Odd expression that, isn't it? Surely if you shoot at a barrel, you'll make holes in it, causing the water to run away and the fish will die anyway, so why bother shooting them?)

A more recent example of prior knowledge arose from my connection with Mark Holder. He was managing a syndicate of owners who had a three-year-old filly called Siberian Mystic in training with Pat Murphy, Mark's brother-in-law. The filly had had endless problems with minor injuries, health scares and to that point had proved an expensive purchase for her owners. Pat Murphy was convinced on the evidence of her homework that she had a modest level of ability, but she had never been able to produce her form on the racecourse, including when well backed once as a two-year-old. As often happens, her problems had produced a benefit in the form of a lenient handicap mark. The handicapper can only rate a horse on public evidence and on her past performances, Siberian Mystic was hopeless. Soon after I started working with Mark, the filly ran in a one-mile maiden handicap at Bath after a four-month lay-off. She produced a promising run in the straight, until tiring in the final furlong, and was also affected by losing a shoe during the race. As she was now fit and sound for the first time in her career, the prospect of a win seemed on the cards.

The race chosen was an apprentice maiden handicap over ten furlongs at Beverley on a Saturday afternoon at the end of August. My involvement was limited to advising on the choice of rider, as the race conditions excluded any apprentice who had ridden more than five winners. I put forward the name of Royston Ffrench, who at that time had only ridden four winners, but had impressed me on two or three occasions. The next problem was getting a run – one of the problems of a very low handicap mark (Siberian Mystic was rated 33) is that the horse is often eliminated from races as horses higher in the handicap take all the available places. This time we were lucky, and she got in as the last runner inside the safety limit of 18. A bonus was an excellent draw, in stall 16, close to the inside rail. I talked tactics with Mark the day before the race, and Ffrench was told to stay on the rail, saving ground and waiting for an opening. If no gap appeared and he lost as a result, there'd be no criticism, but that would be better than coming out wide on the curving 'straight' at Beverley.

With the benefit of hindsight, the choice of Ffrench was inspired – not only did the filly have a bit in hand of the handicapper, the rider was lengths better than any of his rivals. Siberian Mystic never left the rail until the whole field fanned out at the two-furlong pole, leaving a gap as big as the Red Sea, which she accepted readily, running on to win by two lengths. The owners got on at the opening show of 10-1, and so did I, watching from Goodwood. I don't usually become emotional at the end of a race these days, but I can guarantee that everybody in the Goodwood betting shop knew that I was on Siberian Mystic. Inside information? Well yes it was, and the first clue the general betting public had was when the filly shortened from 10-1 to 5-1 in about ninety seconds after the first show. But unfair? No it wasn't. Some shrewd judges unconnected with the horse backed her at fancy prices in the ring at Beverley before the first show, presumably on the strength of the jockey booking. There is almost always a clue if you're prepared to look closely enough, and the presence of a Newmarket-based apprentice (attached to Luca Cumani) at Beverley for one ride on a day when there was a meeting at his home course was enough for some people.

And of course both of my examples, Comrie and Siberian Mystic, were very much operating in the basement. On a day with four or five meetings, it's hard to find much sympathy for a punter who bets blindly on an 18-runner apprentice maiden handicap at Beverley. In neither case was there any cheating, beyond the running of the horse in a race it couldn't win as a warm-up for the main event. It was just a case of applying the trainer's knowledge of the ability of the horse to the task for which the trainer is employed in the first place – winning races. If you want to find the trainers with the real ability in hiding the true merit of their charges from the handicapper, you have to look a good deal higher up the scale.

Whatever my view of the merits of 'whispers', 'gossip', gallop reports or any other form of information, it isn't going to disappear. And I've no doubt from my own experience that there are occasions when I've bet on horses who weren't 100 per cent committed to success. Equally there have been other times when I've probably stumbled on something I wasn't supposed to know, and unwittingly found myself part of a gamble. But I think the punter always has to ask himself one question:

- If this information is so good, how come it's available to me?

And remember that the more people who know something, the shorter the price will be by the time you can get a bet on. Let's return to that ante-post gamble on The Grey Monk for the 1998 Cheltenham Gold Cup. The inspiration behind that was a service run by a professional punter, who was interviewed by the *News of the World* in December 1997. Two quotes from this article show how even the shrewdest of punters can be confused by the lure of information:

- "Too much information and disinformation. It can be very misleading and most of it's useless. When did you ever see a rich stable lad for instance?"

- "The information we have received suggests this horse is a world-beater on softish ground. He works with One Man and Addington Boy and is in a different class."

I haven't had a bet in the Gold Cup for several years, as I think it's one of the hardest races to solve and the excessive publicity means that every angle has been considered by the media pundits. I know that I'm just as vulnerable as the next man to the idea of an easy route to winners, and whenever a 'tip' I receive wins, I'm as annoyed as anyone that I haven't had a bet. I just try to remember all the losers I would have backed as well.

Over the past fifteen years I've made my betting pay by ignoring information, other than that I've acquired by my own efforts. I've never used stable contacts, never taken any notice of jockeys or trainers, and I don't listen to racecourse rumours. It's a duller way of working, but it ensures that when I back a loser, I have nobody to blame but myself – 'they' don't enter into the equation.

# Who is the trainer?

In early October, I was analysing the card before racing for a group of people in a corporate box at Warwick. One of the races was a two-year-old maiden auction race, in which the forecast favourite was a filly called Atlanta, trained by John Dunlop. I advised my audience not to back this filly, as she was almost certainly not trained by Mr Dunlop, and would start at a false price as a result. After I had finished my talk, I was challenged by one punter to explain my view about Atlanta. I pointed out that the filly had cost just 1,000 guineas at auction and was housed in a stable containing up to two hundred horses, many of them bred in the purple and owned by members of the Maktoum family. If you had a fleet of two hundred cars, I asked, most of them Rollers, Bentleys, Mercs, etc, how much time would you spend tinkering under the bonnet of the au pair's Ford Fiesta?

Atlanta justified the warning by drifting from an opening 7-4 out to 7-2, before finishing sixth. There is no criticism of John Dunlop implied by my comments, simply a recognition of the reality that no man running a business of that size can possibly give detailed individual attention to every horse nominally under his care. And, of course, I may be wrong about Atlanta, who may be the apple of his eye – but it's much more likely that she is really being trained by one of the several assistants who are essential in a yard with two hundred horses. I have always been sceptical about punting methods that rely on studying trainer's methods, principally because I don't think that those who support such ideas have really thought about what the job of racehorse trainer involves.

Leaving aside those jumping trainers who keep a few horses as an adjunct to farming, the job of a trainer puts him or her at the head of one of the most complex small business operations imaginable. Consider the number of different roles he has to fill:

| | |
|---|---|
| **Managing Director** | Head of the business, sets policy and takes the credit or the flak, depending on results. |
| **Finance Director** | Obtaining start-up capital, financing major purchases, billing customers, talking to banks, paying suppliers. |

| | |
|---|---|
| **Personnel Director** | Employing staff, paying wages, housing staff. |
| **Marketing Manager** | Attracting and keeping owners. |
| **Public Relations Officer** | Dealing with the media. |
| **Compliance Officer** | Ensuring the rules of racing are followed. |
| **Transport Manager** | Arranging movement of horses and staff to and from racecourse and sales. |

And all of those jobs have to be performed before he can even start to worry about the actual training of the horses, let alone the feeding, grooming, security and wellbeing of the company's only assets. And what assets – temperamental, nervous, genetically unsound, thoroughbred horses, prone to multiple ailments and injuries – and still easier to deal with than most of their owners! The only surprise is that anybody in his or her right mind would choose to set up such a business in the first place.

How should punters respond to this analysis? In my view, the first thing to realise is that a trainer is only as good as his staff. As you can see from the list above, no one person could possibly perform all the roles in any stable with more than a few horses. Crucially, the trainer cannot feed, groom and ride every horse himself. He has to rely on the opinion of others, and that means he has to place his trust in their ability. The most modern and well-equipped stable in the country will only produce winners with a settled and confident staff. So probably the most important task in any trainer's business is recruitment – finding the right people and establishing an environment in which staff turnover is kept to a minimum.

During the course of a season, punters will read a good deal of comment about stables in and out of form. There is no doubt that this phenomenon exists, although I have long been uncertain as to why the performance of one horse in a yard should affect others. I have seen it at work personally inside the last stable to train a horse wearing my garish orange and green colours. During the winter of 1990/91, I owned 25 per cent of a chaser called Liam's Pride, who was trained just outside Swindon by Stan Mellor. In the course of that season, Stan sent out over 30 winners, including a success in a desperate novice handicap chase at Leicester for

Liam's Pride. It was typical of the luck that the stable enjoyed all winter that an initial entry of 21 dried up to just five runners at the overnight declaration stage, leaving us to claim one of the weakest races of the season.

The following season, however, saw a complete reversal. Liam's Pride ran steadily worse and worse, ending with a defeat in a selling chase at Fontwell, after which he was sold and ended up as a point-to-point horse in Wales. Other horses in the yard also seemed to be running way below their previous form, but there was no obvious physical or medical explanation for this trend. Looking back on those two contrasting seasons, I now feel that the key factor was the form of the star horse in the stable, Kings Curate.

Prior to the 1990/91 season, everybody in the stable knew that he was a potential champion and his presence lifted spirits and raised hopes. He won handicap hurdles at Cheltenham on New Year's Eve and at Ascot in January, and speculation began about him as a possible Cheltenham Festival winner. It was in the weeks between those two successes and Cheltenham, that most of the 30-odd winners were achieved, including a hat-trick one afternoon at Taunton. Even horses that had looked ordinary in the extreme were managing to win, Liam's Pride amongst them.

I eventually concluded that it was the confidence flowing through the people in the yard that was transmitted to the horses and produced this surge of success. I confess to being no horseman myself, but I can see a logic in the idea a horse surrounded by happy, cheerful people – a horse that gets Polos and carrots, rather than abuse and sticks - is more likely to deliver the goods on the racecourse.

Conversely, a miserable atmosphere at home produces miserable results on the racecourse. This theory would certainly explain why these trends seem to be self-generating.

But although I'm quite attached to that theory, it certainly can't explain the sudden changes of fortune, such as that experienced by the stable of Nigel Twiston-Davies over the Christmas period in 1997. Prior to the Boxing Day card at Kempton, the yard had sent out 72 consecutive losers, enough to try the patience of all involved, and a massive deterrent to punters. A stroke of fortune provided a winner in the final race at Kempton, when Haile Derring was left clear by a faller at the last flight. Add two winners at Hereford on the same afternoon and it was as if the barren spell had never happened. On the next day, the stable won the Christmas Hurdle with Kerawi and the Welsh National with Earth Summit. Nobody connected with the yard could offer any clues to explain the change of fortune and, frankly, neither can I.

All the punter can do is remain alert and watch for the change to happen. I was at Chepstow on December 27 and saw another Twiston-Davies runner, Borazon, produce an improved performance to finish second in the Finale Hurdle. If I'd been sharper, that might have persuaded me to support Earth Summit, at a generous looking 25-1. But I was conditioned in advance by the long losing run and had dismissed him without a second thought. As with most aspects of betting, flexibility is crucial when you evaluate horses on the basis of stable form.

Having stressed the importance of a settled staff, it's worth noting that the loss of one or more key individuals can have an impact on results. The punter will still see the same name on the racecard, but things can change behind the scenes that cause a loss of form. Nobody is immune to this sort of thing as we can see from the experience of Henry Cecil in the weeks after Julie Cecil left to set up her own yard. Some of the staff moved with her and it probably took a few weeks for things to settle down at Warren Place. There were certainly fewer winners than usual during that period – the loss of his wife seemed to cause Cecil more problems than the loss of Sheikh Mohammed's horses.

At a lower level, the effect of such a change can be dramatic. Down in the West Country, the stable of CJ 'Butcher' Hill had a considerable following in the early nineties. They could be relied upon to set up two or three gambles each season, and punters enjoyed second guessing the trainer and the bookmakers. But, as his nickname implied, CJ had other things to occupy his time apart from the stable and, unknown to most, a man called Tony Newcombe was doing the real training. When he left to set up his own yard, the flow of winners and gambles for CJ dried up immediately. In the last two seasons (1996-7), the name CJ Hill has been attached to just one winner from a total of 56 runners.

Trainer statistics have a role to play in race analysis, but I would never make the trainer's name, or his form, the prime reason for having a bet. I'd be more inclined to use them as a reason for elimination, concentrating on stables having a poor run, or on trainers with a specific weakness with certain types of horse, or at certain tracks.

To give an example of that reasoning, look at the trainer's records at one of my local tracks, Salisbury.

There are two trainers who I'm always keen to oppose in handicaps there – Toby Balding and Peter Chapple-Hyam. Both have very poor strike-rates in such races at Salisbury, and I suspect the reason is similar, though as usual my theory is purely personal guesswork. For both men, Salisbury is the closest track to their stable. I reckon this prompts them to see it as the ideal place to run horses who they think are unlikely to win, either because they are badly handicapped, or out of form, or whatever. Knowing that the run isn't going to produce a return, they enter the horse locally in order to keep down costs. If a victory is in prospect, they will happily send a horse far and wide, with the hope of recouping their owner's costs. Whatever the real reason, the figures can't be ignored and backing their horses in handicaps at Salisbury would have produced a 100 per cent loss on 29 bets over the last two seasons.

One very important part of the trainer's job that punters can try to anticipate, are the decisions on the placing of the horses. For many horses, that isn't difficult. The very best can only run in the programme of pattern races set by the BHB, and the trainers have few options. The ordinary 70-rated handicapper, or worse, has plenty of opportunities and the trainer should be able to find a race on a suitable track over the correct trip almost every week. But for horses who fall between those two groups, the options are considerable, and making the right choice will affect the prospects of success.

For example, with a horse rated between 90 and 95, the trainer must choose between:

- Carrying a big weight in 0-95 and 0-100 handicaps
- Concentrating on the programme of major handicaps open to all horses
- Looking for a suitable conditions race
- Trying his luck in Listed races, here or overseas
- Selling the horse to America or Asia

Not all of those options are likely to suit the horse, with conditions races generally featuring small fields and a modest pace, while the top handicaps would have big fields and a flat out gallop. Whichever route the trainer chooses, there won't be many races on the programme that match up, so that he might be compelled to run on unsuitable tracks or going. It's no wonder that many horses of this type end up being sold to countries that provide them with more opportunities.

For a successful horse with form on the Flat and over hurdles, the trainer has to make significant decisions about the long-term programme he prefers. Thanks to my peripheral involvement with the stable of Pat Murphy, I followed the career of Shooting Light with interest.

He was bought for £21,000 at the July Sales at Newmarket in 1997, with the specific intention of running in the 1997 Triumph Hurdle. After a couple of modest efforts on the Flat that autumn, he made his hurdle debut at Sandown and delighted all concerned with a win. That was followed by a second, giving weight, to eventual Triumph Hurdle favourite White Sea at Newbury, and then another win at Cheltenham in January.

His trainer had learnt that he ran best when fresh, so he was given a break until the Triumph, and showed the benefit when finishing third after being hampered on the turn away from the stands. At that point, the trainer had a range of choices, which I reckoned included:

- Hurdle races at Aintree and/or Punchestown

- A switch to the Flat and take advantage of his fitness in early-season handicaps such as the Queens Prize at Kempton and the Chester Cup

- A break and return to the Flat in time to run in the Ebor

- A longer break and target the Cesarewitch

- Miss the entire Flat season and target the 1997/8 hurdle season

Even within those five major options, there are different possibilities, such as missing the first half of the NH season and aiming only for the Champion Hurdle. The major concern for connections was the lack of obvious targets for Shooting Light as a five-year-old hurdler. That age group has a poor record in the major races, but his third placing in the Triumph would give him a handicap mark that limited him to taking on the best older handicappers. I think I would have favoured option two, with the prospect of some decent prizemoney as the main incentive. But I'm not a trainer, and the choice eventually made was a variation on the fourth option.

Shooting Light immediately showed that Pat Murphy knows a lot more about his business than I ever will, by winning on his return at Sandown in a one-mile six-furlong handicap. A tentative plan to run at Ascot in the race made famous by Mr Dettori and Fujiyama Crest was dropped, and his next run was over hurdles in the Tote Silver Trophy at Chepstow, where he finished second to Marello. His last run of 1997 was fourth in the Bula Hurdle. In total, five runs during the year produced two wins, and three placings in major hurdle races. A tremendous record, and it's hard to imagine a way the horse could have been better handled. But having taken that option, nobody will ever know if he could have won the Chester Cup, or even the Ebor. Hence the fascination for a punter of trying to second guess the trainer. If you had been responsible for Shooting Light, what path would you have chosen after the Triumph Hurdle?

If you think about horses you are following in this way, coming to the same conclusion as the trainer will reinforce your confidence when it comes to having a bet. The same thinking can also be used in the shorter term. I've already talked about trying to assess where maiden race winners will next appear and what I think they can achieve. But that same process can be applied to any winner. For example, when Merlins Ring won the seven-furlong nursery handicap on the final day of the Goodwood July meeting, I was impressed with the way he'd overcome a poor draw, and with the ease which he'd travelled through the race. I felt he must be better than a handicapper and suggested in my column in *Odds On* magazine that he'd be worth consideration in Listed company, and that a drop back to six furlongs might also suit him. His next run in the seven-furlong Acomb Stakes at York seemed to confirm that he'd be better off at six furlongs. He was only fifth in that Class B conditions event, but as every runner had Group entries, it looked a hot contest.

He next ran in the Sirenia Stakes at Kempton on September 10, a six-furlong Listed race. With my opinion confirmed by trainer Ian Balding's choice of race, I backed him confidently at 7-1 and 13-2. From a good draw in stall eight (stalls far side), he couldn't go the pace and had to be switched wide, finishing well to snatch third on the post.

I bet you were expecting a happy ending, weren't you? I'm sorry to disappoint, but that's the nature of betting – this isn't a Hans Christian Anderson book! The Kempton run suggested that I'd over-rated Merlins Ring, but he eventually justified my initial assessment by going on to win a six-furlong Listed race and a six-and-a-half-furlong Group 3 race on his next two starts. Unfortunately the first was at Maisons-Lafitte and the second at Saint-Cloud, and my local pub hasn't yet installed a French Pari-Mutuel ticket machine.

But to demonstrate the point, I should show how it can work in the punters' favour. During late June and early July, I twice saw a two-year-old called Lord Smith win seven-furlong claiming races on softish ground. He showed determination to win the first under pressure, and then easily won at Warwick eight days later. Martin Pipe had claimed him after the first of those wins, and after backing him at Warwick, I was confident he would be a good bet in a seven-furlong nursery. A number of shrewd trainers use claiming races as a way of getting their horses fairly handicapped, and this looked a good example.

After another eight-day break, Pipe ran Lord Smith in a nursery at Chester, and with the added advantage of the number one draw, he looked a cracking bet. He made all and rewarded a bet of £1,250/500. Had I not been looking out for the horse under just those circumstances, I probably wouldn't have even looked at a seven-furlong nursery at Chester on a day when I was at Salisbury and there were four other meetings staged. But when I saw his name among the declarations with stall one, I knew that it didn't matter what else was running – this was the right horse in the right race. This rather undermines the popular view of a professional punter slaving over a hot formbook, but in this case the work, or at least the thinking, had all been done in advance.

I accept that the trainer should be a factor in deciding whether a horse is worth considering as a possible winner, but I'd never make the name of the trainer the major factor in any bet. A slow horse will remain a slow horse, no matter who trains it, but with proper management it's more likely to be correctly placed in races with other slow horses. And if there is one thing British racing in the nineties isn't short of, it's slow horses.

# Jockeys

The top jockeys get the best rides, and therefore they ride lots of winners. Because they ride winners, the punters follow them and the prices are shorter. Because the prices are shorter, the punters back lots of winners, but still lose money. I think it's called a vicious circle. If Frankie Dettori or Tony McCoy is aboard a horse I plan to back, I certainly accept that as a bonus which marginally improves my chances of collecting, but I also know that it will be reflected in the price. No matter who is the current champion, they invariably show a level-stake loss on all their mounts.

The only way that a sharp punter can obtain an edge from the jockey booking, is to look out for the next champion while he is still claiming an allowance. Given his current rate of success, it's hard to remember that McCoy was barely known outside the circle of regular racegoers as recently as 1995. I saw one of his first rides in this country, on a reluctant mare called Anna Valley, at Worcester in September 1994.

She had run twenty times without success, and had made fools of several good riders with her unwilling nature. On this occasion, McCoy got her jumping fluently, making ground at every flight, and showing superb balance in the saddle. In front turning for home, I expected that she would stop, just as she had in every previous race, but he kept her going to the line and simply wouldn't let her be beaten. For the next two weeks, I told anyone who cared to listen that I'd seen a star, and checked his rides every day looking for betting opportunities. It was about two months before the press started to realise what was happening, and then the value disappeared.

On the Flat, the most recent example of the same phenomenon was Royston Ffrench. I saw him twice riding winners and showing a fine mixture of aggression, balance and pace judgement. He has no weight problem at present and will make it to the top if he is able to land a job with one of the big stables. From a punters' point of view, the only problem with following these young future stars, is that they tend to come to prominence much more quickly than would have been the case ten or twenty years ago. That is mostly due to the rise of the jockey's agent as a force in British racing. In the past, a rider like Tony McCoy would have had to work hard to establish himself with a range of trainers, and landing a big job might have been due to good fortune – being in the right place at the right time. Nowadays, he has an agent from day one, and that ensures him plenty of opportunities to show his talent. He still has to be good to reach the top, but the agent guarantees that everybody hears about him.

The rise of the agent also means that a favourite punter cliché no longer holds water. The idea of backing a horse because "Dettori has chosen to ride it" is now pure hogwash. Dettori goes where his agent tells him and rides the horses that his agent has booked, and the same applies to all the leading riders. Only when there are two runners for the same trainer, or the retaining owner, might the rider's choice be significant, and even then they get it wrong more often than not!

Checking back through my 1997 records, I can't find a single bet that was made primarily, or even partly, on the grounds of the jockey booking, with one exception. That was Welton Arsenal, at Newmarket in May, ridden by Royston Ffrench. I remember thinking that this horse, with a history of ducking the issue after coming through on the bridle, might benefit from the forceful style that I associate with Ffrench. But he did also look extremely well handicapped in one of the weakest races he'd contested for a long time. It worked out well, with the horse running much more prominently than usual and pushed clear with a furlong to run, whereas previous riders seemed intent on putting his head in front right on the line.

I can't of course leave the topic of betting on jockeys rather than horses without reference to Saturday 28 September, 1996. On a day to remember for blind followers of Dettori, every mug punter's dream came true. There were several amazing stories that reached the papers from the big winners, but I can pass on one that didn't make headlines. One of my sisters works as a part-time cashier in her local betting shop, and the regular customers include a West

Indian lady of uncertain age and weight. Her usual penny stakes that day produced a return running to several hundred pounds, and the staff were concerned for her safety with such a large sum in cash. She reassured them – "You no worry bout me, I stuff it down my knickers. Ain't nobody gonna fight to get it off me then".

She's still placing the same bet, but I think the Lottery is more likely to produce a pay-off before we see a repeat of that performance.

# The media

I had some fairly harsh things to say about the standard of racing journalism in my first book, and little has changed in the subsequent years to alter my view. The press coverage of racing suffers from a major contradiction at its heart, with journalists unable to decide whether they are primarily sports writers or tipsters. There are a few who concentrate on the second function, but even within their ranks, little has been done to educate the punter about the game. One honourable exception was the work of Henry Rix for the *Racing Post*. During 1997, he not only generated remarkable profits from his tips, but also wrote in plain terms about the analysis of races that led to his recommendations. His columns were not only profitable, they were also educational.

His performance was all the more remarkable when you realise that it was achieved without regular visits to the racecourse, and to an early evening deadline the day before the races in question. Having undertaken to deliver a service at a fixed time in the morning, several hours before the first race, I know from personal experience that things can change before racing that alter my betting plans. Sadly, Rix stands almost alone in the category of writer who provides betting advice without offering opinion on the politics or personalities of the sport. Far too much of the tipping provided by the national and trade press falls into two equally useless categories:

- The racecourse reporter who offers tips based on gossip, speculation, and no more than a passing acquaintance with the formbook or the importance of price.

- The office-bound pundit, still tied to the belief that racing can be beaten by detailed study of form, using the tired old formulae of pounds and lengths as justification for a selection.

Several of the first group can write quite lyrically about racing as a sport, producing material to match anything printed elsewhere about cricket, golf, etc. But the nature of the game leaves them feeling compelled to offer their opinion about the outcome of future events, despite often acknowledging in their own writing that their past record is hopeless. This desire to look forward actually spoils some of the best writing in my view, because it treats even major races as mere trials for later events. This attitude is prevalent on television as well as in the press, and must irritate sponsors intensely.

Imagine that you have supported the Group 2 Dante Stakes at York in May, the most valuable ten-furlong race for three-year-olds in the entire season. As the winner goes clear inside the final furlong, the commentator is telling listeners that this is a great trial for the Derby. All of the post-race TV coverage revolves around the Derby prospects of the runners in today's race. The ante-post betting changes for the Derby are discussed, and bookmaker representatives are interviewed. The press will take the same line the next morning, and the Dante Stakes is never discussed as a significant event in its own right, merely as a rehearsal for the later race.

This happens throughout the season, particularly in NH racing, where the endless hype about the Cheltenham Festival races gives the impression that nothing run from November to March really matters at all.

The second group are stuck in a time-warp, seemingly having read nothing of the new literature on betting, having carried out no research of their own, and having no new ideas to offer. The sheer volume of racing hasn't helped, and there aren't enough hours in the day for some tipsters to do more than gloss over many races at the minor meetings. Readers are offered a recommendation based on five or ten minute's analysis, with no guidance on price or level of confidence. But the old order persists, and editors seem to expect a tip for every race.

Let's look at an example of what happens as a result of this policy. I attended a Saturday evening meeting at Wolverhampton, which would obviously have been bottom of the priority list for any newspaper tipster. The second race was a five-furlong claiming event, with nine runners. The tipster box in the *Racing Post* showed that 14 of 15 'experts' recommended Chemcast to win this race,

8888

and as a result, he opened at 5-4 favourite on the course.

I suspect that most, if not all, of those 14 pundits had based their decision on a swift perusal of the comparison between the official BHB handicap marks of the runners and the weights they were carrying in this claimer. That method gave Chemcast 13lbs in hand of his nearest rival, so surely their confidence was justified? Well, not in my view, and in fact I was adamant that Chemcast would be beaten, for three reasons:

- He had run seven times previously at Wolverhampton without winning, always racing prominently and then fading in the final furlong. In American parlance, Chemcast is a 'one-dimensional speedball'. He runs flat out from the stalls, but is unable to resist challengers if they appear. His only two AW wins were at Lingfield when making all the running from stall one – actually he was caught the second time but the 'winner' was disqualified for causing interference at the start.

- His handicap mark was indeed higher than that of his rivals, but he hadn't shown an ability to win or even run close off that mark in recent races. His best run was his latest, when he was beaten by five and a half lengths over five furlongs. By comparison, his rivals included two that had already won five furlong handicaps at Wolverhampton during the winter season.

- My speed figures told me that Chemcast had never run a time any faster than either Aljaz or Village Native had produced in recent races over course and distance. Chemcast was almost certain to be taken on for the lead by Aljaz, and Village Native would challenge late if he could outrun that one.

So here was a horse with a dismal course record, modest recent form, ordinary speed figures, in a race that wouldn't be run to suit him, but still tipped by almost every national and trade paper pundit. The sizeable family crowd at Wolverhampton were happy to go along with the experts, buoyed up by a winning favourite in the first race, and Chemcast traded at 5-4 throughout the betting, though returned at 11-8 favourite. Aljaz disputed the early lead, saw off

Chemcast on the home turn, and ran on to win comfortably at 5-1. Village Native ran on to take third at 13-2, with Chemcast fading into fifth, beaten more than six lengths.

As John McCririck has often pointed out – "when all the hacks agree on something, punters should beware". He's absolutely right, and as punters we can take advantage of a market that is skewed by press opinion, especially at the minor meetings.

# The mug punter

You are given the names of three horses running the next day, all of which your informant says have an equal chance of success. The first two are beaten at 6-4, the third one wins at 4-1. If you lose money on the afternoon, you are a mug. The mug punter will lump on the first two horses and, when they fail, he either loses confidence and fails to back the third, or he blows all his money on the losers and can't raise a stake. The smart punter will either not back the first two horses at all, or he will back all three to level stakes, producing a 66 per cent profit on the afternoon. If you don't recognise yourself in this story, you are presumably the offspring of Spock or Commander Data. Every punter is a mug when he first makes a bet, but the smart ones learn lessons from mistakes like this and turn things around.

The other sort of mug is the punter who plays erratically. Imagine it's Murphys Gold Cup day at Cheltenham, and our mug is one of the many thousands who are having an annual day out with friends. For the sake of this story, we'll call him Fred, and his home is in West London. On Saturday morning at 8.30 a.m., Fred boards the coach outside the working men's club on the corner, armed with the racing page torn from his wife's copy of *The Sun*. During the journey, Fred consumes eight tins of pasteurised gnat's piss masquerading as Australian premium lager, followed by four pints of ice cold Murphys in the racecourse bar. On the coach, he tells all his mates that he's brought £60 as betting money, and he's going to have £10 on each race. He says he'll be really happy if he breaks even, as it's a good day out.

On arrival at Cheltenham, he invests half his betting stake in a Lucky 15 in the racecourse betting shop, combining a 33-1 outsider in the big race, Trap 6 in the next two races from Monmore, and Brentford to win away from home in the first round of the FA Cup. Somebody tells him that Monmore is in Wolverhampton, but he dismisses that as a stupid idea, because they wouldn't call it Monmore Green in that case.

He puts his remaining £30 on the favourite in the opening race, but it falls at the last when about to take the lead. Fred spends the rest of the afternoon in the bar, telling his hard luck story to anybody who wants to listen, and to quite a few that don't. Every second sentence begins with the words "If only ....". Back on the coach at 4.30, Fred tells everyone that he's broken even, and amazingly enough so have 90 per cent of his mates. The other ten per cent have won on the day. This makes it all the more mysterious that on their return to the club, nobody can afford a round, and the steward has his quietest Saturday night of the year. Fred has just enough small change in his pocket to call in at the garage on his way home for a Lottery ticket.

That might sound extreme, but there are ten thousand like Fred at Cheltenham on that day every year, and the same at Royal Ascot, the Grand National, etc. They might strike lucky occasionally, but they are doomed to lose overall, because they don't know what they are doing. They have no more chance of profit than a man sitting down in a poker club, believing a straight is a man who prefers women and a full house is cinema with no spare seats. But Fred doesn't just go racing once a year, he also visits his local betting shop.

On one of my few trips to the local Ladbrokes last year, I went to watch the races from Cheltenham that weren't shown on C4 or the Racing Channel. Waiting for the Kim Muir to start, I watched as a man in painter's overalls came in, looked at the paper on the wall for ten seconds, wrote '£5 Win Fav Fontwell' on a slip and placed his bet. He returned to sit between me and a friend, turned to the other man and the dialogue went as follows:

Painter - *"Which one's the favourite?"*
Punter - *"Vicosa."*
Painter - *"Which one is that?"*
Punter - *"The grey."*
Painter - *"The one out the back?"*
Punter - *"Yes."*
Painter - *"What the hell's he doing so far back?"*

I could have intervened with a lengthy character assassination of

Vicosa, but I didn't feel it would help. When he fell at the fence in front of the stands, with a circuit to run, I was sure that my silence had been sensible. The painter offered us a detailed dissertation on the jockey's abilities and parentage, although his case was somewhat undermined by having to return to the paper on the wall to find out his name.

Okay, it's easy to patronise the Freds and the painters that make up the mass of punters in this country, especially as I can be confident that neither type will be reading this book. It's one of the odd things about gambling that it's one of the only two things most men think they can do without needing to take lessons. (If you're still thinking that one through, you're presumably a flush rather than a straight.) But the day I first picked up my pencil in Bruce's betting shop in the north London suburb that I called home, I started from the same position of total ignorance as Fred. I certainly wasn't born to be a professional punter, and I suspect my parents would have demanded a recount if it had been suggested that I would end up plying this trade.

The transition from mug to professional was a lengthy process, and I never assume that it's complete as yet. There is always something new to learn, and that is one of the fascinations of the game.

To revert to the parallel I used in the introduction, the attitude of Nick Faldo is one I admire and seek to emulate (although I can't run to a 23-year-old blonde and a house in Florida!). Despite reaching the top of his profession, he has never relaxed his work-rate and his quest for perfection. I don't make any claim to be his punting equivalent, but every mug could learn from him. The reason that they don't, is because they expect to lose and don't believe it's possible to win. That is the mug's justification for continuing to treat betting in an erratic and casual fashion.

The fact that you are reading this indicates that you've already decided to make the effort to turn your betting to profit. The first thing you must realise is that even if you reach your objective, society isn't going to regard your achievement as praiseworthy.

Spend your leisure hours tuned to the Open University and you'll be rewarded with a degree and the approval of your peers. Put the same effort into study of the Racing Channel, and you'll be considered beyond redemption. Search the New Year Honours list and you won't find any awards for 'services to punting'. The personal satisfaction of beating the most challenging intellectual pastime available to man is still a goal worth pursuing. But it will be a private pleasure, because your claim to beat the bookies will either be dismissed as lies, or ignored as worthless.

# The sucker horse

One of the most alarming behaviour patterns of the average punter is their enduring fascination with a group of horses who are regularly well supported and just as regularly fail to deliver. The backing of these professional losers takes on a desperate air that resembles the fanaticism of the dedicated follower of the bottom team in the Football League. Confronted with the reality of the formbook, these supporters know that they are going to lose again, but have to bet 'just in case' today is the day.

The type of horse who attracts this following is usually one who always threatens to deliver the goods – next time. A perfect example of this failure to make the connection between the brain and the wallet is the eight-year-old sprint handicapper Bayin.

During the 1997 Flat season, Bayin ran 17 times and recorded just one victory. That came in a Limited Stakes over five furlongs 167yards at Bath in June, when his normal late flourish took him past a bunch who managed to register just one victory between them in the remainder of the season. His other 16 starts all came in sprint handicaps, and he lost every single one. Despite this dismal record, he started at odds of less than 10-1 in 12 of those 16 races. So easily were punters fooled by his regular tactic of producing a strong finish, they failed to notice that it always started from too far behind to succeed!

Defying logic, he was actually well supported in three of his last four runs in 1997. He was backed from 8-1 into 11-2 in a field of eighteen at Yarmouth on September 18, where he finished sixth. Another sixth place followed, in a field of 15 at Kempton, where as usual the formbook reported he was "slowly away and never nearer, keeping on well from the rear". That bluffed persistent punters into another try at Leicester on October 5, where a Sunday crowd celebrated three earlier winning favourites by backing Bayin from 6-1 in to 7-2 jolly in a field of 21. He rewarded their faith by finishing tenth – "could only run on into midfield having been slightly hampered at the start and (as usual) in rear".

Undeterred by this dismal showing, Leicester regulars went in again on October 27, knocking Bayin down from 8-1 to 5-1 favourite in a field of twenty-two. Overwhelmed by this continuing show of affection, Bayin did what comes naturally, and let them down by finishing a distant 18th, this time acquiring the dismissive comment "never in it".

To the obvious relief of his growing fan club, that was his last run of the season. I hope by now that the vast majority of readers have adopted a knowing smile, happy in the knowledge that they knew all about Bayin and were never sucked in to backing him. Worst of all would be the smart Alec who backed him at Bath, but not in any of his 16 defeats – we'd all like to know his secret, wouldn't we? But behind that smile, I'm prepared to bet that even if you didn't fall for Bayin, there would be two or three just like him hidden in your accounts for the year.

It might not have been a persistent handicapper, but a one-paced top class horse that invariably finished in the frame, whether he ran in a Classic trial or a gaff track maiden. Or it could have been a chaser with a nasty habit of clouting a fence just as he looked on the verge of success. You'd be amazed how many punters think that it's a good idea to back a horse who fell last time out, on the grounds that he might have won if he'd stood up! Whatever the category, it's one of the key moments in a punting life when you realise that following winners is a much smarter policy than chasing losers again and again.

I certainly fell for one during 1997 - a good class staying three-year-old called Winter Garden. I saw him throw away a clear cut opportunity in a 12-furlong handicap at Newbury, and blamed the jockey for being over-confident.

I saw him fail to see out a race at Royal Ascot, where he led two furlongs out but could only finish fourth. That time I blamed the jockey for taking a wide course on the home turn and then hitting the front too soon.

When he ran in a 15-furlong Listed event at the Newmarket July meeting, I lumped on at 100-30. This time he cruised up to join the leaders at the foot of the hill, but as soon as he was asked to go on and win his race, he put his head up, hung away from the whip, and generally looked about as trustworthy as Bill Clinton! I won't fall for him again, and if he wins a race, I'll just look on and shrug my shoulders.

It's worth remembering that horses are essentially herd animals. In the wild, they establish a pecking order, and the majority become followers. Those characteristics can still be observed in the thoroughbred racehorse, with the individuals at the front of the herd usually being identified as having the will to win. But they probably only represent about five or ten per cent of the total thoroughbred population. The remainder are quite happy to finish in the ruck, where they feel safe – just like humans really. If a horse is still a maiden after half a dozen races, then think of him as the horse that, in the wild, at the first sign of a predator, is volunteering to stay behind and look after the foals. Put him in a photo-finish and he, quite literally, won't 'stick his neck out'!

Of course, the racing programme regularly brings together entire fields of followers. They're called maiden handicaps, or sellers, or 0-60 handicaps, or something similar. Something has to win those races, but very few horses make a habit of winning at that level. I used this explanation when talking to a group of racing beginners in a corporate box at Warwick, to justify making no selection in the opening race, an 18-runner maiden handicap. For those who couldn't resist a bet, I offered the name of an outsider with less poor form than most in the race.

The host had arranged a raffle and, before leaving the box, I was asked to draw out the winning tickets. I didn't know, but the prizes were £10 Tote betting vouchers, and two of them were won by ladies with zero gambling experience. They walked to the nearest Tote booth and put the entire £10 on my first race 'tip', win only. To my utter amazement, the horse won and returned 33-1 at SP, and paid £35 on the Tote. The ladies collected £350 in cash, and one later proposed to me, on the grounds that her husband had never in their entire married life given her so much money at one time. She was quite happy to divorce him, if I was available – in the spirit of the *News of the World*, I made my excuses and left.

Needless to say, I didn't have a penny on the horse, although I don't think that claim was believed by too many of the people in the box.

It's another argument in favour of concentrating your betting at the better class end of the game, and only supporting proven winners when venturing to the lower levels. Try going through your records and checking the performance of bets on horses who had a win within their last three runs, against the rest. I think you will be convinced.

# PART 6

## ODDS AND EVENS

## The price is right

The previous sections of this book have all been about analysing races and attempting to identify winners. If that was all that was necessary to be a profitable punter, there would a notable shortage of bookmakers. Anyone, on his or her day, can find winners. The successful punter is the one who makes the right bets. One of the first clichés ever quoted to me about betting was:

> "It isn't how many winners you back that counts,
> it's how many losers."

That over-simplifies the issue, but it isn't bad as a starting point. When you examine your records at the end of the year, there are sure to be bets in there that look appalling and embarrassing with the advantage of hindsight – the "why the hell did I back that" wagers that reduce profits, or worse still, increase losses. Opening my 1997 account book, I found encouragingly few bets that I wouldn't have been willing to detail in the previous chapters, but there are still some horrors that slipped through my fingers when my brain was asleep. Consider this dire indictment of a bored punter looking for some action:

**21/08 Salis 1m 6f Hcp**    **COURBARIL**    **Unpl SP 11-2**
**£2200/400**

This was a run-of-the-mill 0-70 grade race, with 15 runners, on fast ground. Courbaril was wearing a visor for the first time – warning sign number one. He was a beaten favourite over course and distance last time when wearing blinkers – warning sign number two. He was trained by Martin Pipe, whose record on the Flat is dismal by comparison with his NH form – warning sign number three. This was a race in which I couldn't possibly claim an edge, since it was a flag start, and the horse had no speed figure or pace advantage – warning sign number four. But inside every serious punter there's a mug fighting to get a bet on, and for whatever reason, I released him for this race.

So before you start worrying about the nineties' buzzword 'value', your first step toward profits should be to eliminate the bets that look bad in the records. It's impossible to reduce this category to zero, but that should be the target. Now I've broached the issue of value, I'm only going to repeat a couple of points I made in *Against The Crowd*, which if I were given to grandiose language, I might describe as universal truths:

- Value is a matter of personal judgement, so there is no such thing as a value bet that will appeal equally to every punter.

- The only valid measure of your ability to achieve value is the figure in your accounts at the end of the year.

The final race of the day at Ascot, on which Frankie Dettori rode all seven winners, provides an object lesson on the need to look at value as a long-term issue. That final winner, Fujiyama Crest had been offered at 10-1 generally in the early-price exchanges. By the time the Ascot bookmakers came to price up, they knew that most of the punters and all of the office reps would want to back the horse. The price soon settled at around 2-1 to 9-4. Several of the larger bookmakers in the ring took the view that laying 9-4 about a genuine 10-1 shot was a guarantee of profit and continued to accept bets from all and sundry without bothering to take the usual measures to balance their books. Their argument was that any 'real bookmaker' would cheerfully go on laying that price, whatever their liabilities. This overlooked two things.

Firstly, they ignored the fact that even genuine 10-1 shots do win about one time in every 15 tries. Laying 9-4 about a 10-1 shot would be a certain route to riches over one hundred races, but if this was that 15th race, then they were going to be hurt. Secondly, they ignored the fact that, under the circumstances, Fujiyama Crest was no longer a 10-1 shot, regardless of morning prices. Not only was Dettori riding on the crest of a wave of confidence, it was also quite likely that many of the other riders in that final race would be just as keen as the punters to see Dettori win. I'm sure that quite a few felt that to be the jockey who prevented such a famous result would ensure them of unwanted notoriety for years to come.

As everybody knows, those bookies came unstuck, and with the exception of Pat Eddery on the runner-up, few of the other riders seemed to make it hard for Dettori, who was gifted a five-length lead in the back straight at a modest pace. I neither blame nor criticise those jockeys, and the result has proved a huge bonus for racing. But there were two or three bookmakers who learnt the hard way that value couldn't be measured in just one race.

One of the statements I made in *Against The Crowd,* that has produced the most comment from punters I've met on the racecourse, was "don't bet at under 2-1". I don't follow that as a golden rule, but it's true that I very rarely back a horse at less than 2-1. Of the 350 bets I made in 1997, only 12 were under 2-1 and three of those were away bets placed at SP on-course after the Levy Board had ruled that Tote Credit could no longer lay board prices. Those three were all over 2-1 when I placed the bet, and I then sat and suffered as the price shortened. I think very hard before making a bet at such a short price, and the criterion is that I'll only take 7-4 if I rate the horse an even-money chance, or less if I rate it an odds-on chance. Since seven of those 12 bets were winners, I seem to be getting it about right.

I expounded a theory previously to explain why I dislike betting at short prices, but there are simple practical reasons as well. In *Against The Crowd,* I argued that an even-money favourite is prone to all the ills of the thoroughbred, and is just as likely to fail to show his form for physical reasons, as is a 33-1 outsider. But I also see little point in backing an even-money shot because in the long-term, it just isn't going to make any difference. I see punters at the racecourse shouting home an even-money favourite, leaping up and down in excitement, bragging to their mates about their cleverness, and dragging everyone off to the bar. And I wonder if they can actually do the simple arithmetic that should tell them all they have achieved is a profit that will pay for their next losing bet.

If backing such winners was a quick route to fame and fortune, either there would either be no bookmakers, or the winners would be offered at 4-5, not even-money.

If you back one hundred even-money favourites, and find 51 winners, you have made two per cent profit on your turnover, or a loss if you're betting off-course and paying tax. It requires a phenomenal strike-rate to make real money backing short priced horses, and even then a worthwhile profit is only possible if you bet on-course. Not only does that eliminate the tax problem, it offers the chance of finding 11-10 or better if the punter is sharp. That might sound a very small difference in price, but it provides a crucial boost to the profit margin. Take those same one hundred bets, and if you can get 11-10 about all the winners, you're making five per cent instead of two per cent.

Those celebrating even-money punters are happy to back a winner. They certainly wouldn't be interested in the party pooper who points out that they could have got 11-10 if they'd looked around the ring. Even in my work with Mark Holder, I've talked to clients who are convinced they are bound to make a profit, so long as I recommend winners, regardless of their price. It's another one of those old betting clichés that I suspect I first heard when working behind the counter at my local betting shop as a teenage boardboy:

*"It's better to back an odds-on winner than a 10-1 loser."*

I doubt I have to persuade any reader of the fallacy contained in that statement. But it's worth giving an example that highlights just how narrow the margin is when deciding to bet at a particular price. Consider a sequence of one hundred bets, each of one hundred pounds, of which 20 are winners:

- If you bet them at 7-2, you back 20 winners and lose £1,000.
- If you bet them at 4-1, you break even.
- If you bet them at 9-2, you win £1,000.

If you're honest, I'll wager you've taken that 4-1 or 7-2 when you really wanted 9-2, because you didn't want to miss a winner. To quote from one of my American textbooks: "punters should learn to love bets, not horses". In other words, if the price is too short, stand aside and watch. You have to grin and bear it if the horse wins, but don't fall into the trap of thinking about how much you might have won. Always remember that we're playing a game that is never ending, and there'll be another chance in thirty minutes.

There is no secret formula I can give you to help you decide what is the right price for any horse. As I've already stated, the value in any bet is a matter of personal judgement. In conversation with other professional punters, they often use phrases such as "I couldn't have that on my mind at the price". More often than not, I just nod sagely and don't tell them if I backed the horse and thought it excellent value. There isn't much mileage in arguing value with the other professional punters, because their views are fixed and not amenable to discussion. If you don't think your own opinion is best, you aren't going to make it as a professional!

One way to establish whether you are finding sufficient value to make your betting pay is to analyse your bets and establish your strike-rate at different prices. This chart shows my own percentages for all bets during 1997. The columns are:

A  the percentage strike-rate needed to break even
B  the actual strike-rate of all runners returned at the price (i.e. SP) on the Flat in 1996/7
C  the winner-to-bet ratio of my own bets
D  the percentage strike-rate of my bets

| Price | A | B | C | D |
|---|---|---|---|---|
| 7-4 | 37% | 34% | 5–9 | 55% |
| 2-1 | 33% | 30% | 10–15 | 66% |
| 9-4 & 5-2 | 30% | 29% | 11–29 | 38% |
| 11-4 & 3-1 | 26% | 24% | 13–38 | 34% |
| 10-3 & 7-2 | 23% | 20% | 16–43 | 37% |
| 4-1 | 20% | 18% | 9–28 | 32% |
| 9-2 | 18% | 16% | 1–24 | 4% |
| 5-1 | 16% | 14% | 2–16 | 12% |
| 11-2 > 13-2 | 14% | 12% | 9–36 | 25% |
| 7-1 > 9-1 | 12% | 9% | 3–39 | 8% |

It's instructive to note how the actual strike-rate of all runners returned at a specific price always falls just below the level needed to break even, confirming the efficiency of the market. It also highlights the fact that the Starting Price is the best indicator of the true chance of a horse winning a race. It's a crude system based on a small percentage of the total amount bet, but it works.

As for my own figures, the strike-rates for 7-4 and 2-1 are flattering, but definitely a statistical blip. The same can be said for the miserable performance at 9-2 and 5-1, as I know from previous years that that price range has been very successful. These quirks confirm that drawing conclusions from a sample of just 350 bets is risky, and that's why I haven't given the figures for those over 9-1. A more realistic picture would be obtained from looking at five years' worth of results, a sample of about 2,000 bets. Given the excellent strike-rate at all prices from 7-2 downwards, readers may wonder why I bother betting any horse at longer odds. If I can manage better than 50 per cent winners at 2-1 and 7-4, why not back lots more horses at those sort of prices. The answer is, of course, that more bets means reducing the selectivity, which would automatically reduce the strike-rate. Because I only bet at short prices when I believe I have a substantial edge, that means that such bets are few and far between.

I also have to admit that I find it much harder to assess value prices at the low end of the market. As we saw earlier, it can make a substantial difference to profit margins, backing winners at 11-10 rather than even-money. But I have never been able to find any workable method of deciding that a horse is worth a bet at 11-10, but not any shorter than that. This probably stems from the fact that I'm always looking for 11-10 shots that I can bet against, so my view of short-priced favourites is generally negative. Betting at that sort of price presumably suits the type of punter who likes to have the reassurance of regular winners, whereas I have always preferred a more aggressive approach. The figures also show that there are not as many runners to choose from at the short prices, which must make selectivity more difficult. For example, during that two-year period on the Flat, only about 600 horses started at prices from Evens to 5-4 inclusive, whereas 1,500 went at off at exactly 7-2. In my view it must be easier to find one hundred value bets from a choice of 1,500 than from 600.

Balanced against that view is the startling fact that betting some short-priced horses blindly during that two-year period would have produced a profit. These are the returns for runners starting at less than 7-4:

| Price | Winners - Runners | % Profit/Loss |
|-------|-------------------|---------------|
| Evens | 87 - 176 | - 1% |
| 11-10 | 71 - 157 | - 5% |
| 6-5 | 38 - 79 | + 6% |
| 5-4 | 96 - 194 | + 11% |
| 11-8 | 91 - 208 | + 4% |
| 6-4 | 100 - 296 | - 16% |
| 13-8 | 65 - 228 | - 25% |

I confess to being both surprised and somewhat bemused by the discovery that backing every 5-4 shot over a two-year period would have produced a substantial profit to level-stakes. It may reflect the competitive nature of the current betting market, with the heavy losses at 6-4 and 13-8 balancing the books for the racecourse layers. Certainly there are bookmakers on the rails who operate more like punters, and are content to lay short-priced favourites without balancing their books, and this may be the reason. After all, most punters lose, and one presumes that any bookmaker regularly laying 11-8 about horses returned at 5-4 is now down to his last Mercedes! Whatever the cause, I doubt that operating a system based on these figures would produce anything other than a loss in future years.

Continuing this theme, and looking at the same two-year period, the results for odds-on favourites are also instructive:

| Price | Winners - Runners | % Profit/Loss |
|-------|-------------------|---------------|
| 4-5 | 51 - 122 | - 25% |
| 4-6 | 41 - 81 | - 16% |
| 4-7 | 25 - 62 | - 37% |
| 1-2 | 44 - 63 | + 5% |
| 2-5 | 25 - 28 | + 25% |
| 1-3 | 22 - 33 | - 5% |
| Less than 1-3 | 66 - 77 | + 3% |

That would certainly suggest that any favourite at a price between Evens and 1-2 is worth opposing, because you're certainly going to go broke very quickly by backing them. The figures for the very short-priced 'good things' seem to support the method adopted by two or three professionals, of concentrating on these horses and seeking a very high strike-rate. Mind you, I also checked on losing runs, and there was one occurrence of three consecutive losers at 1-3. That might shake the confidence of even the most successful punter!

I've actually adopted the policy of betting against odds-on favourites for many years, and it has provided me with some decent winners. If you look at the figures above, which show only 25 winners from 62 runners at 4-7, that means there were 37 races in which the winner must have been odds against. If you could identify even half of those beaten 4-7 shots in advance, you would have found some great betting opportunities.

Many punters regard a race with an odds-on favourite as a waste of time – the favourite is sure to win, but isn't worth backing. As a result they don't spend any time analysing these races, but move straight on to the bookmaker sponsored handicap of the day, with 16 runners and betting at 5-1 the field. I never pass up a chance to oppose a horse at odds-on, and regard such races as well worth the time and effort spent on them. The approach is relatively simple. I look at the favourite and try to find weaknesses which mean that he is worth opposing. For a horse to be a genuine odds-on chance, he has to pass all the tests discussed in earlier chapters. If he's running on an unsuitable track, over the wrong trip, or if he has never recorded a fast speed figure, or even if he's just a short price due to hype, then I'm willing to take him on. If the favourite looks a good thing, then I pass on the race, and nothing has been lost. But if I think he can be beaten, I move on to look at the other runners.

What I hope to find is a horse with a clear chance of beating the rest of the field. In effect, I analyse the race treating the favourite as a non-runner. If the remainder produce two or three contenders of equal merit, then the decision has to be to let the race pass. But if I can find a horse who is a strong contender to finish second, even if the favourite wins, then I've got a chance of making an excellent bet. In most cases, I'll be getting better than 2-1 in what I see as a two-horse race between the favourite and my selection. Here are some examples from 1997:

| 10/06 Salis 1m 4f Hcp | SHALATEENO | 1st SP 13-2 £3,000/400 |
|---|---|---|

The favourite in this modest fillies handicap was Timissa. She was trained by Luca Cumani and had won a maiden race over ten furlongs at Lingfield. That race had been run at a modest pace and in a slow overall time, and Timissa had the advantage of a prominent position throughout. Her only other run had been at Doncaster, when she finished second over a mile, again in a relatively slow time. For her third career start, she had been allotted a handicap mark of 80, and was taking on experienced handicappers for the first time. Her starting price of 8-11 had more to do with her trainer's record at Salisbury, and the presence of Frankie Dettori, than any logical assessment of her form.

Shalateeno stood out for me from the remaining six runners, as she seemed almost certain to be allowed a free ride in front. She had shown her best form in the past when front-running, and had also shown a good attitude, running on well even when headed. I had anticipated that she would be around 9-2 second-favourite, and was delighted to obtain 15-2 in the ring. With Timissa out of the race, I reckon Shalateeno would have been sent off at around 9-4 favourite.

Shalateeno made all the running, pressed through the final furlong by the 20-1 outsider Dramatic Moment, but holding on gamely by a head. Timissa was back in fourth, with Timeform stating that "the obvious conclusion is that the handicapper has her measure".

| 18/06 Wolv 5f Seller | RISKY WHISKY | 1st SP 7-2 £3500/1,000 |
|---|---|---|

Two of the best reasons for opposing a horse at odds-on are:

- The first time wearing blinkers or a visor
- The first run on an AW surface

This race provided both those factors on the same horse. The filly Sun In The Morning had won a claimer on turf, but had been beaten in a seller at Goodwood last time. Not only was she a very opposable odds-on favourite, the race included a horse who had caught my eye on his last run in Risky Whisky. He had finished ninth of ten in a six-furlong seller on the AW at Southwell, coincidentally having opened at 4-5 and in first-time blinkers on his AW debut. He had shown blazing speed on the long bend at Southwell, opening up a clear lead, but stopping quickly after being headed at the two-furlong pole. With the drop from six to five furlongs, and running on a track much more suited to front-running tactics, I felt that he would win if he could show the same speed again. The blinkers had been retained, but he would be less likely to run too freely in them with the benefit of experience. All my American books had emphasised that a horse that 'flashed speed' the first time on dirt would run well next time.

Sun In The Morning opened at 4-5, but was friendless and eventually went off at 6-4. This can happen, but it doesn't really affect the logic of this strategy, so long as the selection is available at the expected price. My confidence in Risky Whisky was reflected in the stake, although to some extent, it was a test of how much I could get on at a midweek Wolverhampton meeting. Risky Whisky didn't tear off in front this time, but ran close up throughout and just got the better of a duel in the final furlong by a short-head. Sun In The Morning finished seventh of eight runners.

**31/07 Gdwd 6f Group 2     LINDEN HEIGHTS     4th    SP 7-1**
**£4750/600**

This was an example of opposing a favourite who went off at 8-13, a price based mainly on his reputation. That was the Henry Cecil trained two-year-old Daggers Drawn. He had won his only race to date, a six-furlong maiden at the Newmarket July meeting, in which he started at 4-11. He didn't impress me in any way that day, being green in the paddock, moving poorly to post, and only finding his stride on the rising ground at the furlong pole. On fast ground at Goodwood, I felt there was every chance that he'd be unsuited by the downhill run. When he once again cantered down with all the athletic grace of a wildebeest with lumbago, I was compelled to bet against him. From the remaining five runners, I felt that Linden Heights stood out on the strength of his second in the Group 3 July Stakes, on the same day as the favourite's debut, but run in faster time. He was a much more athletic colt, and a free mover who should act at Goodwood. He also had the advantage of the position against the stand rails, drawn in stall two, but with stall one empty due to a non-runner.

Of course, this strategy doesn't always work, and Daggers Drawn lived up to his home reputation with a convincing success. Linden Heights was well beaten in fourth.

**28/11  Nwby  2m 4f Hcp Ch  CALLISOE BAY       1st    SP 9-4**
**£1350/600**

Only four runners in this race and the favourite was Challenger Du Luc, forecast at around 10-11. If there is one horse running over fences at present that punters should be keen to oppose at a short price, it must be Challenger Du Luc. With Gales Cavalier unsuited by the soft ground and Dublin Flyer apparently past his best, this looked a chance to take 9-4 in a definite two-runner race. Callisoe Bay had won over this trip at Uttoxeter last time, and had always shown his best form on flat left-hand tracks.

It was close, but Challenger Du Luc's nature asserted itself when he took the lead on the run-in, and Callisoe Bay got back up on the line to win by a head.

This approach won't throw up a bet every day, but usually once a week there is an odds-on favourite who can be realistically taken on. It has certainly proved a useful addition to my betting armoury over the last ten years.

# Not the win single

## 1 Each-way betting

Des O'Connor tells a story against himself that I've always liked. After a show at the London Palladium, he's leaving by the stage door, when an elderly lady tugs at his arm and pulls him into the shadows. She proffers a five pound note and says "I enjoyed your singing Des, can you send me a copy of your latest LP." O'Connor explains that the record only costs £3.99 and she can buy it at any shop, and then hands back the fiver. The old lady recoils and explains "Good grief, I don't want anybody to see me buying one of your records!" I share that feeling of embarrassment every time I succumb to an each-way bet.

I know that it's just a safety first instinct. I know that it's taking a short-term view on the outcome of a single wager. I know that at the current place odds, there is hardly ever any value in an each-way bet. But still I have these occasional lapses, amounting to a total of 14 bets during 1997. They produced just one 14-1 winner and, despite some place returns, I would have been considerably better off if I'd invested the place portions as win stakes.

For me, an each-way bet is a pre-race admission that you don't really expect the horse to win. The place half is an attempt to acquire some sort of return on outlay. That's what I mean by saying that it's a short-term option.

I can only see any logic in this approach when the place price exceeds 4-1 – that's to say 20-1 or more at one-fifth the odds, 16-1 at one-quarter the odds. At those odds, the win-only punter has to expect long losing runs, and the each-way bet then seems a reasonable method of limiting the losses during the run. But it is still a prime essential that you really want to back the horse to win, and aren't placing the win part of the each-way bet simply because you can't have a place only wager.

One factor in my avoidance of each-way betting is that it isn't generally available in the ring at the racecourse. Those bookmakers who offer the option are rarely the most competitive when it comes to pricing up the longshots that are likely to attract each-way interest. My own each-way winner from 1997 demonstrates what can happen. I backed Imshishway (£250 each-way) on my Tote Credit account in an eight-runner two-year-old event at Goodwood. He was on offer at 16-1 in the ring, but a bet of that size would have been hard to place at all, let alone at the best price. After he won, the SP return was only 14-1, even though I'd seen 20-1 offered and taken with one of the main ring bookmakers betting win only. It was still a handsome win, but there is a big difference between £250 each-way. at 14-1 and £500 win at 20-1. And why was I betting each-way at all? To be honest, I can't really explain it, since the horse was an instinct bet based on a good draw and paddock inspection, plus a couple of fancied runners failing to impress on the way to post. He certainly didn't justify a potential loss of £500 if, as was most likely, he failed to make the first three. A bet of £5,000/250 in the ring would have made more sense.

There is another argument against place betting that isn't often mentioned. That's the fact that the second and third places aren't always filled by the second and third best horses in the race. In many races, especially on the Flat, the second best horse is the one who puts the winner under most pressure at the decisive stage of the race, from the two-furlong point to near the finish. But we've all seen plenty of races in which that horse tires inside the final furlong, and is passed by runners who have never been in with a chance of victory. Add to that the problem of beaten horses eased down by their riders and conceding any chance of a placing, and the element of luck in place betting starts to look unacceptable. At least when betting win only you know that, in the majority of races, the best horse does actually win.

I am by nature an aggressive punter, and I've a resolution for 1998 to totally cut out each-way betting.

There will be a time when a run of second places will cause me to question the decision, but as I have the capital to sustain me during losing runs, there is no sense in my betting each-way. But I know I'll be tempted!

## 2 Multiple bets

Under this umbrella, I include all the combinations of doubles, trebles, accumulators, up and down and 'any to come' that are the preferred option of the average betting shop punter. If your total stake is a couple of pounds, then I can fully understand the reason for the choice of a multiple bet to produce a worthwhile return on a small stake. The logic is the same as the Lottery player's, and so long as the regular losses can be accepted, it's not a problem. But for the serious punter, and if you're reading this I assume you don't bet £2 per day, multiple bets should only be used as part of a considered strategy. After all, if win singles weren't the smartest way to bet for profit, don't you think Ladbrokes would include a 'Lucky One' slip amongst their offerings?

As we'll see later, I work on the basis of win singles, my stakes contained within a narrow band. My strongest objection to doubles and bigger is that they impose erratic staking. For example, consider a win double in which the first leg obliges at 5-1: suddenly the stake on the second horse is six times greater than that on the first, although it's highly unlikely that the punter considers it a six times better bet. And if it doesn't oblige, then the 5-1 winner is wasted, which should be anathema to any serious punter. The more selections you include for a single stake, the worse this equation becomes.

If you consider the effect of a win double alongside the equivalent two win singles, it's the same as the undisciplined punter who increases his stake after a winner. That's a punter who every bookmaker loves, because he never retains his winnings for long enough to justify calling them profits. Having said all that, I did place one double bet during 1997, and to make it worse it was an each-way double. That's nearer to buying a Teletubbies record than anything by Des O'Connor! The two horses involved both ran at Newmarket in consecutive races, on a day when I was attending Newbury. Because the race times were close together, I wanted to avoid the Newmarket bets getting in the way of paddock watching at Newbury. So I placed the following bet with Tote Credit in their racecourse shop:

| £200 Win | WELTON ARSENAL | 2.30 Newmarket |
| £100 EW Double | WELTON ARSENAL | 2.30 Newmarket |
| | SOOJAMA | 3.00 Newmarket |

If Welton Arsenal was beaten, I would have placed a win single on Soojama immediately after the 2.40 race at Newbury. It was a lazy way around the problem, but I got much better than I deserved, with Welton Arsenal winning at 5-1, followed by Soojama at 13-2. My one and only multiple bet of the year and it produced over five and half thousand pounds profit. There were times during 1997 when it seemed as if anything I tried would succeed, and this was definitely one of them. Early in the Flat season I had secured a win that would almost guarantee me a profitable season. I didn't press my luck by trying to repeat that success!

I know some punters swear by the each-way double as the ideal bet with a couple of selections in the range 5-2 to 5-1. They argue that even getting both horses in the frame ensures a profit. I cannot swallow this, and it must lead to the same sort of safety-first thinking that makes me dislike the each-way single. The dominant thought seems to be finding two selections with a great chance of being placed, with their win prospects taking a back seat. Perhaps fans of this bet are right, but I know it doesn't suit my style.

In the seventies, I used to be a hardened win double punter, putting together combinations of four or five horses every Saturday afternoon in six or ten doubles. Even then I was aware enough to miss out the trebles and four-timers, content to find two or three winners and make a decent profit. But I eventually realised that I was finding winners and losing money at the same time, and I haven't placed that sort of bet for at least fifteen years. Once again the question is simple: if the Yankee was a good bet for punters would the Big Three print special slips to make it easier for us?

## 3 Forecast Betting

The American authors I've read make it clear that forecast betting (called Exacta in US) is a popular and potentially profitable method for many of them. They all make the point that the pool contains a proportion of money inspired by lucky number punters that offsets the considerable deduction made by the tracks. The US pools are also boosted by the average punters' habit of reversing every forecast bet, or playing all the combinations of three or more horses.

Sadly, I can't advise readers to try to make a profit from forecast betting in this country, although given the right conditions, I'm sure it would be possible. The bookmakers Computer Straight Forecast is calculated using a complex mathematical equation that has been the subject of much sarcastic comment in the trade press over the years, but has never been properly explained. What is certain is that every time punters have spotted a potential loophole, the formula has been changed to shut the door long before any horse has bolted. I used to make the occasional CSF bet when I felt that the draw would heavily favour two or three horses favourably drawn, but the value has long since disappeared.

I haven't carried out any scientific survey, but the CSF dividend appears to me to be at its most miserly when a short-priced favourite is involved, whether in first or second. Running that a close second would be any dividend with a longshot paired with a fancied horse. If you do play the CSF, It seems to me that the best option is only to include horses priced in the range 3-1 to 8-1, when the dividends do at least look to bear some relation to the SP. One factor that shouldn't be overlooked is that the formula deducts the betting tax before the dividend is declared, so for a true comparison, it would be right to add nine per cent to the actual amount paid out. Then again, is there any evidence that the formula was ever adjusted when the rate of deduction was cut from ten per cent to nine per cent? If that change was made the bookmakers were strangely coy about publicising the fact.

That inbuilt tax makes the CSF a particularly unattractive bet for on-course punters, who are left with the pathetic offering from the Tote — the Dual Forecast. If you can explain to me why our Tote doesn't offer a straight forecast bet, you can probably resolve the problems of the welfare state. With the possible exception of the Quadpot, the dual forecast is the most unattractive bet in their portfolio from the point of view of value, with a massive 29 per cent deduction and tiny pools. As currently set up, the Tote forecast bet should be avoided at all costs.

I have experimented with the CSF under one set of circumstances when I think it can be used to extract some value from races with small fields. It requires a race in which one of the runners has perennial seconditis. The SP of such an animal will reflect its true chance of winning the race, which is not great, but will not reflect its chance of finishing second. The CSF formula works off the SP, and this is about the only circumstance left which allows the punter to take advantage of that method. A good example from the last two months of 1997 would be Challenger Du Luc, with a run of four second placings, culminating in the King George chase at Kempton, where a bet on him to be second to each of the main challengers would have produced a healthy profit. But since you might only find one or two of these opportunities each month, it's hardly a sure-fire method of making a living. It can, however, provide a means of playing a race that would be unattractive for single win betting.

# One for the pot

## Not my idea of fun

In order of rip-off, I think the three worst ways of having a bet available in this country are:

- The National Lottery
- The Football Pools
- The Tote Placepot

It says much about the British education system that those are also the three most popular bets in this country! I'm sure I don't have to offer any explanation for trashing the Lottery or the pools, but there remains a substantial body of opinion that the Placepot is 'fun', and that it provides 'an interest throughout the afternoon'. And I accept that playing a couple of lines for two pounds isn't the greatest crime a racegoer can commit. But to suggest that the Placepot should be taken seriously as a potential source of profit strikes me as ridiculous.

There are five reasons why, as a professional punter, I wouldn't touch the Placepot with a borrowed bargepole:

1   As I explained in the earlier piece on each-way betting, the second and third best horses don't always finish second and third. If a jockey easing down near the finish has never beaten you out a Placepot, then you haven't been watching closely enough.

2   The rules regarding non-runners mean that you can select a horse who finishes third, only to find that the withdrawal of a 50-1 shot means that it needed to be second. Once a meeting has started, the number of places paid on this bet shouldn't change. It doesn't bother the Tote, since their cut is guaranteed anyway. Even worse is the rule that puts you on the favourite if your own selection is a non-runner, when the logic of your bet might have been to oppose the favourite.

3   There is no way of estimating the value of your bet in advance. The dividend paid out is highly variable and depends on which

other horses are placed alongside your own selections. You can find six 10-1 shots to finish in the frame, but still get paid less than ten quid if all the favourites are also placed.

4    The deduction of 27 per cent from the pool before the dividend is calculated is a massive edge to have to overcome. It would be impossible to beat a Tote system that deducted that much from a win pool. If there was ever a carry-forward from the previous day, that would solve the problem, but such an event is as rare as a Godolphin runner in a selling hurdle.

5    The pools are too small to handle the sort of stake required to generate a turnover sufficient to make winning worthwhile. Even with the increase in Tote Direct terminals, the daily total rarely exceeds £100,000, often spread over three or four meetings. Only at the major festival meetings does the pool grow to a size that can absorb a £20 winning line without seriously damaging the dividend. Consider a pool of £50,000, a typical amount for the main meeting on a Saturday at present. After deductions, the total to be paid out is £36,500. If there were £100 worth of winning tickets, the dividend would be £365. But if I've also won with a £20 line, then that cuts the dividend to just under £305. If you backed a 12-1 winner, how would you react if your betting shop told you they were only paying out at 10-1 because one of their other branches had taken a £20 bet on the same horse?

That last objection can be overcome if you can bet outside the pool, so that your result doesn't affect the dividend, but that's increasingly difficult as Tote Direct is installed in more shops.

## Hitting the Jackpot

Some of the objections I have to the Placepot can also be made to the Tote Jackpot, especially the provision for replacing a non-runner with the favourite. But on the days when there is a substantial carry-forward in the pool, then the issue of the deduction and the value doesn't arise. Since I wrote about a Jackpot win in *Against The Crowd*, I've been fortunate enough to collect another £11,000 win, under almost identical circumstances.

I've also uncovered some more efficient ways of staking a Jackpot bet, based on material produced by several American authors.

The latest win was on a meeting at Folkestone on the Friday after the Cheltenham Festival, when there was a healthy amount left in the pool after it was only partly won on Gold Cup day. I adopted the new policy of dividing my selections for each race into A and B categories, with A meaning a banker and B meaning a back-up selection. For each of the six races, there should be one, or at most two, A selections. The number of B selections need only be limited by your willingness to invest, but it makes it cheaper if there are one or two races in which you are happy to leave it to your banker, and have no B selections. I won't bother with a list of actual names, but here is an example of how your list should be drawn up:

| Race 1 | A1 A2 | B1 |
| Race 2 | A1 | B1 B2 |
| Race 3 | A1 | |
| Race 4 | A1 A2 | |
| Race 5 | A1 A2 | B1 B2 |
| Race 6 | A1 A2 | B1 |

If you enter a full perm covering all those selections, that amounts to:                **3 x 3 x 1 x 2 x 4 x 3  =  216 bets**

The problem with that simple approach is that all 216 bets carry the same stake, despite the fact that you must feel more confident about the line that includes your six most fancied selections, than about the line that covers the ones put in just in case. The AB system means that you make a number of entries at different stakes that more accurately reflects your idea of the chances of success with each combination. The above set of selections would produce five different perms, as follows:

| Race | 1 | 2 | 3 | 4 | 5 | 6 | |
|---|---|---|---|---|---|---|---|
| Perm #1 | A1+A2 | A1 | A1 | A1+A2 | A1+A2 | A1+A2 | 16 bets @ 2pt |
| Perm #2 | B1 | A1 | A1 | A1+A2 | A1+A2 | A1+A2 | 8 bets @ 1pt |
| Perm #3 | A1+A2 | B1+B2 | A1 | A1+A2 | A1+A2 | A1+A2 | 32 bets @ 1pt |
| Perm #4 | A1+A2 | A1 | A1 | A1+A2 | B1+B2 | A1+A2 | 16 bets @ 1pt |
| Perm #5 | A1+A2 | A1 | A1 | A1+A2 | A1+A2 | B1 | 8 bets @ 1pt |

Those perms mean that you will have a winning line for a one-point stake, so long as at least five of your banker (A) selections are successful. The total outlay is 96 points, considerably less than the 216 points for a full-cover perm. You can extend this further to include the perms that would provide a win with any four successful bankers. That would require another six perms, each including four sets of A selections and two sets of B selections. For the cautious, another option is to use the perms above, but add a full-cover line of 216 bets at a lower stake, say half a point. That brings the total stake up to 204 points, but does distinguish between your confident and back-up choices, by placing the most money on your bankers.

The latter was the option I chose for the Folkestone meeting, and with five of my bankers winning, I collected the return to a £1 stake. If all six bankers had won, I would have had two £1 winning lines, but less than five bankers would have only produced a 50 pence winning ticket.

Regardless of the staking system used, I still only play the Jackpot when two conditions are met:

- There is a carry-over of at least £100,000 effectively to eliminate the punitive 29 per cent deduction from the pool.

- The card has at least one and preferably two races in which I can identify a confident banker selection.

I also ensure that my selections don't include any combination that would be likely to pay more as a SP accumulator, than through a winning Jackpot ticket. Even if there is a million pounds in the pool, it makes no sense to invest in a line that includes a couple of 20-1 shots. One last piece of advice about playing the Jackpot – the stake has to match your ambition. If there is £100,000 carried forward, then it's likely that the same amount will be bet again to produce a £200,000 pool. If you are going to play, then remember that a 10p stake is only aiming at a maximum £14,200 return (one-tenth of the total paid out after deductions). The big wins are only available to the punter who plays to the full £1 stake. I don't get involved very often (only three times during 1997), so I prefer to play high when the opportunity arises.

I suspect that two wins in the same decade is stretching things a bit, but the realistic odds about such a win are probably a lot less than you might think. For example, the starting prices of my selections for that Folkestone card were:

| Race 1 | 9-2 | 11-2 | 6-1 | | Combined | 11-10 |
|---|---|---|---|---|---|---|
| Race 2 | 9-4 | 10-3 | 6-1 | | Combined | 1-2 |
| Race 3 | 1-12 | | | | | 1-12 |
| Race 4 | 7-4 | 3-1 | | | Combined | 8-13 |
| Race 5 | 7-2 | 6-1 | 8-1 | 10-1 | Combined | 4-5 |
| Race 6 | 5-2 | 5-1 | 5-1 | | Combined | 8-13 |

The accumulative odds were only 15-1 against my having all six winners. Even taking out the bookmakers' profit margin contained within those starting prices, I can certainly say I had about one chance in 20 of winning. My total investment was £208 plus tax paid on, and the return was just over £11,000. That's a 50-1 return on a 20-1 bet – good value, however you slice it! But without the carry-forward from Cheltenham, the return would probably have been about 10-1, though the real odds would still have been 20-1. That's why the Jackpot is never going to attract serious punters on a daily basis.

# Making the right bet

Finding winners is only the first step in making your betting pay, and in many ways it's the easiest part of the job, because emotion doesn't get in the way of your analysis. When it comes to laying out the readies, all sorts of conflicting thoughts can prevent a punter from making the right moves. I used to be just as vulnerable as anyone to mistakes such as:

- Increasing stakes after a winner
- Staking what was left in my wallet
- Trying to recoup the day's losses on the last race
- Large stakes on favourites, small stakes on longshots
- Not keeping records

That last category is perhaps the most common, and offers a losing punter the opportunity to deceive himself, if nobody else, that he isn't really losing at all. The only way to overcome these problems is to have a plan, so that when you go to place a bet, your stake is already decided by your long-term strategy. I have been operating in this fashion for the past ten years and it ensures that I only enter the betting ring, or pick up the phone, when I know the answers to the two key questions:

- What is my target price?
- How much will I bet at that price, or a longer price?

In the hustle of the betting ring, things don't always work out exactly as planned. I might decide that 6-1 is my target price, start betting, only to find the price disappears as soon as I've struck part of my bet. For example, if I've placed a bet £1,000/160 and then find that 5-1 is the best offer, the only option is to stop betting. If 6-1 doesn't reappear, then that leaves me with a bet less than I wanted; but there is no mileage, long-term, in continuing to bet at the shorter price just in order to place my entire planned stake. I could of course place all my bet in one go, but if I want to back a horse to win £3,000 or £4,000 at a price like 6-1, I know that most bookmakers in the ring will only accept a bet to take out £1,000 or

£2,000. Hence the need to spread the bet around. It also means that I can take advantage if I've misread the market and the price lengthens. I can then get part of my planned bet at 13-2 or 7-1, rather than feeling frustrated that I've taken 6-1 for the whole stake.

For the calendar year 1997, my strategy was to operate in a band between £300 and £600 for the majority of my single win bets, with the option to bet up to £1,000 in strong markets when it looked right. I had a target of 350-400 bets, with a projected turnover of around £150,000. The actual figures, compared with those for the previous two years were:

| 1995 | Turnover £110,000 | Average Stake £380 |
| 1996 | Turnover £140,000 | Average Stake £420 |
| 1997 | Turnover £160,000 | Average Stake £480 |

The gradual increase represents increased confidence, increased capital and the normal growth required to combat inflation. During 1997, I exceeded the nominal £600 ceiling on 30 occasions, just under ten per cent of all bets placed. Those bets included ten winners and produced a profit of approximately £6,000 from a stake of £24,000. I've brought those larger bets into the discussion because they demonstrate the perils of trying to use staking systems, with fixed rules that decide the bet size regardless of your confidence about the value of the bet.

The first rule of systems is that no staking system can consistently turn a level-stake loss into a profit. Any system can work that miracle, given a perfect sequence of results, but in the long run, a losing punter will lose just as much, just as quickly, by following a staking system. The American literature I've studied has plenty to say about staking, with the most popular approach being the one that requires the punter to bet a fixed percentage of his current bank. For example, if you set up a pot of £1,000 for your betting, then you might bet ten per cent of that each time you play. If you win and the bank grows, then the stake size grows as well. This works well, so long as your winners arrive at frequent and regular intervals. But as soon as you hit the inevitable losing run, your bank disappears quite quickly.

If you've done well over a three-month period and doubled your bank to £2,000, then your standard bet is now £200. Back five consecutive losers and you're back to square one! Let's try this approach on my 30 most confident bets of 1997, in the sequence in which they happened. For the purpose of this experiment, I'll ignore the impact of the betting tax.

| | Result | Price | £ Stake | £ Return | Balance |
|---|--------|-------|---------|----------|---------|
| 1 | Loser | | 100 | - 100 | 900 |
| 2 | Winner | 11-4 | 100 | +275 | 1,175 |
| 3 | Winner | 3-1 | 110 | +330 | 1,505 |
| 4 | Loser | | 150 | - 150 | 1,355 |
| 5 | Loser | | 150 | - 150 | 1,205 |
| 6 | Loser | | 150 | - 150 | 1,055 |
| 7 | Winner | 7-2 | 150 | +525 | 1,580 |
| 8 | Loser | | 150 | - 150 | 1,430 |
| 9 | Loser | | 150 | - 150 | 1,280 |
| 10 | Winner | 3-1 | 150 | +450 | 1,730 |
| 11 | Loser | | 170 | - 170 | 1,560 |
| 12 | Winner | 7-2 | 170 | +595 | 2,155 |
| 13 | Winner | 7-2 | 210 | +735 | 2,890 |
| 14 | Loser | | 280 | - 280 | 2,610 |
| 15 | Loser | | 280 | - 280 | 2,330 |
| 16 | Loser | | 280 | - 280 | 2,050 |
| 17 | Loser | | 280 | - 280 | 1,770 |
| 18 | Loser | | 280 | - 280 | 1,490 |
| 19 | Winner | 3-1 | 280 | +840 | 2,330 |
| 20 | Winner | 11-4 | 230 | +630 | 2,960 |
| 21 | Winner | 13-8 | 290 | +470 | 3,430 |
| 22 | Loser | | 340 | - 340 | 3,090 |
| 23 | Loser | | 340 | - 340 | 2,750 |
| 24 | Loser | | 340 | - 340 | 2,410 |
| 25 | Loser | | 340 | - 340 | 2,070 |
| 26 | Loser | | 340 | - 340 | 1,730 |
| 27 | Loser | | 340 | - 340 | 1,390 |
| 28 | Loser | | 340 | - 340 | 1,050 |
| 29 | Winner | 2-1 | 340 | +680 | 1,730 |
| 30 | Loser | | 170 | - 170 | 1,560 |

At first glance it looks good, with a 56 per cent profit on the starting bank. But remember I was placing bets of over £600 on these horses, so my starting stake would have been higher. If we assume that my first bet in this sequence was £600, then by the time we reach line 22, I have to stake over £2,000 on each selection. Apart from the obvious problem of getting that bet on at an acceptable price, do I really want to be betting that much on a single race. It's certainly going to make me more selective, even if only subconsciously. It's a safe assumption that if the amount of your bet is affecting your decisions on what to back, then the stake is too big. Every punter has a comfort zone, but you only discover what it is when you exceed it!

And note that the run of losers from 22 to 28 would cost me over £14,000 if I start with a £6,000 bank. If bet number 29 doesn't win, I'm facing the loss of my entire bank in just two more bets. At that stage deciding on your next bet must become really nerve-wracking.

Of course there are variations on this theme that can remove some of those problems. You can cut the stake after each loser, as well as recalculating after each winner. But that way, if you drop below your starting total at any stage, it becomes increasingly difficult to get back into profit using smaller stakes.

A better alternative is to stop after the bank has doubled, withdraw your profit, and start again from £1,000. That has some merit, but still looks dreadful if you reach £1,900 before hitting eight or nine straight losers. In the end this method imposes erratic staking on the punter, leaving no scope for judgement on value or confidence. There are half a dozen other ideas contained in the American literature but they are all essentially variations on this theme. They all have the same basic idea, which is that every bet is of equal merit, and the stake is decided by artificial means.

A couple of the authors offer the idea of a standard bet on your strong fancies – or 'prime bets' as they call them, with the option to place smaller stakes on other horses in order to provide sufficient action to avoid boredom. I suspect that scheme says more about the nature of a day at the races in America, than being a worthwhile staking plan. It does, however, suggest that you can have different options for different types of bet. If you do want to play forecasts, multiple bets, etc, then it makes sense to have some sort of staking plan for those areas.

So I prefer to stick to my own 'system', which allows me, within defined limits, to decide the appropriate stake for each bet. I'd recommend that punters should have their own plan, setting realistic targets and with staking levels that match the amount available for betting. If you have a £1,000 bank, then an average stake of £50 should minimise the risk of losing the lot. But even if you make 500 bets in a year, staking at that level you cannot expect to make much more than £2,500 to £3,000 before tax. Having set a strategy, stick with it for at least six months and preferably longer. Even if you are successful, it is a mistake suddenly to double your stakes overnight. That will only ensure that the next losing run will wipe out your profit in half the time it took to achieve.

The issue of staking has also been brought to prominence by the use of betting points in the price-related columns in the trade papers, such as Pricewise and Beat The Book. Both of those, along with Henry Rix, now use a scale from one to 20 points. I think that is too wide a disparity between the minimum and maximum stake. If any bet you are considering is worth only one-twentieth of your maximum bet, then in my view it's a bet you shouldn't be placing at all. I'll spare the blushes of the perpetrator, but one of those columns once tipped a 20-1 winner - but had a losing day. The stake on the winner was one point, but there were two other bets, including 20 points on an 11-8 loser. I wouldn't be backing the 11-8 shot anyway, but using my scale of three to ten points (equivalent to £300 - £1,000), that 20-1 winner must produce a profit of at least 50 points. If I ever backed a 20-1 winner and had a losing month, I'd be upset, let alone a losing day!

## Savers

There are plenty of professionals who like to back more than one horse in a race, and this method warrants some discussion. It isn't my choice, but I can see the logic in such an approach. I find that I rarely have sufficient time actually to make the necessary bets, as I like to see the horses go to post before I move into the ring. Neither does it suit my aggressive nature to be placing bets to save my stake. I have tried this way of working but I found that it distracted me from the business in hand.

There are two reasons for betting multiple horses in the same race:

- Backing one or two dangers to small amounts in order to recoup the stake placed on your main selection.

- Backing any horse who exceeds the target price set in your personal tissue, with the stake decided by the price difference.

As an example of the first – if I back my main selection at 4-1 (£2,000/500), then I can bet the horse I consider the danger at, say, 3-1 (£600/200). If my number one choice wins, the profit is £1,800. If the danger wins, the profit is £100.

As an example of the second, if I have two horses on my tissue at 3-1, and both are offered at 4-1, then I bet £1,200/300 on both. If either of them win, the profit is £900. In effect, by backing two horses at 4-1, I've had a bet of £900/600 in this race. One of the skills needed by punters who adopt this method is the knowledge of the combined odds they are achieving when backing two or three horses.

Compared with my own 'six or out' style, these methods produce a larger turnover but reduce losing runs. The punters who work this way are generally looking to find one or more short-priced horses to oppose, and they then back against those horses. It requires tremendous concentration in the ring and long hours working on the tissue before racing. You can see these punters working with the bookmakers, calling bets in with no cash changing hands until after the race. I admire their work-rate, but I'm happy to continue operating in my own 'idle' fashion.

## The betting tax

One of the common misconceptions of the life of a professional punter is that he pays no tax. Well, it's true that betting profits don't attract income tax, but leaving aside the council tax, VAT and excise duties, I still have to pay the tax when I place an off-course bet. During 1997, I coughed up £3,660 in tax paid on with my stakes. If I could bet tax-free and be sure of getting on and getting paid, I'd take that option. As things stand, I prefer to bet where I know there won't be any problems of that nature, and accept the nine per cent charge. I take the tax into account when deciding the price at which I'll be prepared to bet off-course, looking for enough edge to cover the extra outlay. For example, if I'd be looking for a minimum of 4-1 about a horse to back it on-course, I'll want at least 9-2, and preferably 5-1, to back the same horse off-course.

The mathematics of the betting tax are quite simple but can be relied upon to defeat most mug punters. Try this question on your betting friends:

- You place a bet of £100 Win on an Evens favourite and pay the tax on. The horse wins – what is your profit?

I hope readers know that the correct answer is £91 – you hand over £109 and receive a return of £200. But I suspect that most betting shop punters will answer £100, and quite a few won't be convinced even when you explain the calculation. Place the same bet without paying the tax on, and your return will be £182. Those same betting shop punters will also tell you that you lost £18 by not paying the tax. That's because they can't cope with the idea that £100 Win, tax paid, is a bet with a different stake to £100 win without the tax.

**Stake £109      Profit £91      Return on Investment   83.5%**

**Stake £100      Profit £82      Return on Investment   82.0%**

So it is more profitable to pay tax on, but the difference is not great and the extra outlay of £9 means that your turnover is effectively nine per cent higher. Over a period of a year, it is beneficial to pay tax on if you are a winning punter, but if you lose, it increases your losses. For most punters, therefore, it would be better not to pay the tax with their stake. It suits the betting shops to have punters pay the tax with their bet, as it increases their turnover and their recovery of the duty they have to pay to Customs and Excise. If they didn't want punters to pay tax on, they wouldn't make it easy, would they?

To summarise my suggested approach to the finances of betting:

- **Make a plan**

- **Set realistic targets**

- **Bet within your means**

- **Be consistent**

- **Keep records**

- **Keep your betting bank separate from your everyday finances**

# Winners and losers

Betting should be enjoyable, but it can often be a miserable experience if you are losing and have no idea when the next winner will appear. It's a fact that the punters I talk to about working as a professional are much more interested in how to handle losing runs than coping with success.

We've all said, or at least thought, what an easy game this is when you're winning, but I'm of the opinion that punters are just as likely to go wrong during a winning run as during a losing one. Both bring their own pressures, and I think it pays to have thought about how you will handle either situation.

In December 1995, I was interviewed by the *Sporting Life Weekender* for their Betting Boots column, and was amused that one of their standard questions was:

*"What do you do during a losing run?"*

As a question, this begs a simple answer to the effect of, "I lose". It's symptomatic of the general approach to betting that losing runs are common to every punters' experience, because most punters expect to lose. For a column that purports to educate readers, I felt it would be more useful to talk about winning, although I hadn't the wit to query their agenda at the time.

My own answer to the question above was, "to keep employing the methods I knew had been successful over many years, in the confident belief that I would return to profitable betting in due course".

Although as we've seen in the opening section, that approach hadn't helped me during the 1995 Flat season, and I had eventually accepted the inevitable and started to question my methods. I think there are a couple of other things I do which can also help:

- Keep all your betting records and look back at profitable periods from the past to check that you are still working to the same standards.

- Keep a scrapbook with cuttings from the trade papers of your best wins, or alternatively keep video recordings of the races.

- Take a break from betting for at least one week, to clear your mind of the constant thoughts about recent losses and start afresh when you return.

All these ideas are aimed at reminding you of your own ability to make a profit and to concentrate attention on the things that have worked for you in the past. It's also important to stick to your staking plan and not to start cutting back. If you lose £500 betting in approximate £50 level stakes, it won't help if your next bet is £20 on a 10-1 winner. That's a combination guaranteed to make the end of a losing run feel worse than the run itself. If you've set up your staking correctly in the first place, in line with your resources, then there should be no need to reduce stakes.

My own experience over seven years of full-time punting is that the most common experience is a gentle plodding progress in which I neither win much, nor lose much. This can go on for two or three months at a time, but is then followed by dramatic periods of a few days or weeks in which the account moves rapidly one way or the other. As I've commented in earlier chapters, the profit/loss figure at the end of the year can be massively influenced by the outcome of a single bet. But that will never be apparent at the time – I have never placed a bet with the thought that "this will decide my year".

When the winning runs arrive, it is just as important to handle them correctly as the losing spells. Once again, it's essential to maintain control of the staking and not to start betting more and more from profits. Never, ever refer to winnings as the bookmakers' money. Never assume you've got the game 'cracked' and can't be beaten, just because you've backed a few winners in succession. I'm actually more likely to take a pull and cut back my betting when I'm winning than vice-versa. If I have a good win on the racecourse, I prefer to pass on the next race and let the adrenalin settle before getting involved again. And if I put together a run of success over two or three weeks, I'll be quite content to take a break for up to a week, just as I would during a losing run. It's too easy to fall prey to the 'Messiah' complex and start making bets because you don't want to risk missing another winner.

Far better to step aside and enjoy doing something different – spending some of your profits. After all, there has to be a point to making all this effort. For me, it's to make a living, but even then I will treat myself or members of my family when things are going well. Either way, whether winning or losing, it will pay to have thought in advance about how to handle your emotions. Unfortunately, most punters tend to attribute such runs to the one thing that has no influence on betting at all – luck.

In my time I must have responded to hundreds of people wishing me good luck and I usually point out that luck has nothing to do with it. Profitable betting is a matter of skill, judgement and hard work. I accept that luck in the sense of good fortune or misfortune can decide the outcome of a single bet, but it won't make any difference in the long-term. If I back a chaser who falls at the last when it's ten lengths clear, that's a misfortune. But I remember the occasions when I've backed a winner who might have been beaten but for the falls of other horses during the race. If I back a horse who fails to get a clear run in a Flat race, I could claim that was bad luck, but I prefer to analyse whether I should have foreseen the trouble before I made the bet. Too many punters remember all their apparent bad luck but regard every winner as their just reward and never admit that they benefit from good fortune as well as bad.

There's an old American blues number that the sixties supergroup Cream performed on one of their albums, that would serve as an anthem for the average betting shop punter: The song is called *Born Under A Bad Sign*, and the chorus goes:

> *Bad luck and trouble, been my only friend,*
> *I been down ever since I was ten,*
> *If it wasn't for bad luck,*
> *If it wasn't for real bad luck,*
> *I wouldn't have no luck at all.*

Then again, if you have a bet on the 49's every day, what sort of luck should you expect! If it isn't luck that turns a loser into a winner, what exactly is the quality that achieves that transformation? Personally, I'm inclined to put most of it down to a mixture of experience and effort. It isn't hard work in the physical sense, nor in my case do I spend long hours sweating over a hot formbook. But it is necessary to put time into research, reading, watching and thinking about racing and betting.

The American authors are very hot on the mental approach to their betting and some of the books include reams of psychobabble about the power of positive thinking, visualisation, etc. Try this example from Dick Mitchell's *Commonsense Handicapping*, in a chapter with the same title as this one of mine:

"Winning is an attitude. It's about not being denied. Winners do what losers refuse to do. A loser refuses to keep records. A loser refuses to do original research or in fact read the research of others, never mind validate it. A loser doesn't read books on the subject of handicapping. A loser doesn't seek out a winner for advice. A loser views a losing day at the track as money irretrievably lost. A winner views the money left at the track as an interest-bearing loan that he'll be back to collect.

Losing is also an attitude. A loser wants something for nothing. He wants to win without doing the requisite work. A loser tends to have his ego invested in his selections. If his horse wins, he's a certified genius, and if it loses, he's a low life ignoramus. Hence the need to find an excuse when he loses.

Winners strive for excellence, while losers strive to get by. Winners have goals, and plans to get them to their goals. Losers have daydreams. They dream about winning the lottery or about a long-lost relative dying and leaving them a fortune. Losers believe that winners are 'lucky'. They believe that external forces are responsible for their destiny.

Most people view wealthy people as successful. People are not successful because of their wealth – they are wealthy because of their success. By our behaviour we choose to be a winner or a loser. We each have a success mechanism and failure mechanism built into us. Unfortunately, if we choose not activate our success mechanism, our failure mechanism goes off automatically."

That's just an extract from an entire chapter along similar lines. I wonder if his deal with the publisher meant that he was being paid by the sentence. I can't write like that and keep a straight face, but there is nothing in those extracts that I'd disagree with, even if I wouldn't use quite the same words to express the ideas. Once you've gained enough experience to be able to analyse races with sufficient accuracy to find a decent percentage of winners, it's only attitude that can prevent you from making profits. As with golf, it's the six inches between your ears that will ultimately decide whether you win or lose.

Having got this far, I hope that you are already thinking of new ways to approach your betting. When I was searching for a title for this book, I looked up 'inside track' in my dictionary, where I found the definition:

**An advantageous competitive position**

I hope you now feel that you have a better chance of achieving a place on 'The Inside Track'.